Exceptional Relationships

Exceptional Relationships

Transformation Through Embodied Couples Work

Brian And Marcia Gleason, LCSWs

iUniverse, Inc.
Bloomington

Exceptional Relationships
Transformation Through Embodied Couples Work

iUniverse books may be ordered through booksellers or by contacting:

iUniverse
1663 Liberty Drive
Bloomington, IN 47403
www.iuniverse.com
1-800-Authors (1-800-288-4677)

ISBN: 978-1-4759-5032-8 (sc)
ISBN: 978-1-4759-5077-9 (ebk)

Printed in the United States of America

iUniverse rev. date: 09/19/2012

To our "Couples Pod"

Marsha and Michael Antkies, Barry and Elizabeth Carl, Judy Gotlieb and Neal Brodsky, Sandie and Gerry Rumold, Margo Harris and Craig Thurtell. Thanks for being our beacons in the stormy seas of full-on relationship.

Table of Contents

Acknowledgments

A special thanks goes to all those couples who have ever graced us with their struggles, hearts, vulnerabilities, and unique gifts. Their transformational process which we have witnessed again and again inspires and challenges us to stay honest in our own relationship. We never cease learning through every couple we counsel, every workshop we lead, and every class we teach. You have given us more than you know.

We would also like to thank, in no particular order, Judy Gotlieb for her careful eye in proofreading and editing our manuscript; Jorge Galindo for bringing the embodied couples training to his post graduate students in Mexico; Loly Sierra Finke who, along with Jorge, have opened their hearts and home to us; Anna Timmermans for introducing our work to The Netherlands Institute of Core Energetics; Ann Bradney for her support in bringing this work to the world; Jeanekke Kempen and Gerard Janson for setting an example of what it means to have an Exceptional Marriage. Stuart Black whose wisdom is sprinkled throughout this book; and John Pierrakos, the father of Core Energetics.

Cover graphic: Perry Pennick
Cover design: Marcia Gleason

Foreword

Brian and Marcia Gleason are brave souls. For me they are in the vanguard of a new movement to bring the emotional aspect of our humanity back into the conversation. And as far as I am concerned, this is not only important for relationships but for the future of our world. As the creator of Radical Aliveness, a process which welcomes vibrant expression as the pathway to wisdom, I have come to place great value on trusting emotions and energy in group process. By offering enough room for divergent reactions to emerge growth occurs. Trusting in the innate intelligence of the shared energy, be it a couple or a group, helps each individual to flourish.

The concept of using the relationship to open up all the way—to "bring it all" is sacred and profound. I envision a world where we use our relationships to become all we are meant to be, where passion stays alive and we don't settle into safe, deadening patterns. Where we can grow into the complete human beings we are capable of becoming by using the crucible of the relationship as our source.

Exceptional Relationships: Transformation Through Embodied Couples Work is more than an innovative handbook for helping professionals. It invites anyone who works with couples to take stock of what they do and consider jumping into the deep end of the pool. Here you will learn to welcome the passionate, erotic, chaotic truths that are often kept under wraps in the therapy room. You will learn to trust in the non-rational, non-linear ways in which all couples operate. Beyond problem solving and conflict resolution, Brian and Marcia will show you how to awaken couples to their great potential.

Key to this work is the professional's ability and willingness to hold the space for the expression of life force as embodied in the full range of human emotions. In Exceptional Relationships: Transformation Through Embodied Couples Work you will be introduced to a variety of new possibilities for supporting couples to move beyond blame, to take risks with each other, to re-discover eros, to unearth their power and passion, and to ride the waves of authenticity. This requires more of you as the therapist than school ever teaches.

Here is a roadmap for just that. Does it take courage? YES! Does it take heart and sexuality and breath and commitment? YES! And isn't this what most of us would want if someone would show us the way? Isn't that what you want to bring to your work with couples?

For too long the therapeutic world has ignored the vital aspect of energy (as embodied in our emotions). For all you who would like to help your couples to bring heart and soul and sex together for the long haul—this is for you. I am proud to call Brian and Marcia colleagues and excited that this work is getting out there to be shared with more and more professionals.

Ann Bradney, Venice California

Introduction

"Why are we together?" Most couples in long term committed relationships will eventually confront this very challenging question. Indeed it is often the central motivation that compels couples to seek help. It is precisely this query that has directed the two of us to our life's work. In this book we hope to open you to new possibilities in your work with couples, possibilities that arise from expanding your perspective on this fundamental question.

This book is meant as an introduction to our approach to helping couples invigorate their relationships. It is directed primarily toward therapists and counselors who work with committed partners. It is designed to offer both practical information on how to work with couples in a more "embodied" and transformative way, and to inspire you to stretch your limits and bring more creativity and aliveness into your work. If you are like most therapists "in the trenches," you work with couples at all levels of development and individuation. Our approach can be effective for most couples, and is particularly effective when partners are looking for more than the abatement of conflict or pain.

We call our approach to couple's intervention **Exceptional Marriage Mentoring (EMM)**. The word mentoring was chosen (after much debate) for a couple of reasons. First, we believe that the concept of therapy is too limited and misrepresents the actuality of the work we do. Therapy falls under the rubric of the medical model and is not consistent with our view of relationship as a vehicle for transformation. Second, mentoring suggests a collaborative effort which relies on the experience of the mentor in communion with the couple's own innate wisdom. We recognize that the term mentoring may suggest to some that this work does not attend to history, wounding, and deeper psychological realities. As you read this book you will discover that this portrayal is certainly not the case. EMM embraces the entire spectrum of human experience from early injuries to non-ordinary states of consciousness. This is precisely why we move away from adherence to the counseling/therapy paradigm.

EMM has emerged out of our own relationship of over three decades and our involvement with the body-centered psychotherapy movement, in particular, Core Energetics. Together and separately the two of us have participated in and experienced a breadth of modalities of couples, individual and group therapy. Much of our respective lives have been dedicated to our personal evolution.

For all the experiences we went through, however, we still found ourselves struggling in our relationship. We would sometimes flounder, returning to habits of relating that only made us feel separate and alienated from one another. Overall, we never doubted we had a good relationship, but was it good enough? Was there a better play-mate, soul-mate, sex—mate out there somewhere? At times we seemed to be holding each other back, our rhythms out of sync, our aspirations colliding. Something inside of both of us kept saying “yes” to our marriage, but we wanted to know precisely what it was we were really saying yes to.

A Broader Vision for Couples Work

This book offers what we believe is an exciting and dynamic approach to working with couples. It begins by posing a challenge to you as therapist. Do you really know what you are trying to achieve in working with couples? What the two of us have discovered is that, while some couples are looking to “stop the bleeding” or overcome a specific problem (*He doesn’t take me seriously. All she ever wants to do is discuss things. She never initiates sex. He works all the time.*) many couples come in with a more nebulous, harder to pin down unhappiness or ennui in their relationship. They want something more and they are keenly aware of its absence, even if they cannot quite articulate what it is.

When, as a therapist, you attempt to identify the couple's problem in concrete terms, you are apt to narrow your focus and miss the larger opportunity. Because many therapists are trained in a specific model of treatment or intervention, there is a built-in narrative about what the couple needs, and a prescribed set of rules about how one should proceed. While nearly all models add to the collective body of knowledge, each holds the danger of dogmatism. Whenever a therapist becomes wedded to a particular treatment model, therapy proceeds in the orderly direction of that model's operating tenets. Every new psychological theory, even those grounded in rigorous research, has a tendency to be fiercely defended as the penultimate therapy by its adherents. From primal scream to Polyvagal Theory, from transactional analysis to EMDR, from dialectical behavioral therapy to attachment theory, every construct adds something to the collective knowledge, but there is always more. Even in neurobiology, as we learn about the crucial role of the limbic system, neuropathways, and heart/brain communication, we still are left with more inscrutability about the human condition than answers.

The two of us are more interested in untying your hands as marital specialists and bringing a wider vision to your work. Over the past 15 years, we have had to challenge some cherished assumptions about what couples need. First and foremost is that strong emotions need to be tamed. Safety is ultimately achieved not by learning to modulate feelings but by making adequate space to get to deeper truths. This often only happens when couples learn how to "mix it up" emotionally with each other. More couples are harmed by the neglect of emotions than by a surplus of them. Emotions are the language of intimacy, the collagen of commitment.

Couples generally want (and simultaneously are afraid) to take more risks in order to bring greater aliveness, juice, and spontaneity to their relationship. The unique opportunity in long term relationship is that it provides space to meet the need on both extremes of Maslow's famous hierarchy. At the bottom, relationship can be our secure base that allows us to have the fortitude to reach higher. It is our safe haven in which we can shed our ersatz bravado and gain comfort in our most tender places. At the pinnacle of Maslow's hierarchy, the potential of an exceptional relationship is that it can support each person's self-actualization. In the EMM approach we never lose sight of this ultimate potentiality. This is the new era of the committed relationship—to bring forth the best in both partners and to make a difference in the world.

Second, couples don't need explanations, they want experiences. There is a deep longing in each partnership to transcend habitual, characterological modes of operating. In our sessions, we like to take risks to challenge deeply entrenched patterns of relating by having couples actively explore various parts of themselves that typically remain hidden and denied in normal life. A dispassionate, left—brained individual conceals an outrageous, irrational side that is yearning for some air time. Couples grow, not by adopting new language but by opening to an inner guidance, a non-rational, or transrational sensing of what needs to happen. Intuition is the forbear of intellectual comprehension. Our work emphasizes the innate wisdom of each person as it longs to emerge from an ever evolving consciousness.

As a couples therapist we suspect that you may have set your sights too low. There is one common denominator we have found in most relationships when partners truly want to stay together. All such couples are seeking to discover the best within themselves. Each person at some point had a window opened to the experience of pure love, deep connection and heightened pleasure. Mirrored through the other, each had at least glimpses of his/her higher self. Though such glimpses have a propensity to fade into shadow, most couples sincerely long to reclaim the ardor of their unrefined, wide open "higher selves." The self wants desperately to evolve along with and through the evolving other, spontaneously ever after.

What motivates many couples to keep trying even though commitment is, at times, profoundly difficult, is the often unarticulated sense that this other person can give me what I need—and what I need is to be seen clearly, fully and deeply. For it is the warp and woof of our humanity to be seen beneath, behind, and beyond our multiple masks. Each of us longs to be apprehended because, in order to become fully who we are, we need others to see clearly what we ourselves are blinded to.

As basic as the needs for food and shelter are, they are rivaled by the infant's requirement to have a parent who reflects back to him emotional understanding. For the first several years, his not fully developed brain is reliant on her to provide him with the essential awareness of the inner, subjective world of feeling. Psychiatrists and authors Thomas Lewis, Fari Amini, and Richard Lannon in their book, A General Theory of Love [(20)] put it this way: "Emotional experience begins as a derivative; a child gets his first taste of his feelings secondhand . . . A parent who is a poor resonator cannot impart clarity . . . If she does not or cannot teach him, in adulthood he will be unable to sense the inner states of others or himself."

It is equally true that we have a deep longing to see. What intimacy entails is the capacity to see the whole truth in ourselves and in our partner. While most mates settle for fairly narrow definitions of each other, the evolutionary desire is to know the other more and more. This aspect of couple's work is too often ignored.

The paradigm of couple's therapy keeps the bar well below what most couples long for. So, while we have worked with numerous couples who have been helped in previous therapies, they often come to us with a similar refrain. It goes like this: *The longer we're together the more separate we feel. We've done lots of therapy but we are stuck.*

Twelve Guiding Ideas

The problem seems to be that the work that couples do often does not challenge them to evolve into uncharted territories with each other. There are a number of crucial factors that the two of us have identified as essential to the work we do with couples. Some of these factors fall outside the norms of conventional approaches to couples therapy. We will briefly identify them here and go into greater detail in the body of the book.

1. Emotions are fundamental to a growing, maturing relationship. Central to our work with couples is the *support* for and *elicitation* of the entire range of human emotions. We believe it is essential for couples to not only become aware of their respective emotions, but to "embody" them. **By embody, we mean that emotions need expression, not just to be witnessed, but to be released, (as every child knows intuitively.)** While the prevailing approaches to emotional work stress a mindful consciousness of our feelings, we have come to the realization that there is a place within the committed relationship where feelings such as anger, hurt and fear need to be openly and passionately expressed—in communion with an observing "witness self." Losing a degree of control, for many couples is experienced as liberating. The relationship is, after all, built for passion.
2. A relationship is an evolving organism. Yet, most couples quickly fall into habits of interacting that are designed to maintain a status quo. Change is experienced as threatening. But in order to evolve, each partner must become the other's guide. Your partner has the privileged position of seeing aspects of you that no one else is privy to. In our couples work we seek out the wisdom each person has to offer the other. This wisdom comes in the form of the capacity for empathic connection, "entrainment" of each other's energies and an evolving resonance between each person's limbic brain. Partners can learn to challenge each other to come out of hiding and show up in newer ways. Evolution requires an ongoing reorganization of each person's identity. Thus each will go through many "deaths and rebirths" of an evolving self over the course of a long term relationship. This is both frightening and humbling and therefore typically avoided.
3. Couple's therapy is generally limited to a mostly passive interchange between the two partners and the therapist. To sit and dialogue for fifty minutes severely restricts the possibilities for deeper connection. What couples reveal in this format does not resemble the real-life interactions that

are part of their existent world. In the EMM approach we typically have the partners out of their chairs and relating to each other in a myriad of forms. Communication occurs on multiple levels. We attempt to create adequate space and a safe holding environment for two human beings to meet each other in various ways. Couples are invited to work with breath, sound, movement and energetic expression in novel ways. We utilize equipment (from large foam cubes to stuffed animals) in order to support the work couples are here to do.

4. In the Exceptional Marriage approach there are occasions when we support one of the partners in "losing control." There is such a taboo around getting out of control in this culture that most couples live under the hegemony of rationality where intensity is frowned upon. Under the right conditions, as you will learn, it can be profoundly important for one of both partners to allow their bodies to thrash, kick, shout, tremble, vibrate, and open up to non-rational, uncontrolled movement. This helps to create neuro-muscular connections for spontaneity, greater passion, and creativity.
5. Couples move through time in their interactions with each other. Sometimes they are operating from one or the other's history, sometimes from the vibrant reality of a present moment, and sometimes from their future potentialities that are longing to be expressed. Thus at any given moment one partner may be operating from a "regressed" consciousness, a very present adult space, or through tapping into a wisdom that seems to be emerging from a "higher self." While therapy by its very definition focuses on evaluating what is not working and taking corrective action, EMM creates space for each partner to, in C. Otto Scharmer's words, "learn from the future" [(32)], by releasing emotions which block access to our creative source.
6. Most therapies offer a "heart up" form of intervention. That is, the goal is to bring the hearts and minds of both people into deeper contact. Or, conversely there is an

exclusive focus on sexuality when it becomes problematic (as it frequently does). There tends to be a split between sexual connection and heart and mind connection. The two of us have seen that many couples, over time, build a larger and larger divide between compassion and passion—ultimately weakening both. Sexuality is one of the most fundamental means of communication and it is too often relegated to a secondary status behind verbal communication problems.

7. The goal of our work is to help each person in a committed relationship discover a radical acceptance of the other's "otherness." Most of us (consciously or not) are ceaselessly trying to get our partners to change. It is a very difficult challenge to surrender this impulse and begin to see the other exactly as she is. To get there, each partner must uncover the immature need for the spouse to provide something that is a leftover from childhood experience. One person cannot accept the other when she is unconsciously seeking a partner who isn't there.
8. It is not simply the lessons we learned in our families that need to be understood or healed, it is our complete cultural conditioning which teaches us to seek approval and external acceptance rather than to be spontaneous, playful, sensual, emotionally honest and curious. Couples are often in struggle because they have sunk down into life-denying habits that cannot be overcome by the same cultural consciousness which created them. Couples need help in breaking away from these spirit-crushing routines that are reinforced everyday by the prevailing culture. Our approach supports partners in liberating themselves from the deep conditioning to "be good" and to claim their individuality. In doing so, curiosity trumps approval-seeking.
9. Instead of adhering to a particular therapeutic modality, all of which have their benefits and limits, the therapists we train are encouraged to utilize their own particular gifts to help the couple find their own way. While there is a large body of research which can guide therapists

in helping couples, there is also the creative unknown which exists beyond the frontier of a scientific body of knowledge. In our approach we work both with what we know from the sciences (including the wealth of emerging knowledge about the brain and neurological factors in human development) and with what we imagine, sense, feel and intuit within a broader, wider, deeper field of human consciousness.

10. In the EMM approach, neither the clients nor the mentor are the experts. It is through the synchronicity that growth occurs. The couple and the mentor each play their part in this larger drama. Central to our approach is the understanding that we each evolve through an unruly process of human interaction that gradually leads us toward increasing inner wisdom and love.
11. While the Exceptional Marriage approach does employ a small number of its own concepts, the essence of this approach is to help couples have **experiences**. It is not in the appropriation of a new language or terminology that couples evolve, but through having deeply healing and transformative experiences.
12. In our work we view conflict as essential to an evolving relationship. It is through conflict that each person must challenge the tendency toward security as the overarching goal. Conflict engagement replaces conflict resolution as the objective of this work. Conflict engagement emphasizes the *process* of conflict rather than the resolution or outcome of conflict. Conflict that is not avoided creates an *emergency* of sorts that, if followed through, can lead to the couple to *emerge* into a higher state of consciousness and emotional awareness—an "Ah-ha!" and an "Ahhh!"

Theories That Inform Our Approach

We rely on several developmental theories to guide us in understand ing the influences of each partner in relationship. Most notably we draw from character theory, attachment theory, transpersonal theory, and multiplicity theory. There are others (such as David Schnarch and Bradford Keeney) who eschew developmental theory in their work, but whose contributions influence us as well.

From **character theory**, first articulated by Wilhelm Reich, there are several archetypal character structures that children embrace as a way to cope with relational breaches. What character theory offers us is an understanding of how the child develops both psychological defenses and *physical armoring* in order to cope with environmental conditions. The human organism is geared first toward survival so the child adapts by suppressing vital life energy that becomes too threatening to express. The body literally contracts away from feelings that are deemed too intense or which threaten the relationship with the all-important caregiver.

Character formation as posited by Reich was still cleaved to Freud's construct of suppressed sexual and aggressive impulses. Subsequently, others (Alexander Lowen, John Pierrakos, Stephen Johnson) have recognized that children are adjusting to imperfect environments which cause them to protect themselves through constricting normal emotions of anger, fear, and sadness. The human body—muscles, tissues and brain all conform to an environment to which they are indebted for their very survival. The child, over time, learns she must conduct herself, as a maestro will conduct the symphony, by *directing* her emotions rather than *allowing* them and learning from them. She has learned to pull back her organic responsiveness because it no longer feels safe to be herself. In character theory we recognize four critical incursions or threats a child experiences. To each of these she will energetically, physiologically, and neurologically adapt and create cognitive narratives to explain.

The four environmental threats are:

1. **Danger** to the child's very wellbeing and sense of self. This typically involves the child entering into an unsafe environment where caregivers are either hostile or so terrified themselves that they "transfer" their terror into the child.

2. **Abandonment** or inadequate attention from the caregiver. When a child is "undernourished" or emotionally deprived there is a deeply felt sense of despair, emptiness and collapse.
3. **Control** or the sense of being dominated and smothered. Such children feel stifled and become reluctant to express their autonomy needs openly.
4. **Betrayal** of trust. This occurs when a child's innocence is manipulated and utilized for the caregiver's own wishes. Such children learn to mistrust others as well as their own instincts. As Stephen Johnson describes it, "The injury is a deep wound to the experience of the real self." (15)

In couples work each of these threats to optimal development ultimately lead to distortions in a spouse's intersubjective experience with his partner. If he was tricked and manipulated by a caregiver, chances are high he'll be wary and mistrustful of his mate. Likewise if he was born into an unsafe world, he will bring this deep-seated terror into his relationship.

The term "character" is used to denote an overall psychological *and* energetic expression toward the world (as understood by the child in her particular circumstances). Character theory does not have the same extensive body of research to support it as attachment theory does. But in our experience it can be tremendously helpful in comprehending how an individual in a relationship is postured toward life and mate. It is also valuable because it alone focuses on the somatic experience and chronic patterns of muscular constriction in each person. Reich, in his book Character Analysis (37) said this: "To be able to cope with this world people had to suppress what was most beautiful and true, what was most basic in themselves; they had to strive to annihilate it, to surround it with the thick wall of character armor."

One partner, who is emotionally undernourished, for instance, reveals a depleted energetic expression, while his mate exhibits a highly charged "can't sit still" nervous energy that is fused to her childhood exposure to a volatile father. In EMM we are not looking to change these basic character structures so much as helping partners flow together and learn from what emerges between them, that is, to embrace the other's otherness. Instead, we want to help them break free of unconscious "enactments" or conditioned responses which are fused to their character stance.

Through **transpersonal theory** the committed relationship can be viewed as an evolutionary progression and a spiritual practice. Developmentally, in transpersonal psychology (as articulated by Ken Wilber, Abraham Maslow, Jean Gebser, Michael Washburn, David Nelson, Michael Kegan, Jorge Ferrer and many others) we are all evolving from narrow, egocentric levels of consciousness toward a more unified sense of wholeness and participation in a larger reality. Children are energetically alive and vibrant, but lacking in a broader awareness of the internal subjective state of the other as distinct from self. As a child matures, she becomes more conscious of the other as separate, but simultaneously, her energetic expression constricts. She loses much of her freewheeling spontaneity, both in order to take direct action in her environment and because the culture is very wary of intense expression. As a result, she loses contact with innocence, with her unfettered expressiveness. The progression is inevitable. As intellect and self-awareness flourish, emotional fluidity desiccates.

When we refer to the Exceptional Marriage, our aim is to help couples envision the possible. Marriage is, in our view, an ideal environment to cultivate the highest potentialities of our humanness. Through the energetic experience of deep relationship we can open up to discover the mystery of this life. Perhaps Jorge Ferrer [(7)] put it best when he said, "I believe that we are in direct contact with an always dynamic and indeterminate Mystery through our most vital energy. When the various levels of the person are cleared out from interferences (e.g. energetic blockages, bodily embedded shame, splits in the heart, pride in the mind, and struggles at all levels) this energy naturally flows and gestates within us, undergoing a process of transformation through our bodies and hearts, ultimately illuminating the mind with a knowing that is both grounded in and coherent with the Mystery."

The "Mystery" includes all that we still do not know of, our untapped potential, and how we are related to the larger unseen realities. Science helps us to make sense and comprehend a great deal about our nature, but so much is still part of the greater Mystery. We know far more today about how energy, consciousness and biology play together to create our uniquely human experience than we ever have, and this knowledge contributes significantly to the work we all do helping couples. But it is still insufficient to explain all that is occurring within the boundaries of a long term relationship. We can bring what we know from developmental psychology, anatomy, and neurobiology into our work with couples, but we still need to be open to the mystery of life, and to work within this field of uncertainty. This is where the artistry of couples work resides.

Nelson [22] tell us, "The transpersonal perspective views 'normal' consciousness as a necessary and useful, but defensively contracted, state of reduced awareness that enables the individual to live in a world but blinds him or her to greater spiritual potentials that lie beyond the ego or world-self." In a long term committed relationship partners will be challenged by each other to discover more and more of who they are and to transcend normal levels of consciousness. This can happen in a variety of ways such as through sexual encounters, conflict, life transitions, child-rearing, shared spiritual practices, and opening up to each other more and more over the years.

The committed relationship as an evolutionary practice means that, through the crucible of commitment to another human being, we are challenged to look deeply into ourselves and face all those places that we had to exile from awareness as children, and confront the vulnerable reality of our own limits. **Thus evolution is a continuing process of first defending the self as we have come to know it, and then surrendering to a deeper, broader consciousness of a newer self.** Emotions are central to this process. As Michael Kegan [20] writes, "I am suggesting that the source of our emotions is the . . . *experience of evolving*—defending, surrendering, and reconstructing a center."

In marriage, when a spouse confronts his partner with a strong reaction to her behavior (e.g. You can be so critical!) there is an affront to her self-image. She will most likely defend against his characterization and argue with him about whether he is right or wrong. Surrendering would involve the acceptance of a newer definition of self which, in this instance, would mean that the wife begins to see the truth of herself as someone who *can* be critical. This expanded definition of self is the evolution of consciousness that emerges through the tempest of emotions and the sometimes shocking reflection we see through our partner's judgments. The "ouch" that is felt when a partner challenges our dearly held self-characterization is the jolt of growth. Long term relationship in this regard might be described as an ongoing process of becoming more fully human—both more autonomous and more intimate, a process Kegan calls *interindividuation.*

Attachment theory opens us to the understanding that we are all energetically attuned to each other in ways that go beyond words. A child needs to *feel* the connection to the caregiver on a deep level in order to experience a safe world. The attunement between caregiver and child is not about how the parent acts, but about how she energetically relates to the child. Not about how often she picks him up, but whether she knows when he wants to be put down. It is not just about being accessible, but emotionally responsive. There is an inborn biological drive toward attachment that has children seeking out the caregiver whenever need or danger arises. **This attachment drive is still very alive among the couples you work with.**

According to Bowlby [(5)] and his colleagues, there are several major attachment styles. As you get to know them you will see how they influence the adult committed relationship. The first is "secure attachment" where the parent gives the child the secure sense of connection that allows her equal access to the impulse to explore when she feels safe and to seek solace in contact when she does not. Such children grow up to be more spontaneous and free of predictable rule-like thought patterns.

Second, is the "avoidant attachment" style. When the parent is energetically unavailable the child learns inhibition of emotional expression, aversion to physical contact, and an outward indifference to relationship, although internally he reveals a heightened sympathetic nervous activity. Such a child learns to stop crying upon separation and will actively avoid or ignore the parent upon return. But inwardly, his autonomic nervous system is in overdrive.

Third, is the "ambivalent attachment" style. This arises from a relationship where the parent is unpredictable in responding to the child, sometimes being available and often disappearing energetically, being caught up in her own emotional world. Such children have difficulty containing themselves, often getting demanding and clinging. This child is preoccupied with the whereabouts of the parent and even when she returns remains in a state of distress.

Lastly, is the "disorganized attachment" style. This is characterized by those relationships where the source of nurturance is also seen as the source of danger. When a parent is perceived as either harmful or is herself so fearful that the child senses danger in her presence, then he is caught between a rock and a very hard place being unable to approach or avoid what he both needs and fears. Such children display energetic patterns of chaotic responses, disorientation and trance-like expressions.

Finally, **multiplicity theory** helps us to perceive that there are various internal "parts" or sub-systems each playing an essential function. From a systems perspective nothing in the universe is autonomous. Everything is a part of something else. Even our sense of self can be viewed as have multiple internal "parts." The Internal Family Systems [(42)] model, as developed by Richard Schwartz, postulates an extensive array of sub-systems which are in perpetual interaction with each other. Schwartz writes, "Multiplicity transports us from the conception of the human mind as a single unit to seeing it as a system of interacting parts. This shift permits the same systems thinking that has been used to understand families, corporations, cultures, and societies to be applied to the psyche."

For our purposes in EMM, we find it is sometimes useful to have partners identify young, child parts which seem to be showing up when there are difficulties in the couple's interactions. Or, to name disowned or exiled parts that each person is only vaguely aware of, such as scared, greedy, cruel, playful or sexual parts. Also, to help them embody "protector' parts which can actually allow someone to bring out powerful self-affirming emotions that would otherwise be disavowed.

At our core, our essence, is a witness self, or higher self, which serves to integrate all the sub-selves. Often, emotions that would not otherwise be accessible are revealed and released when one can "give" the feeling to a part of oneself, while the higher self remains in control. So, for example, Carlos grew up with a raging father. He has disowned in himself any connection to his own anger. In one mentoring session he is trying vainly to suppress his hostility toward his partner Rose who was poking fun at him. When he is able to see that he has a *strong* "part" that is wanting to protect another *vulnerable* part from being ridiculed, as his dad often did, he could allow himself to actually stand up and express with power. This is what we call self-affirming anger. By witnessing these distinct parts he was more able to access a very important aspect of his emotional inner world.

One of the most valuable aspects of multiplicity theory is that it allows for the observing self to create enough distance from a highly charged emotional "part" to see it clearly. This is, in effect, the objective of all individuation—to craft enough distance so that one is not overtaken by an external or internal "other." This space between observer and observed can help one to, in John Welwood's [(49)] words, "find the right distance from a feeling." In other words, to be able to experience the feeling but without becoming "flooded" or in IFS language "blending" with a particular emotional part.

The two of us are dedicated to expanding the EMM approach to provide something to all couples who are working hard to keep their relationships radiant and evolving. We have chosen to use the term "approach" rather than "model" because our desire is to keep EMM flexible, evolving and non-exclusionary. In our view the term model conjures a sense of a fixed schema, whereas an approach suggests a "moving toward" without having arrived. The invitation to you, as therapist, is to discover more of yourself in your work. This means finding *your* creativity, leadership and capacity for entering the deep and wild experience of Mystery which is flourishing in every couple that crosses your threshold. We begin this exploration in Chapter One by describing what we mean by embodied couples work.

Lastly, you will notice that, at times, we refer to ourselves in the third person (Marcia and Brian) when we are describing our interventions during sessions. This seems to be the best way to convey with clarity what was occurring during these sessions.

Chapter One

Embodied Couples Work

For those unfamiliar with body-oriented psychotherapy, there is no great secret. What is happening in the client's body is central to the work. Attention is paid to the living reality of how the body protects against unwanted feelings and movements. The autonomic nervous system, the muscular-skeletal system, the limbic system, the respiratory system, and more are all vital realities that cannot be ignored in the therapy room.

Some models such as Hakomi and Somatic Experiencing focus more on subtle energetic expressions and help the client learn to attend to and work with such energies. Other models, including Bioenergetics and Core Energetics, work directly with more powerful energetic expression. The aim in these models is to use what is happening in the body to help the client transform trauma, depression, anxiety, and other problems which are now viewed as expressions of a psychosomatic unity. The work of Bessel van der Kolk in particular, has been groundbreaking in its focus on the somatic aspects of trauma.

Classic body-oriented psychotherapy deals with the ways in which early impulses are thwarted and leave the child with contracted, rigid and conflicted somatic states. For instance, a child is caught touching his genitals and is admonished and told to stop. The pleasurable sensations are immediately countered by an intense fear of parental negativity. The body quickly cuts off the pleasure and tightens the pelvis to stop the sensations. Over time the individual is left with conflicting internal realities.

The free flow of pleasure and arousal is greeted with contraction and inhibition of this energy.

Embodiment, in this regard, involves helping such a person to reclaim the pleasure in his pelvis and would be accomplished through working directly with releasing the contractions in the body through breath and movement. More recent approaches to embodied psychotherapy display somewhat less focus on muscular and respiratory release and more on developing greater consciousness of subtle internal experiences. Increased emphasis is placed on altering the body's non-productive responses to stress, trauma, and habitual emotional patterns which lead to unhappiness or difficulty functioning in life.

The embodied work we espouse here includes both subtle and more florid expression and release of emotions and energetic impulses. As you will learn later, embodiment goes beyond gaining greater awareness of what is happening from the neck down. It also includes assisting individuals to reclaim the open and sometimes riotous expression of a wide range of emotional potentialities. **Through embodiment we help people to cry more fully, laugh more deeply, vibrate more openly with both fear and pleasure, express aggression more cleanly, and encounter love, sexuality, passion, gratitude and creativity more directly.**

Sometimes it will even serve an individual to overwhelm her "observer self" and enter into the flow of emotional energy. Just as a child might cry robustly without a witnessing part, we have found that embodying an emotion fully may only occur when one is free of the obligation to stand back from it. As one person we worked with put it, "I am always so aware of what I am doing that I can't seem to ever let go." This does not mean we support unconscious emotional expulsion. On the contrary, it can be through fully embodied affective release that greater consciousness emerges.

Couples often seek counseling with a desire for answers that speak to their cognitive propensities. They want to know what is going on and what to do about it. This is the result of a lifetime's worth of enculturation into a world of logic, abstract thinking and action-oriented "solution-focused" consciousness. The underworld of murky emotions, taboo impulses and unclassifiable sensations is often foreign terrain. The tightly wrapped stories or narratives constitute the bulk of what they share with each other. Yet with most couples there is an often unarticulated longing for something deeper.

In EMM we redirect the focus of each partner's awareness toward their own lived experience. Transformation is largely a "bottom up" experience. The mentor brings a great deal of attention to energy that shows up in the form of emotions, sensations, impulses and through the buildup and release of tension. So much of what is occurring between partners is implicit or beneath the level of the conscious, linguistic neo-cortical brain. It is what Christopher Bollas [(4)] has called the "unthought known." Neural traffic flows "upward" from the limbic brain to the neo-cortex at a much greater rate that the reverse. As a result, John Nelson, M.D. tells us, "So the domain of reason can exert only limited power over its emotional forebears. This anatomical shortcoming corresponds to the troublesome human experience of having greater awareness of our fiery emotions than ability to control them through higher reason." [(29)] Emotions and implicit experiences are apt to dominate the landscape of the relationship far more than the intellect would care to believe.

Thus it is often a bit uncomfortable for couples new to this work to begin opening up to a different way of relating. It can feel awkward for partners to just look at each other, or to pay attention to their breathing, or to bring awareness to a rapidly tapping foot. **Most couples would rather just talk about themselves than inhabit themselves.** But as David Wallin aptly points out, "The pursuit of meaning may short-circuit the deepening of experience." [(47)]

As we suggested above, central to this body-oriented model is the concept that each person learns to hold back vital life energy (emotions, creativity, intuitions, curiosity, sexuality and playfulness) in order to accommodate to both familial and cultural influences. It is not simply our psychological development that has been stymied. Every one of us has also been conditioned to hold back our life-affirming, unhindered impulses toward connection, exploration, spontaneity, and the state of pure love. Thus we are helping couples to step fully into relationship and life, to discover what each of them is truly capable of.

Alexander Lowen, in his seminal book Bioenergetics [24] tells us, "The emphasis on the body includes sexuality . . . but it also includes the even more basic functions of breathing, moving, feeling and self-expression. A person who does not breathe deeply reduces the life of the body. If he doesn't move freely, he restricts the life of the body. If he doesn't feel fully, he narrows the life of his body. And if his self-expression is constricted, he limits the life of his body."

The embodied approach helps each person to both re-establish a direct connection to their innate capacities to express themselves fully, and to elicit the wisdom of the individual's evolving consciousness. Thus each one becomes more ***alive*** and ***aware***. The alive part occurs through three distinct pathways—physical movement, breath, and sound; all in the context of relationship. What this approach adds to the field is its clear emphasis on the open ***experience*** and ***expression*** of various somatic states and emotional correlates.

Going beyond the mindful awareness of interior states, or the verbalizing of emotional experience, embodied couples work supports and instructs partners on the active expression of a wide range of emotions. In the Core Energetics model Dr. John Pierrakos, M.D. [27] speaks of the twin dynamics of energy and consciousness. In the transpersonal world it is said that "energy flows and consciousness knows."

When we make space for couples to move and release tightly contracted emotions, new awarenesses will often emerge. For example, one partner unconsciously raises her hand, palm facing her partner, as she is responding to his complaint about her lack of affection. We ask her to make the hand gesture more pronounced. She then brings up her arm, like a traffic cop with a firm gesture that says "Stop!" As she does this for a minute or so, she becomes aware of a voice that declares "I won't let you control me!" By following the energy of her somatic expression (the hand gesture) she becomes more conscious of her resistance to being controlled. This opens a whole new arena of possibilities for this couple to explore.

In relationship, there is almost a universal need for couples to learn self-protective modes of interacting when differences arise, as they surely will. **The love of one's life is the most dangerous person on the planet.** As bizarre as it may sound, most couples live under a constant threat of potential abandonment and therefore learn to move into self-protective interactions when the smell of rejection is in the air.

We believe that it is sometimes necessary to help a spouse to experience the fullness of her self-protective emotion in her physicality, as a means to energetically soften the boundaries that have become firmly rooted over years. **Just as sex can soften boundaries between partners, so too can the open expression of sadness or anger.** And to get to sadness there needs to be ample space for the power of the more self-protective states (blame, demand, resistance) to be released. At the forefront of the EMM approach then is the capacity to experience and express the entire spectrum of human emotion. In EMM we refer to this as "Full Self Expression." You will be learning more about this in Chapter Seven.

Adapting the Core Energetics model and the work of Reich, Lowen, Stanley Keleman, Stephen Johnson, Ron Kurtz, Peter Levine, and others to a specific couples' approach proved challenging for us. Early on we discovered that with all the powerful body-oriented work clients may have done *individually*, it was not translating into better *relationships*. This was deeply disturbing to us and really forced us to confront what was missing. These body-oriented approaches were conceived as intra-personal models and by and large ignored the interpersonal world of the committed relationship.

The embodied approach we espouse here also draws from various treatment methodologies as well as other disciplines and philosophies, from shamanism to organizational development. In particular we have been influenced by Arnold Mindell's work on state and process consciousness, and group dynamics; David Schnarch and his notion of "self-validating intimacy"; Susan Johnson and her adaptation of attachment theory to couples work; Daniel Wile's couple's therapy; John Gray's Total Truth process, and many others. Ann Bradney's Radical Aliveness group work has also influenced our understanding of emotional freedom in the context of relationships. Additionally, we work with music, the arts, eastern philosophy, Bradford Keeney's contributions on opening to the ecstatic and more.

In EMM we place great value on both ends of the energetic spectrum—arousal and relaxation. In our opinion too little attention is paid to arousal in couples work and the result is often an over focus on awareness and gentle emotional expression. This is not what real relationships are like. Each individual needs to have room for both the sympathetic and the parasympathetic. As Bradford Keeney puts it, "The copresence of arousal and relaxation must be acknowledged when we speak of the self-regulating process of the human body, mind, and soul." [(19)]

In this chapter we will introduce you to critical aspects of embodied couples work. These are:

- The Shared Energy Field
- Mirroring and Entrainment
- Charge and Discharge
- Shaping
- Working with Shared Energy
- Objectives of the Embodied Approach

Shared Energy Field

A primary component of embodied couples work is the concept of a "shared energy field." (SEF) Simply put, two people in an intimate relationship become keenly attuned to each other's every nuance, with most of what gets exchanged occurring outside of consciousness awareness. When a couple arrives at your office there is a palpable energy exchange between them which results in their interacting in highly ritualized and restricted ways. They are largely unaware of this incredibly dynamic exchange of energy that is reverberating right there in your room and in every moment of their lives together. In a shared energy field each partner is continually resonating with the other in a perpetual dance of undetected emotional ebbs and flows.

While the analytic neo-cortical brain operates with a consciousness of linear cause and effect, the SEF displays a multi-directional causality. **There are numerous influences on**

any given interaction that go far beyond the narrow stories or "narratives" each spouse constructs. Transpersonal author Christian de Quincey writes, "There are just too many fine details, connected by too many complex relationships, for anyone person to hold it all in awareness using rational concepts. An intuitive element is always involved, aiding us in grasping the pattern as a whole." [(6)]

The SEF invites couples into an exciting new world of authenticity, emotional availability and profound intimacy. The reason that most of us resist change is that we have come to mistrust our instinct, impulses, and inarticulate emotions. We stay stuck in our controlled styles of interaction because the leading edge of change is always irrational. Once we try to intellectualize what troubles us we avoid stepping out into the netherworld of uncertainty. Yet this is precisely the place where couples need to go if they want to grow. "Analysis," as Irish author and scholar John O'Donohue points out, "is always subsequent to and parasitic on creativity." [(25)]

The SEF is also, to borrow psychologist Daniel Stern's [(44)] term, "polytemporal." It encompasses the influences of our history, the in-the-moment energy exchanges and the evocations of our future potentialities, that is, the higher self within each person striving to evolve. Past, present and emerging future enfolded into each moment. **What you witness in your office is usually two people discussing a present problem that is highly influenced by historical factors but is seeking and longing to reach toward a higher wisdom.** Though trapped in history, every moment has the potential for a "breakthrough" experience. In his book Theory U, C. Otto Scharmer suggests that there are two selves in each one of us. "One self is the person . . . we have become as a result of a journey that took place in the past. The other self is the person . . . we can become as we journey into the future. It is our highest future possibility." [(39)] In Core Energetics this is referred to as the Higher Self.

Take, for instance, Adrian and Maura. Each attempts to tell us their version of the story of their relationship struggle. As they both take turns describing in detail what the problem is (Adrian is reluctant to further commit to the relationship and Maura is pressuring him because her biological clock is ticking) neither is aware of what is occurring in the moment.

Maura leans forward with what can be described as a 'forcing current," where she is challenging Adrian and on the verge of overwhelming him with her intensity. Adrian grows more muted, in word and physical expression. She is unaware of how her intensity is received by him, and he is equally disconnected from the way his withdrawal triggers her. When Maura challenges him to explain his ambivalence, Adrian can only say "I'm not sure." He means this in two ways: "I'm not sure about moving forward with you" and "I'm not sure why I'm not sure about moving forward with you." Together, they co-create a dynamic of increasing frustration on her part and mounting contraction and confusion for him. Neither is aware of what is happening in the SEF.

Both Adrian and Maura are reacting, not only to the present issue, but from their respective histories. He is protecting himself from being controlled, and she is fighting valiantly to be received. These are patterns of response that each has brought into the relationship from previous times. In the SEF, his self-protective habit of withdrawal "triggers" her urgent need to persuade. Simultaneously, her forcing energy current "triggers" in him an almost instinctual withdrawal, like a hand that wants to pull away from a hot flame. Neither of them is aware of the wide range of feelings that exist concurrently not far below the surface. Just south of this pattern they engage in, lies a wellspring of various emotions. Fears, anger, needs, and hurts are all swirling simultaneously in the SEF. The task for the mentor is to elicit contact with these vital energies.

The concept of energy is often dismissed today as too vague and non-scientific from a therapeutic standpoint. In EMM, however, the notion of energetic expression is most useful. **We view energy as "movement" which manifests, through emotions, muscular-skeletal expression, the plasticity of the brain to form new neuropathways, limbic resonance, and the influences of all that surrounds us**. In our couples work the concept of energy is applied by working with all of the above. Couples "move" in this work. Our sessions invite a lively exchange of energy as voices get louder, bodies move and emotions surface.

In addition to what is occurring between a couple, the SEF is larger than the sum of each individual's contribution. In the EMM approach we perceive of a broader source of energy that is available to draw upon than either person's distinct biology. It appears that the energy each couple shares comes from *within* them, *between* them and even from *beyond* them as they are able to access from a larger energy field that encompasses all things. This mysterious force is sometimes referred to as "collective intelligence." The two of us like to refer to it as the "creative edge" or the space where each person can draw from the collective intelligence and discover something new and important about him or herself. The SEF is the *whole* being more than the sum of the parts.

Just as each person is a human being, the SEF can be viewed as a "relationship being." That is, partners are each individually humans ***being*** human, and together a relationship ***being*** a relationship. This relationship being is the source of wisdom that transcends either partner alone. It is the job of the mentor to trust and respect the wisdom that is available (though often bypassed) in the collective energy of the relationship. There is deep intuitive knowing that can be tapped into if the mentor can learn to support a more active flow between the pair. In any given mentoring session there are moments (sometimes brief) where one partner or the other has a spontaneous awareness or gut feeling. Trusting and following these is often the most important part of the session. Likewise, one person's somatic expression is often trying to share something even as her words are saying something else.

A couple we recently worked with was gridlocked in a hostile power struggle over money. He believed that she would never be happy with how much he made and she was angry at him for being consumed with work. He would beseech her with plaintive arguments about how hard he works to support her. We became aware that his arms cramped up every time he tried to convince her. His arms were offering a different story than the one he kept repeating with his words. So we suggested he stand a few feet away from her and reach out with his arms toward her. As he reached we invited him to try the words "I need you to accept me." As soon as he did this, a flood of emotions poured forth and he collapsed into her arms. The intelligence that was speaking through his arms offered us a direction, a creative edge, in which his understanding increased profoundly. The cramping up of his arms signaled a holding back of a need he could not let himself consciously feel. In reaching, he was able to feel, for the first time, how much he truly needed her. And until that moment, she had never felt important to him. She thought he only saw her as this "ungrateful bitch" that he had to take care of.

In this respect, embodied couples therapy works with what is happening on a somatic level, beneath the linguistic brain, and invites each partner to discover his or her, in Joseph Chilton Pearce's words, "original wisdom" which speaks loudly and forthrightly through the body. It also draws from the shared energy, the collective intelligence or what Pearce calls the "mind-at-large."

Energy is the lifeblood of relationship. **A mentor's job is, in one way or another, to get energy moving**. When couples come to you they will do everything possible to prevent energy from moving, at least outside of a familiar pattern of manageable energetic exchange. We refer to couple's restricted (and intelligently choreographed) energy exchange as a "Control Pattern" and we'll return to this later. But the heart of the work in EMM is to get energy activated.

Shared energy begins in our first relationship with our primary caregiver. Mother and child relate on such a primal sensual, experiential and energetic level that it is probably impossible, as adults, to once again experience the full extent of this. Communication prior to the advent of language in the child is sensate and sensual. The dialogue of taste, touch, sight, sound and smell is both intricate and intimate.

Even as mature conscious adults, we still operate with a very high-intensity energy exchange. We are more affected by the visceral than the vocal, but we are distracted by the seductive and lulling effect of speech. In addition to the distracting effects of language, early attachment and character styles prevent us from accessing the fullness of the shared energy field that exists with our partners.

Mirroring and Entrainment

Entrainment is the process of energy from two different sources moving toward synchronization or resonance (as when the vibration of one tuning fork "entrains" the other). Pearce writes, "Resonance [entrainment] is relationship and relationship, again, is all there is." [(33)] All relationships are defined by how two entities affect each other. From an attachment perspective, mother and child resonate in accordance with the mother's capacity to really **feel** her child. She can do all the right things, but have no resonance. Same with the couple who arrive at your office, they can learn to behave appropriately and yet still feel empty and disconnected.

In character theory, the child who senses his environment is dangerous entrains to a disorganized and frightening world. As an adult, he has great difficulty making any kind of energetic contact with his partner. The child who was abandoned is entrained, as an adult, to meet her own needs, or compulsively attempt to be "filled" by her partner. The one who was dominated and smothered entrains to submissiveness with his partner. One who felt betrayal learns to respond with caution and suspicion.

Take, for instance, Bert and Norma. They came to us after several years of gradual drifting apart, culminating in Norma leaving their bedroom and moving to another. She told us that Bert never even acknowledged her departure. She was astounded by this. Indeed, a main reason she left the bedroom was to "get a rise" out of him. Because Bert grew up in a chaotic and what he described as a "totally crazy" family, he displayed a disorganized attachment style and the characterology of someone who was born into danger. He said that he "lived in his head" and never really felt his body. He couldn't understand why people liked to dance and he was largely disinterested in sex.

There was tremendous dissonance in the energy between the two, Norma complaining all the time and Bert disappearing. This couple, like most couples, really long to connect, to feel a resonance, but struggle to find their way. Bert hides to protect himself from Norma's anger, and she criticizes him as a way not to feel her deep pain and fear of abandonment. Norma's pain and fear are the leftovers of a childhood replete with tragic losses in her family. Though they had done much therapy and were well aware of the effects of one another's history, they could not break the cycle—they were entrained energetically to respond as they have.

A simple goal we had with them over time was for Bert to get louder and Norma to get softer. His fear of being "crazy" like his family, had caused him to hold back his expressiveness. We had him dancing in one session, and invited him to complain about Norma's abandoning the bedroom in another. Norma explored telling Bert that she felt hurt when he disappeared rather than expressing judgment and bewilderment. She also experimented with being curious about where he would go when he checked out.

As couples learn to break from their habituated entrainments, the energy in the room enlivens. When two people learn to respond not to history, but to the actual person standing there, it is easy to feel the resonance in the SEF. To feel resonant energy in the room as a couple begins to feel each other more is truly a rewarding experience.

Another example of this is discussed above. Maura expresses an intense energy trying to persuade Adrian, and he responds by withdrawing. His impulse to withdraw and her urge to pressure him are unconscious ways they control against connecting to more raw emotion. If Adrian were cued into his inner experience he might say to Maura, "I'm feeling overwhelmed by your energy. Or, Maura could say "I'm feeling frustrated by your shutting down." This then could begin a movement toward resonance. Both of them bring into their relationship *tendencies* to respond as they do (withdrawal and persuasion) and neither is actually causing the other's response in spite of how they define it.

Our goal is not to get either partner to change, but to assist them in becoming more aware of how each is affected by the other. In the SEF, Adrian's withdrawal, for instance, is likely to alter Maura's energy which, in turn has a countervailing affect on him. As we will explore later in depth, the process of entrainment completes itself as a couple is able to utilize dissonant states as an impetus to open up to increasingly "softer" emotional truths. In doing so, they cultivate empathy rather than self protection.

Most of the time this process of entraining from dissonant, harsh and conflictual energies to more vulnerable and connected feelings becomes blocked by the couple's tendency to avoid disowned emotions. Instead the partnership creates ritualized, tightly formed modes of interacting (what we are calling a Control Pattern).

The natural process of entrainment in our culture is nearly always muted by a couple's control pattern. We have discovered that even highly sensitive people are likely to react to a partner's moods by enacting a control pattern rather than just staying with what is emerging is the SEF. For example, if Peter senses Annie is upset, he may be apt to avoid her or cajole her rather than letting himself feel how he is really affected. His primary emotional reaction to her upset is fear, but he responds in ways that cut off awareness of this fear. Instead of trying to change her, which is motivated by the fear he feels when he believes she is angry, we would help him to identify and experience in real time his primary feeling. This can then instigate a process of deepening resonance.

Just as a mother who is attuned to her child mirrors her baby's energetic expressions with exquisite resonance, couples can develop their innate capacities toward mirroring through the process of entrainment. **Mirroring is not the mimicking of another as an exact reflection, but rather the ability of one human being to attune to what another is expressing and to be directly affected by that person**. In a truly stunning example of the power of mirroring, Lewis, Amini and Lannon describe a research study; "Imagine a double video camera setup, in which mother and baby can see each other, but not face-to-face; each sees the other in their respective monitors. In real time, mother and infant look at each other, smile and laugh, and both are perfectly happy. If a baby sees a videotape of his mother's face instead of the real-time display, he quickly becomes distraught. It isn't just his mother's beaming countenance but her *synchrony* he requires—Their mutually responsive interaction. Restore his mother's face in real time to his TV monitor, and his contentment returns. Introduce a delay into the video circuit and the baby will again become distressed." [(24)]

True mirroring requires (to as great a degree as possible) affective responsiveness to another's immediate internal state—resonance. Ideally, one's response to another is unmediated by one's own history. However, a purely unmediated response is not the norm since we all "bring our baggage" into our interactions. So every couple you work with is, in effect, distressed like the baby in the study by not feeling in harmonious resonance with each other. Much of what show up as complaints, withdrawal, judgments, and other forms of acting out are really just more sophisticated ways of expressing distress. Both blame and withdrawal are forms of protest.

In our work with couples, we know that every interaction will be colored by history and the *narratives* that each person construes. (We will go into more detail about narratives later). We ask ourselves, "Is this partner reacting directly to the other or to her narrative of the other?" When one partner is reacting to the story he has constructed about his mate rather than to the present reality, it is again like the child seeing her mother on tape delay video—it creates distress. The partner does not "feel seen."

In the world in which we live, it is not possible to have a pure reaction to one's partner that is unmediated by one's narratives. Yet, the closer one can come to responding directly to the other's present subjective state, the greater potential for transformation. Responding primarily to one's narrative of the other, conversely, leads not to transformation but to self fulfilling prophecy, or as EMM mentor Barry Carl put it "self-fulfilling lunacy."

Much of what we do is to help the couple to move from their separate narratives and resulting dissonant states toward a greater capacity to experience an unmediated reaction to each other. So, for instance, Jesse is angry and critical toward Margot because he believes she is irresponsible with money (his narrative of her). She, in turn, is critical of him for being cheap (her narrative of him). Of course they could argue their respective narratives endlessly. Instead, we help them to feel more deeply into their direct experience of the other's blaming judgments. When partners are in a highly charged blame cycle they need a way to move through the charged up "protective" energy until they are ready to release into contact with what they feel *beneath* the blame. Margot's unmediated response to Jesse's hostility we learn is fear and hurt, but she quickly and deftly circumvents these unsavory emotions by firing back her own salvo of blame. Jesse's unmediated response is to feel the sting of shame and hurt at Margot's unflattering characterization of him.

Charge and Discharge

As couples begin to notice more acutely what is occurring in their bodies, they gradually can open to mirroring one another and to living more spontaneously. Mirroring is the end result of a gradual disintegration of control patterns which are designed to protect each partner's sense of self-integrity. In bioenergetics this is referred to as a process of *charge* and *discharge* of vital energies. Charge is experienced as mounting tension, discharge as relief. In the SEF of a relationship a couple is undergoing a continual building up and releasing of tension. This is their bodies' way of searching for contact, synchrony and ultimately a deeply felt sense of profound human connection. The two of us have come to see this state as what we would call love. Entrainment leads to love as a couple learns to mirror each other. They mirror each other when they learn to "feel each other." This then, is a primary objective in EMM, for partners to deeply feel both self and other—with acceptance and empathy.

Unfortunately, most couples actually drift away from their energetic ability to mirror each other and cut off from the moment-by-moment flow of vibrational exchanges. They tend to rely far too much on their explanatory capacities and the narratives which accompany this proclivity. Most couples seeking help are trapped in either unconscious enactments of their control patterns, or their cognitive descriptions of their woes.

The SEF is continually evoking multiple reactions between each partner, resulting in a very distinct style of interaction with each other that differs from how they relate to others. In the SEF energy is exchanged and held in ways that sustain a balance in the couples system (or the relationship being). So, for example, what one partner may *suppress,* the other is apt to *express*. So, going back to Adrian and Maura, as he suppresses his deeply felt resistance to being controlled, she expresses the charged up energy for both of them. She literally feels his resistance (which has a much higher charge to it than he lets on) and she can hardly contain herself. The more he learns to express his resistance outwardly the more likely it is that she will feel some relief. If, for example, Adrian could express, "I feel this big resistance and I want to run away" Maura will at least feel some relief by experiencing his truth. She could exhale and begin to feel what lies beneath her tendency to persuade Adrian.

Shaping

As partners entrain to each other's narratives, they are actually shaping one another's responses. This is so because over time each party learns to *anticipate* a particular reaction from the other when an interaction unfolds. The way one responds to a request, for example, will be shaped over time by how that person comes to predict the way the other will react back. In this way reactive cycles don't take place in real time, but are laced with behaviors that have modulated over a span of time—sometimes decades. So, for instance, if Chelsea asks Neal to empty the garbage and she anticipates annoyance from him, she becomes more inclined to have a hard "edge" when she asks. His response is then shaped by the tonality of her request. What comes first, his annoyed response or her hard edge? Each believes it all began with the other.

With Maura and Adrian, his withdrawal and contraction is shaped by his *anticipation* of her pressuring him. Adrian grew up in a family where he was often pressured to conform. Maura's intensity is shaped by her *expectation* that Adrian doesn't really want her. She learned early in life that she had to work hard to get any attention from her father.

The implications of this idea that partners shape each other's responses are significant. Both partners in a long term relationship are intimately involved in each other's personal evolution. Partners are deeply influenced by the shared energy field they create together. It is a misunderstanding, for instance, to believe that we marry our parent in order to heal our past. More accurately, we collude with our partners to evoke in them aspects of our parents which trigger us in specific ways. In other words, we don't magically find someone who is so remarkably similar to a parent, even though we didn't see it at the time. We bring out in our partner those qualities or traits which we project onto her. Through "projective identification" we mold our partner as she molds us.

Working with Shared Energy

Let's take a look at how shared energy reveals itself in a mentoring session. Brett and Carla seek help because Brett is questioning whether he wants to remain with Carla. The energy between them can best be described as cautious and calculated. In our third meeting Brett announces that he wants to let us know that he has been emotionally involved with another woman. He had revealed this to Carla before the mentoring session. She was noticeably unemotional about the betrayal. She said "I know I'm angry but I can't find the place in me where I want to throw dishes." They continued to discuss the situation in reasoned and polite tones. But as we poked a bit deeper there was a wild and turbulent undercurrent of intense energy that spoke of buried passions. In marrying, each of them chose a partner who was "safe" in certain ways. This allowed them to keep strong emotions at bay. Brett grew up with a violent and volatile father. Carla learned very early from her mother not to express upset. She recalls her mom frequently saying, "Leave and come back to me when you can talk rationally."

Together Carla and Brett learned to keep a tight grip on their emotional expressiveness. The constriction in their energy field was causing their love to atrophy. We asked Carla if she would be willing to find the place in her that *wanted* to throw dishes, and to release the energy into a foam cube. (We utilize such equipment to facilitate the physical expression of strong emotions which can never be adequately transformed by words alone.) Essentially, through the hitting of the cube, we were saying, "It is OK to let out some of that anger you feel at being betrayed." (Hitting a foam cube is also a more economical alternative than busting up the china.) As she began to move her body and hit the cube she declared, "I feel like I did when I was four years old." She said she hadn't allowed herself to be this "out of control" since that age. Yet, to us, she was still only cautiously moving her body.

At first, she liked being able to show some of her anger, but as she continued to explore this energy of "throwing dishes," her movements became even more stilted and mechanical. As we pointed this out to her we asked what she sensed her body was conveying by holding back. She stopped momentarily and turned her awareness inward. In short order she told us, "I know why I am pulling back. I don't want Brett to know that he can get to me." By tightening up, it was as if her body was conveying the message, "I'll never show you that you can cause me so much distress." As soon as she saw this, we could feel her energy release. She then said, "I also don't trust that Brett could handle my anger, so I am fearful of showing it."

So she was telling us that some of her anger was about the betrayal, and there was another layer connected to her belief that Brett was weak. In a sense, she was punishing him by not reacting strongly! We asked her then if she would be willing to take the risk to go back to the hitting, but with different words; "You don't want my feelings, then screw you, you'll get nothing!"

This time her energy came out with vitality and vehemence. She quickly saw that much of her anger was really at her mom who had demanded she be reasonable. Brett actually began to encourage her to hit the cube and bring out her anger. We could see both of them started to come more to life. She would never have felt the truth of the way she had chosen to withhold her emotions so deeply unless she had showed it to us through her body. The unspoken "energy dance" between them involved Carla never letting Brett know that he could affect her, and withholding her passion from him. For his part, Brett brought his needs and passion elsewhere, because he was afraid to tell her how upset he was about her dispassionate demeanor. Brett wanted to shake her up, but he was too afraid to confront her directly because of his fear of raging like his dad.

Thus, while the shared energy appeared flat and depressed on the surface there was a vibrant exchange going on just beneath the level of awareness. Brett wanted to believe he cheated on Carla because she wasn't emotionally available, but that linear thinking falls far short of the truth. **In a shared energy field there is no first cause.** There are multiple realities occurring simultaneously. Brett was concurrently bored with Carla's flatness, taking pleasure in provoking her with his expression of dissatisfaction, fearful of her rejection of him, resentful over her tendency to push to get her way, self-critical of the ways he gave into her, needy of her acceptance, and tender toward her innocence.

Meanwhile, Carla was deeply hurt by his affair, enraged at him for his judgments of her, blaming herself for sending him into the arms of another woman, fearful of his leaving, wanting to punish him by withholding her passion, longing for him to accept her as she is and admiring of his willingness to take risks.

As you can see, there are multiple emotional and cognitive realities occurring within each partner and, because they have not been identified, they create a complex interchange which knows no beginning and reaches no end. It is often so overwhelming that each partner is compelled to devise narrow explanations of what is happening between them.

As partners begin to embody their energy within the context of a mentoring session, a wellspring of awareness and awakenings begin to emerge. As you will learn more about later, there are energies waiting to emerge and your task as therapist is to be attuned to what is wanting to happen, that is, to the latent potential. When Carla realized that her holding back was deliberate she came more alive. The voice that said "you get nothing" came to the surface when she was given permission to embody her withholding, which she had learned long ago was taboo.

Objectives of the Embodied Approach

In EMM, the embodied approach has a number of key objectives.

1. Support each partner in becoming more aware of what is occurring somatically and energetically in the moment.

2. Normalize all inner states (memories, images, thoughts, feelings, and sensations.) Help each partner to accept that nothing is taboo.
3. Respect the dignity of each person in their need to protect themselves *and* in their desire to grow.
4. Help each partner to actually embody what her/his experience is as it wants to emerge.
5. Convey a deep sense of trust that each of the partners can "open" to powerful emotional states that were shut down early in life.
6. Support partners in deepening their awareness of the present moment and in conveying what is happening in simple, clear language.
7. Assist a partner in being able to receive the other's strong feelings and to see the value in making space for the emergence of such feelings.
8. Encourage the couple to loosen up the predictable, rigid and avoidance-oriented control patterns of interaction so that energy flows more openly and spontaneously.
9. Bring greater consciousness to the implicit memories that are held as somatic responses to present relationship interactions.
10. Serve as a "caring provocateur," or catalyst to help the couple release the stranglehold of their formalized interactions (control patterns) challenging them to bring forth forbidden or disavowed parts.
11. Support greater access to sexual energy that often constricts over the course of an extended relationship.
12. Help couples move from fear-based sympathetic nervous system reactivity to the expression of more tender and vulnerable states aligned more with the parasympathetic.
13. Ultimately, support the couple in opening up to positive (ecstatic) arousal in the form of expansive emotional states.

In our experience, nearly all couples are frightened by strong intense energies. Powerful emotions are withheld, sexuality is frequently inhibited, laughter is not fully released, pleasure of all sorts is kept in check, and need, longing and desire are swept away from awareness. The challenge in couples work is to help partners feel and express these energies.

Embodied couples work is ultimately an evolutionary model. It stresses that relationships can and need to evolve. We work with couples to help them achieve the "high-end" of intimate relationship. In this model couples can move from Eros to pure love. Along the way they must traverse the difficult times where they will struggle to release the hurts and control patterns stemming from childhood and confront the breaches to human attachment that make it so difficult to remain emotionally open.

Chapter Two

Key Concepts

The EMM approach as we have stated earlier is "experience driven." Consequently, we have no desire to load up either you or your clients with a more contemporary vocabulary to replace an older model of conceptualization. The thrust of this approach is to open up the therapeutic environment to follow a wisdom which transcends any particular cognitive construct. It seems that the more we learn about what makes psychotherapy effective, the clearer it becomes that the relationship is the agent of healing. **No techniques or lexicon can impact a client the way the experience of relationship can.**

It can be useful at times for couples to have a name for something that occurs between them in a way that helps them to have more self-compassion. Ultimately, however, growth occurs through a deeper connection to one's authentic self which results in trusting one's non-rational processes. This occurs most powerfully through the holding space of relationship.

With that recognition, we will devote this chapter to an explanation of a small number of concepts which will help you to comprehend the basics of this embodied couples approach. Much of the remainder of the book is dedicated to bringing this approach to life.

In this chapter we will identify and explore the following concepts as a theoretical framework for assisting couples to evolve:

- *The two basic human drives*

- *Primary restorative feelings*
- *Two levels of consciousness*
- *Control patterns*
- *Historic (childhood) needs and mature needs*

The two basic human drives

The forces that motivate us as human beings can be viewed as inherent drives. In classic psychodynamic drive theory humans were thought to be motivated exclusively by aggressive and sexual instincts. By and large, this depiction of what provokes us to action has been dismissed as either incomplete or erroneous. In the embodied/evolutionary approach, it is more fruitful to conceive of the human experience as encompassing two distinct motivations. We refer to these as: *The Self Preservation Drive* and the *Drive toward Full Self Expression*.

The Self Preservation Drive encompasses the energy and consciousness required to maintain ourselves physically and psychologically. The bulk of our lives are consumed in activities motivated to remain viable (having a roof overhead, making money, preparing food, etc.) Additionally, self preservation means protecting ourselves from harm, humiliation, loss of sense of self, and annihilation. What motivates us under the influence of self-preservation consciousness is fear of loss of self. All our decisions, actions, and interactions are colored by this fear. The energy of our will is the fuel which keeps us doing what we need to do to stay intact in body and mind.

Couples are often bogged down in "survival" patterns of relating to each other that binds them to what's familiar, cohesive, and safe. In large measure what prompts couples to seek help *is* this self preservation drive. Couples look for assistance when one or both partners feel threatened. As you have probably experienced more than once as a therapist, this sense of threat is palpable when new couples arrive at your door.

One of the primary reasons couples "fall out of love" is because so much of their lives begin to revolve around functionality. Love poems are replaced by laundry and sex partners become soccer moms. The stifling effects of a relationship mired in self-preservation are abundantly evident in every therapist's practice. When worry usurps wonder, relationships falter. Our task in helping couples is to place self preservation in its proper context within the long term committed relationship.

Trudi and Rufus came see us because they were constantly fighting about money. He acquiesced all the decision making to her and she complained bitterly about his not making enough to cover expenses. She paid all the bills and was chronically stressed out over the finances. Trudi spent more than they could afford and Rufus kept his mouth shut because, he declared, he "had no say."

Their sex life grounded to a halt and pleasure was a wistful memory. This couple was fully embedded in the self-preservation drive. Fear and anxiety ruled the day, and blame was their only strategy for coping. For them to transcend this deadlock, they needed to confront what was missing. For Trudi, this involved letting go of her tight grip on the finances and for Rufus it meant finding his authority. As we progress through this book, you will see how inadequate it would be in this situation to focus only on behavioral solutions. This couple needed to discover how to risk expressing other parts within themselves, beyond the fear-driven self-preservation energy.

In addition to the everyday type of self preservation consciousness, couples usually enter therapy frightened and hurt. When couples are threatened by each other they operate more from those parts of the brain that are oriented toward survival, most notably the amygdala. Their energy and consciousness are consumed with self-preservation. They cannot hear each other when the threat level is too high. As we will see, couples in self-preservation consciousness will have great difficulty listening to each other and not taking each other's words as a personal assault upon one another's integrity. There is high sympathetic arousal in the autonomic nervous system and the capacity to feel the more tender, connecting and expansive emotions is next to nil. Anger and fear trump compassion and need whenever one feels threatened.

Arnie and Jessica came to us on the verge of breaking up (or so they threatened.) Each of them came from severely inhospitable family backgrounds. Jessica was a highly emotional woman who often expressed her distress through tears. Arnie was critical of Jessica's emotional lability and with great regularity told her she should be medicated. She, conversely, was angry at Arnie and judgmental of him for being disorganized and floundering in his career. Both expressed exasperation about the other's condition. Historically, Arnie's mom would fall into long periods of despair and be completely absent as a mother. Jessica's dad was a cold and critical man. Energetically both Arnie and Jessica were protecting themselves from a deeply felt sense of threat of re-experiencing painful emotions that were still tightly held in their respective bodies. Each saw the other as a threat to their internal sense of control. It simply didn't seem safe for either of them to feel what lay beneath their anger and judgments.

In order for them to transform from a self-preservation mode of interaction to a more open and expressive one, they each needed to acquaint themselves with a primary emotion that was long ago paved over. Neither saw the other as safe, in large part because neither felt safe enough to actually experience their raw emotions of terror and hurt. **We open up to our capacity for full self expression when we make the very fundamental shift from seeing the threat as external, to an awareness of how frightening the potent energies feel within us.**

Life isn't just about avoiding catastrophe and creating safety, it also encompasses the grander urge toward fulfillment and exploration. It includes our curiosity, creativity, spontaneity, emotional expressiveness and sense of spiritual purpose and connection. This is what we refer to as the full self expression drive. Self preservation and full self expression contrast in the following ways.

Self Preservation	**Full Self Expression**
• Reactive	Creative
• Protective	Expansive
• Fear of "annihilation"	Longing for connection

• Pre-individuated	Greater sense of autonomy
• Fixed Imprinted (immature) needs	Mature adult need
• Habits	Spontaneity
• Physically oriented	More emotionally oriented
• Worry—"What if?"	Excitation—"I wonder"
• Control patterns dominate	Creativity & emotions dominate

The drive toward full self expression exists in all couples. Although many opt for staying safe, there is an undeniable urge in most committed partners (indeed in every one of us) toward expansion, creativity and spontaneous emotional expression. In the EMM approach we are consistently exploring the edge between safety and expression. Our goal in every session is to invite couples to take a risk to expose something beyond their self-preservation impulses.

From the perspective of attachment theory the more secure the attachment between child and caregiver, the greater the ease the child will feel in her exploration of the world beyond her "dual-unity." As Daniel Stern [(45)] describes it, "The nature of the infant's attachment to the parent (or other primary caregiver) will become internalized as a working model of attachment. If this model represents security, the baby will be able to explore the world and to separate and mature in a healthy way." Children with insecure attachment histories tend to remain energetically trapped in self-preservation while securely attached infants are more apt to move into the world as they grow with curiosity, spontaneity and emotional freedom.

What makes for an exceptional relationship is the mutual support for discovery, inquiry, risk-taking, adventurousness, and a willingness to occasionally jettison reason in favor of Mystery. The drive toward full self expression is the very real human urge toward self transcendence.

Primary restorative feelings

Emotions are fundamental to relationship. **Our aim in EMM is to support couples in claiming emotional freedom.** This means both reclaiming the childhood emotions that were lost as each person adapted to their unique circumstances *and* discovering the higher level capacities for empathy, remorse, gratitude, mature need, compassion, altruism, awe and pure love.

From very early on, children incorporate three primary "corrective" or "restorative" emotions. These are anger, fear, and sadness. Commonly described as negative emotions these three are actually vital to affirmative and healthy relationships. They are considered restorative because they serve two main functions. First, they signal us that something is amiss. Fear alerts us to danger, anger motivates us to protect ourselves, and sadness or hurt helps us to bridge any breach of relationship. It reminds us that someone else matters. Together they assist us in our quest to navigate the real-world friction between individuation and communion.

Second, the expression of anger, fear and sadness are the ways we cultivate an inner state of harmony. By releasing the energy of these three emotions, we will soon return to a more tranquil inner state—from sympathetic to parasympathetic states. When these feeling states are disavowed we become fragmented, chronically under stress, and cut off from an open, honest and spontaneous flow with our partners.

Each of us learns, in different ways, to put a lid on our primary restorative feelings in childhood. To have a full-bodied cry, to give vent to our natural aggression, or to let fear ripple through us becomes a distant reality. Most of us come to believe that these raw feelings are too intense so we clamp down on their expression. By doing so, however, we cheat ourselves of our very life-force. Consequently, we make it nearly impossible to fully engage our more expansive feelings.

In your work with couples you will find it extremely helpful to first ask yourself, "What primary feeling is this person holding back right now?" Because most partners regulate their primary feelings through physical armoring and patterns of behavior with each other, it is often helpful to them to learn to stick to these three basic descriptors: "I'm angry," "I'm afraid," "I'm hurt.". Nearly all couples tend to overcomplicate their inner world and struggle to fully experience what the basic emotion may be. In your couples work, you are apt to hear such phrases as:

"I feel that he disapproves of me."
"I'm confused."
"I feel abandoned."
"I feel your anger."
"I think . . ."
"I don't understand why . . ."
"I feel like it's pointless."

There are infinite variations of statements that veer the client away from the simple primary feeling. The task of the mentor is to help partners become more aware of basic emotions and to bring these into their communication with each other. When partners are able to make clear feeling statements during a session, there is an immediate change in the energy in the room. So, for example when one spouse shifts from, "I feel like you always take our son's side." To "I feel hurt when I think you are taking sides with our son against me," the energy between the two will shift. It helps the partner who is trying to express what is occurring to have the basic language of primary emotions and likewise, it helps the listening spouse to empathize with the internal world of his partner. Often, the dialogue will be about the outer circumstances (such as who is siding with whom) at the expense of the inner life. Content trumps process. As we begin to help couples open up to the inner world of feelings, deeper connection begins to occur.

As the therapist it will help you greatly to appreciate what feelings each partner has trouble experiencing. Often, Bollas' "unthought known" is one of the primary restorative feelings that a spouse simply doesn't see clearly. By helping him garner a language for the disowned inner life, he can begin to heal the wounding of childhood, as previously unacceptable emotional states are now openly received by his partner.

Don't hesitate to ask a spouse if she is feeling anger, fear, or hurt. The tendency for her to soft-pedal a primary feeling is routine. In an effort to make what she has to say more palatable the emotion is frequently expressed in vague, and neutralized language. For instance, she may say, "I'm a little disappointed that you didn't call." You can help her along by asking, "Does it hurt when he doesn't call?" This increases the vulnerability which is often an intimacy enhancer. Or a man might say "I just feel like giving up." To which you may inquire, "Are you angry at her for not listening?"

Two levels of consciousness

The work you do with couples, from assessing to intervening, always involves an interplay of two prevailing levels of consciousness. What are these two levels? First, our minds are trained to think in discreet, deductive, interpretive and causal patterns. This is called "state consciousness." Arnold Mindell refers to state consciousness as "consensual reality" [(28)], or that which is held as agreed upon truth. In state consciousness we think in abstraction from present experience. We develop and attach to stories about what we experience. This is also called our "narrative." Each partner in a relationship has his/her personal narrative about "the way things really are." Each brings to the session their narrative of childhood existence coupled with their marital narrative. In assessing the relationship, the narrative of each partner offers tremendous insight into where and why emotions and energy gets frozen.

Since we are meaning-making animals we are constantly striving to make sense out of our experiences. Life without understanding on this level would be overwhelming and chaotic. Narrative creates a sense of safety, order and control. You will notice with couples the urge to explain rather than experience what is happening. The explanation brings a sense of coherency to our freewheeling emotions. Yet, the tales we tell can easily be manipulated, our feelings, not so easily. As important as state consciousness is, it alone ultimately prevents partners from truly knowing each other. Its essence is conclusive and exclusive.

While we typically think that in everyday life we describe what we see, when it comes to state consciousness or narrative, as Reverend Michael Beckwith suggests, we *see* what we describe.

The second level of consciousness is referred to as "process" or flow. Process consciousness is, in Mindell's terms, "non-consensual reality." It involves entering into the immediate and unregulated flow of emotional and sensate energy that is perpetually occurring and shifting within and around us. This is, in part, what we have referred to as the "shared energy field." It is both the world within each of us as well as the one that exists all around us. Emotions, intuitions, mystical experiences and all non-rational subjective realities make up process consciousness. In state consciousness conflict arises out of attachment to narratives and an over-identification with one position or feeling state. Process consciousness opens couples to a wider reality of multiple emotional truths and a capacity to flow between seeming opposites.

One of the main goals in the EMM approach is to support couples in discovering the flow of emotion and sensations that allows them to make deeper levels of contact with each other. The non-consensual nature of process consciousness is that one's experience stands separate from fixed ideas and linear thinking. In state consciousness we fear conflict will somehow destroy us or our relationship. In process consciousness we need conflict to help us break through fixed ways of seeing and being.

Entering into process takes partners into an unpredictable expressive experience where narrow and restrictive state consciousness dissolves. Our edges are those places where state consciousness resists giving way to process. To accept process involves a need to surrender the restrictions of our narratives and make room for newer and deeper levels of consciousness. We are all resistant to shifting our narratives because they are indelibly bonded to our sense of who we are, and how the world operates. Much of the conflict in committed relationships arises from the disparate narratives of each partner and the stubborn refusal to see beyond their respective stories. Mindell says this, "It's normal to have a fixed identity in consensus reality, but this identity does not contain the totality of your relationship abilities." (26)

For example, Martin and Ruth are entangled in an argument about what went wrong around their Thanksgiving planning. Martin declares: "You said you made the reservation for the hotel last Wednesday, I heard you!" Ruth retorts "I did not, I explained to you that we needed to decide between the suite or the standard room." They go around and around getting progressively more entrenched in their narratives. We have two highly intelligent people who tell radically different versions of the same objective experience.

If we guide them away from state consciousness ("This is the way it is") and invite them to explore the world of process everything changes.

Marcia—"What is it like to hear Ruth so vehemently disagree with you Martin?"

Martin—"It makes me not trust her. It scares me."

Marcia—"Can you say more?"

Martin—"I'm afraid she will try to make this all my fault."

Marcia—"Keep staying with whatever is here."

Martin—"Well, she gets so adamant that I feel compelled to defend myself. I want to make her take responsibility. I think neither of us wants to be wrong, and it hurts when we make who's right and who's wrong bigger than our compassion."

Martin has shifted from the conclusiveness of state consciousness to a more non-linear flow of awarenesses and primary emotions. Ruth follows suit and ultimately both admit that they do not remember exactly how the conversation went and that it was not really what mattered anyway.

State consciousness is wedded to our brain's capacity for explicit memory. These are the very conscious rememberances of the past, from the sights and smells of grandma's house to where I left my wallet this morning. Explicit memory emerges from the brain's hypocampus. Our explicit memory, while malleable and susceptible to revision over time, is nonetheless very clear to us. Process consciousness, conversely, is betrothed to our implicit memory (or what we call "body memory") as well as our intuition.

In couples work it is crucial to have partners tell their stories but only with a movement back and forth between narrative and process. So a spouse may be talking about her partner as if she wasn't aware of his presence. By having her stop, breathe, and take him in, she moves away from narrative into process. This will subtly alter her continuing story.

The task of the mentor is to help each person begin to see that their stories are partial truths. As Susan Johnson [15] describes it, "Every way of seeing is also a way of not seeing." Even childhood memories are incomplete and to some degree distorted. What is important is to connect to what the story triggers within each person emotionally and experientially. Stories are often used to justify self-protecting stances against being too "vulnerable" and therefore need to be challenged, expanded, or understood as an incomplete truth.

When you help each partner to enter into process consciousness you are essentially guiding them into a state of mindfulness about their immediate experience. This is a crucial skill in learning to reclaim disowned emotions and in making genuine contact with each other. When you assist a partner in becoming more mindful of her immediate "felt" experiences you are, in essence, teaching that person to re-parent herself. Compassionate awareness is the need every child has of her real parent. So, for an individual to enter into the mindful flow of immediate experience is to give to herself that which she probably did not receive enough of in childhood. As couples learn to move together through the fluid reality of process consciousness, their energies entrain much as a securely attached parent and child have learned to do.

Some Key Points

1. All explicit memory is narrative. It is used to explain life and excludes a great deal.
2. Process consciousness includes "felt or implicit memories."
3. Much of what creates our narrative is a way to make meaning around intense feelings.

4. Process is ever-moving energy, narrative is static.
5. Narrative is wedded to safety and survival, while process is about full self expression.
6. As we will see shortly, in the early Eros Stage of a committed relationship there is a higher level of process consciousness, in the later Safety Stage there is much more state consciousness.
7. The Exceptional Marriage flows organically between the two levels of consciousness.

To reside in the world of our linguistic minds is to live in a detached way from our partners and indeed from ourselves. State consciousness leaves us highly susceptible to the creation of myths about our lives. We operate from a constricted worldview and sink ever so imperceptibly into life-denying habits and routines. Energetically, our bodies reflect the myths we have come to embrace like life jackets in a raging sea. To quote our earlier book, Going All The Way—The Heart and Soul of the Exceptional Marriage: (8)

> "Our bodies react strongly when exposed to a world that doesn't always take kindly to our intense childhood expressions. As we incorporate myths to help us manage our own intense reactions, we develop what is called "body armoring." We can view armoring as the physical instrument of our emotional constrictions. The myth reinforces the movement away from full emotional expression. The body then acts as if the myth is real.
>
> "Paul, for instance, tends to be exhausted frequently. He experiences his wife Joanne as very needy. His myth is that he cannot depend on others because they are too weak. As a result, his energy supply is often depleted and he tends to get sick. His body literally looks undernourished. Paul walks through life believing that he is on his own and that people either don't want to support him or are not capable of it. From this myth he lives a life deprived of adequate human support. His body, over the years, reflects that condition."

Energetically most couples resist letting go of hard won narratives. In the couples we have worked with we have detected some common narratives that radically affect the capacity for each partner to be open and alive.

- I'm a bad lover.
- He'll never understand me.
- All men cheat.
- She's just using me.
- I will be humiliated if I express my need.
- All he cares about is sex.
- Nothing is freely given—everything carries a price.
- You should always want to be together—otherwise you don't really care.
- Fighting is bad.
- You are just like my father (mother).
- You should know what I want without my having to ask.
- My impulses are evil.
- My father was perfect.

We could go on, but suffice it to say that each narrative constricts our spontaneity and vitality. To surrender into process consciousness is to challenge our prevailing beliefs and to be willing to inhabit our less predictable ebbs and flows of a more wide open energy field. Many narratives involve the belief that one has more control of life that one truly has. "If I was less demanding my dad wouldn't have drank so much." Or, "If I acted more sexy he wouldn't cheat on me." As children our narratives help up to manage emotions that could be otherwise overwhelming. Again to quote our earlier book: "Prior to the development of our myths, we confront head-on our unadulterated reactions to an unpredictable world. Myth [narrative], in essence, is our cognitive front line of defense. We diminish our own painful reactions to a world we have no control over by employing it."

Surrendering to process consciousness is to release the grip of the analytic mind and to bring what Mindell calls "second attention" to our immediate experience. In a mentoring session we ask Lily what she is aware of. She replies, "I see that Craig is looking like he doesn't want to be here." So we inquire "Are you aware of what happens to you when he looks that way?" This second attention is far more useful to Lily than the simple awareness that Craig looks disinterested. Her state consciousness takes the form of a belief that he doesn't want to be here with her. This is consistent with her firmly held, rock solid "knowing" that she is more interested in saving the relationship than he is. Everything she then experiences is sifted through the filter of this narrative. By bringing second attention to her immediate experience she can gradually begin to open up to that which the narrative serves to protect her from, which we soon learn is a deep terror of abandonment and rejection.

State consciousness struggles to offer an explanation to what is often inexplicable. Early breaches of secure attachment are frequently felt as a swirling chaotic somatic stew of sensations and proto-emotions. No wonder we learn to engage our rational mind in buttoning down these rogue internal states. In our work with couples we have come to realize that dropping into process or flow can sometimes lead backward to a re-experiencing of terror, rage, grief and profound need. Our work supports partners in building a container so that they can finally surrender to these powerful energies and not be controlled or overwhelmed by them.

In contrast to some other therapeutic approaches, our experience is that many individuals want to and are fully capable of moving through powerful pre-verbal emotions. Can people by re-traumatized? Yes, if the person is not held in safety. But when an individual is allowed to flow with energies that have long been disavowed and do so in the presence of a partner and a strong and sensitive therapist, profound transformation within the person and in the relationship occurs.

Often what "re-traumatizes" people is not the surfacing of intense emotional energy, but how these feelings are received. When they are met with fear, judgment, or an attempt to "fix" the problem the individual experiences a re-creation of earlier failures in attachment. **From a characterological perspective, the holding back of primary emotions anchors trauma in the body and leads to movement away from process consciousness.**

Character theory emphasizes the crucial role of the non-rational. It offers us a wider view of the profound responses to early development. In character theory we learn that the body holds a wisdom (a somatic mind as it were) which both predates and transcends reason. As Stanley Keleman suggests, "To be born one must have a body. To die one must give up his or her body. Our bodies are us as process, not us as thing. Structure is slowed down process." [(21)]

From a transpersonal perspective process consciousness allows for couples to move between past, present and emerging future potentialities. As Ken Wilber [(52)] suggests, evolution involves the *transcendence* and *inclusion* of all previous states. Thus we all possess the entire spectrum of evolution from inorganic matter all the way up the complexity ladder to a sublime consciousness of self.

Similarly we transcend and include all levels of human development, we have the infant, the five year old, the adolescent and the young adult alive inside of us. By opening up to feel what is beneath our armoring each of us is capable of experiencing the in-the-moment powerful emotional realities (both painful and pleasurable) of our earlier selves. In EMM we invite couples to surrender to process consciousness and to move with what is always available beyond the analytic mind. This can show up in a couple's session as a frightened child, rebellious teen, pragmatic adult, or wise elder. In process consciousness the couple learns to let go of fixed roles and confining narratives. It has been said that to let go is to lose your foothold temporarily. Not to let go is to lose your foothold forever.

A poem by Marcia captures this:

Wildly Unsure

I've been sleep walking down a hall,
Lined with the same old images,
For far too long.
Photos of phantoms beckon me to emulate,
Mocking me to mimic.
Every day the same hope of redemption.

Such safety in that daily ritual
That narrative of knowing.
Now, I am not unsure.
I am wildly sure of nothing.
My prayer faces the not yet known.
As life opens its bulging wallet
I'll be looking for the brightest colors
Not the ones whispering their worth,
But the ones that make me breathe and smile.
I am the wildly unsure
Waving my arms
Until the right bird lands.

Control patterns

In the beginning, the relationship feels exciting because one's partner is new and unknown. There is a sense of adventure and unpredictability that fills the relationship with what can be described as Eros. In a sense, we energetically lose control and allow ourselves to be swept away by the power of feeling so deeply connected.

Eventually, as the relationship evolves, partners begin to allow themselves to feel a need for each other. When this occurs, they become more and more important to one another. When need is experienced, relationship anxieties begin to surface and as a result, spouses resort to unconscious control patterns to reduce their anxieties. **We use the term control patterns to refer to the habitual efforts on the part of both people to influence and restrict the expression of emotions that are deemed too difficult to handle.** So, if one partner is fearful that he may lose his spouse to another man, instead of feeling the fear he may belittle her, or act as if she doesn't matter. This is his control pattern.

All control patterns allow partners to avoid the primary emotions that were not tolerated in childhood and the deep experience of need that the human condition calls forth in us. Further, as children make the shift from a life of seeking pleasure and comfort through contact and exploration, to a life of seeking validation and acceptance through performance and "should," their worlds change. When a child learns that gaining approval is necessary in order to feel secure, then control patterns are inevitable. The goal shifts from being an "alive self" to an "acceptable self."

The amygdala reacts to anything the self experiences as a possible threat to security well before the conscious mind can even come up with a suitable explanation. Hence, our tendency to avoid having to feel the emotions associated with the threat seems automatic, almost beyond our control. Only afterwards do we apply a justification to our actions. So, for instance, Lars has a propensity to get in his car and leave whenever Tricia brings up her desire to get married. This behavior of Lars is a control pattern which connects back to a deep fear of being smothered the way he was as a child. His rational mind kicks in and says "We talked about this last week, I don't have any more to say." But the reality is he never talks about what the thought of having a child brings up in him, nor his strong reaction to feeling controlled by Tricia.

Like all of us, Lars effectively seduces himself into believing his post hoc explanation of why he does what he does. And if you ask him what he feels when Tricia brings up the subject of marriage, he'll tell you he feels like leaving. Our control patterns evolve from the particular life circumstances each of us was exposed to. If we grew up in a dangerous home we'll incorporate different patterns then if we grew up in a neglectful home or an overbearing one. In all cases though we are reacting to a perceived threat on a very primal biological and neurological level and then we piggyback onto to this reaction our explicit justifications (state consciousness.) If we were to stop doing what we regularly do when our bodies begin to feel something uncomfortable we would then be touching our primary restorative feelings. For most of us this spells danger because we have long ago concluded such strong emotions would lead to even greater hazard.

Control pattern typically fall into one of two categories. We refer to these as passive and aggressive control patterns. Since the purpose of control patterns is to create affect regulation, how this is accomplished depends on the early experiences of attachment and character formation. Those who came from families where there were avoidant attachment problems and characterological adjustments to abandonment and deprivation, there is a greater likelihood of "deactivation" responses. Deactivation results in passive control patterns. Conversely, "hyperactivation" strategies, which are associated with ambivalent attachment histories and characterological adjustments to manipulative and controlling parenting styles, usually result in more active or aggressive control patterns.

Some examples of these two types of control patterns include:

Passive, dismissive patterns:

- *Giving in order to get: false generosity as a way to keep partner quiet*
- *Withdrawal, or literally avoiding one's partner*
- *Withholding: being unwilling to express your emotional fullness, both positive and negative, and particularly your need for connection*
- *Indecisiveness and ambivalence*
- *Guilt*
- *Distraction*
- *Acting weak or wounded*
- *Victimization*
- *Caretaking*
- *Trying hard to please*
- *Humor, smiling, false optimism*
- *Self flagellation*
- *Preemptive actions: doing or saying something as a way circumvent a spouses negative reactions (such as hiding junk food or getting off the computer when you hear your spouse nearby)*
- *Feigned worry or concern*
- *Using illness, exhaustion, injury, etc. to avoid intimacy*
- *Silent treatment*
- *Using spirituality to control against negativity*

- *Getting consumed with children, work, hobbies, extended families or any other relationship or activity that takes you away from intimacy with your partner.*
- *Sexual avoidance*

Aggressive patterns:

- *Yelling or insulting*
- *Using debate and reason to convince partner*
- *Overwhelming spouse with strong non-primary feelings (jealousy, blame, insecurity, etc.)*
- *Chronic demands for reassurance*
- *Psychoanalyzing partner*
- *Nagging*
- *Undermining partner's self esteem*
- *Bullying and intimidation*
- *Using sex to avoid conflict*
- *Making excessive demands on partner*
- *Blame and over focus on partner's shortcomings*
- *Criticism*
- *Affairs*
- *Emphasizing partners limitations in order to avoid how important she or he is*
- *Crying in order to manipulate the partner*
- *Lack of toleration of partner's differences*
- *Abusiveness*
- *Self centeredness*
- *Threatening*
- *Over control of partner's behavior*

A third category of control patterns exists among those who were raised in an environment where the parent was a bona fide threat. Such individuals can often display disorganized patterns of approach and avoidance that come from an inability to feel any authentic emotions other than terror. Such individuals often withdraw from a partner as well as themselves into dissociated states. The so-called borderline personality often exhibits this pattern of dissociating along with a noxious mixture of clinging, periods of hating and extreme judging of the spouse. In our work we have come to realize that even such profound reactions are engendered to ward off intolerable emotional/somatic realities.

In the shared energy field of a committed relationship each partner is continually activated by the other's subtle shifts in affect. One responds to the other in an interlocking display of behavioral reenactments each designed to curtail exposure to unwanted or exiled emotional states. Daniel Siegel [(44)] writes, "In these situations, a historical rut has created the opposite of resonance of states of mind: a cascade of emotional reflexes, and defensive distortions, locking a romantic pair into a series of mutually induced misunderstandings and misattunements. These repeated ruptures in connection are rarely repaired." In fact, they tend to be carried out with increasing regularity and with highly predictable outcomes. Even though the partners may say that they are reacting to each other to bring about change, the ingenuity of control patterns may be best expressed by paraphrasing an oft-repeated axiom; "The definition of a control pattern is repeating the same behavior and expecting the same result."

Siegel goes on to say, "Interlocking states strengthen earlier maladaptive self-organizational pathways . . . At one extreme, these ruts can be experienced as a sense of malaise or deadness, which each member of the pair may feel but may be unable to articulate; at the other extreme, these ruts may be filled with anxiety and a sense of intrusiveness and uncertainty." The former are more likely to be expressed as passive control patterns the latter as aggressive.

When working with couples it is useful to recognize whether they exhibit passive/aggressive, passive/passive, or aggressive/aggressive styles of controlling against unacceptable emotions. The patterns will be pervasive in the day to day life of the couple but will erupt into a more florid state when the relationship is distressed. In a typical distressed state, a couple may display a pattern where, for instance, she nags him about his lack of initiative around things that are important to her such as getting the kids in bed by a certain time. He exudes an attitude of "riding the storm" where he may try to get her to lighten up, or condescendingly invokes the fury-inducing "yes dear" attitude. This is a typical aggressive/passive control pattern.

Aggressive/aggressive patterns are characterized by escalating circuits of blame and accusation. Melody, for example, chides Byron about his inattention to things that need to get done around the house. Byron fires back about how inept Melody is with money. Their exchanges start out as bickering but often end up in warfare.

Passive/passive control patterns may often give the appearance of serenity and acceptance, at least to the untrained eye. But what lies beneath, what lurks in the dark shadows is a Molotov cocktail of resentment, judgment, and disdain. Joshua never outwardly complains about Danielle's lack of sexual desire. Danielle is resistant to expressing her dissatisfactions about Joshua lovemaking. Over time she develops a sense of disgust and he absorbs himself in internet porn. Each learns to withhold love from the other.

While control patterns are fundamentally employed to avoid disowned feelings, it is often the case that emotions are used as a component of the control pattern.

For example:

Anger used to intimidate
Sorrow used to neutralize
Tears used to manipulate
Love used to smother
Forgiveness used to avoid conflict

These are, of course, inauthentic emotions, or perhaps more accurately very small and safe slices of affective reality. They are not expressed to deepen the connection.

The reason control patterns become so intractable is because change is scary. To begin to reveal disowned and vulnerable feeling states is fraught with risk. When a partner forays into an expression of new and unfamiliar parts of herself she can be fearful of being humiliated by her spouse, she can be worried that she is "going crazy," she risks getting flooded with energy she doesn't trust she can handle and she may be concerned that to do so would de-stabilize the relationship. Thus the control patterns serve a vital function and to challenge them prematurely can bring about a serious disruption in the shared energy field.

Historical (childhood) needs and mature needs

One of the greatest sources of conflict for a couple arises from the confusion between needs that are left over from childhood and those that reflect the genuine adult need for connection. When a partner's early attachment experience was erratic or empty, the spouse becomes a surrogate object and together the couple plays out a decades old drama. David Wallin writes, "Throughout our lives we are prone to monitor the physical and emotional whereabouts—the accessibility and responsiveness—of those to whom we are most attached . . . attachment must be seen as an ongoing human need rather than a childlike dependency that we outgrow as we grow up." (48)

Confusion results however when one turns to another in a vain attempt to get what was lost in childhood. For instance, Carrie keeps looking to Malcolm to reassure her he will remain faithful. Her father had numerous affairs and her mother was perpetually consumed with his whereabouts. No matter how much Malcolm tries to assuage Carrie's worries he will never succeed because he would be slaying the wrong dragon. Our attachment needs as mature adults are of a different ilk. Carrie believes that Malcolm can somehow make her feel safe, but from what? In her narrative, if Malcolm remained fully devoted to her, all would be well.

In the shared energy field created between them however, Malcolm experiences both a desire to reassure her and a sense of being trapped. It is not his job, after all, to provide her with something that was lacking from her past. Her looking to him is a way for her to avoid feeling a very ancient dread that she absorbed from her mother. The entrainment to her mom's fear and hurt has become part of her own characterological internal landscape.

The historical need for undying faithfulness will never release her from the shackles of her deeply held fear. What April Benson, author of To Buy or Not to Buy, [3] suggested regarding material possessions is equally valid for historical needs, "You can never get enough of what you don't truly need." The mature need in this regard is to hear Malcolm's authentic reactions. If he were to tell her how much he wanted her to feel safe and yet how trapped he felt by her constant questioning a very real mature need would be satisfied.

Nearly all spouses will harbor expectations that their partner is somehow responsible for satisfying unmet childhood needs that can never really be fulfilled. These residues of insecure attachment are typically expressed as thinly veiled demands that our partner make up for what our parents failed to deliver.

Couples are largely unaware of the nature and strength of their childhood needs. They often do not even express them overtly. But the existence of such needs generates an insidious strain within the relationship that deprives each person of being able to fully see and love the other. Surrogate parenting one's partner is not equivalent to mature love. It is not one partner's duty to rescue the other from the dungeons of the past. The immature needs that are remnants of the past will trap us in preservation-based styles of relating.

As an example, if one spouse had a parent that was unpredictable and erratic, he may place a silent demand that his partner always by calm and available. The partner senses this and may either try to accommodate or act in ways to resist the subtle sense of being controlled. Even the most accommodating spouse however can never fully make up for the unmet childhood need.

Unspoken (and sometimes overtly expressed) childhood demands litter the terrain of most committed relationships. Even though our adult consciousness realizes the absurdity of these demands, we will still harbor resentments when they are not met.

Some typical examples of historical needs (demands) are:

"You should never criticize me."

"I want you to make lots of money so I never have to worry."

"You can never get sick."

"You have to make me feel attractive."

"Don't ever flirt with anyone else."

"I always need to know where you are."

"You must always take my side when there is a conflict with family or friends."

"Drop what you're doing anytime I call for you."

As you can see, the commonality among these demands is a certain childlike self centeredness or narcissism. There is, we believe, a universality to this dynamic. Even among those who were fortunate enough to come from a secure attachment environment there is still a childlike set of unreasonable expectations that each person holds toward a mate.

While childhood needs are remnants from an earlier time in life, genuine mature needs emerge from the awakening of the consciousness of ourselves as being deeply connected. With such an awareness we come to realize that our partner is a real person. She is not a satellite orbiting around us, tied to our gravitational field. It has been said that commitment is the realization that someone other than oneself is as real as we are. Mature need is felt as the desire for authenticity—to know and be known. It blossoms when we awaken to the genuine importance our partner's hold in our lives. In mature need we realize that our partner is vital to us not as a parent is to a child, but as one whole person to another. They are not here to make up for what mom or dad failed to deliver but as a source of honest human connection. It is highly courageous for couples to begin to acknowledge to each other, "You matter to me."

When couples are able to see each other in truth (neither idealizing nor demonizing) they are open to feel mature adult need. To allow yourself to experience the full-bodied, wholly conscious, undefended need for your partner is high up on the list of peak experiences. To feel, to express, to reveal the words "I need you," from the fullness of your heart and soul can transport you to the absolute highest levels of human experience. It can also leave you feeling quite vulnerable.

In our mentoring work we routinely see how partners will diminish each other in order to keep at bay the disquieting realization of one another's importance. Indeed every couple we know (ourselves included) concoct myriad ways of diminishing each other's significance. The way you dress, speak, wear your hair, leave the towel on the bathroom floor, floss in public, organize your stuff, laugh too loud . . . there is no shortage of possibilities for making you less important. It is truly hard to let your partner become central enough that you might have to feel the hurt of rejection. To be open enough to know he matters, grounded enough to want the truth (and to give the truth) are the basic ingredients of mature, adult need.

Further, it is likely that childhood needs emanate from the limbic system in the brain. Thus there is an emotional intensity behind them. This is typically overridden by the higher brain (neocortex) so that the awareness and expression of these early needs is kept in check. The more mature needs emerge from a brain that is conscious of the other as a separate individual and not as an object of transference.

A comparison of these two types of needs:

Childhood Needs	Adult Needs
• Hard	Soft
• Demanding	An awareness that it may not be met
• Survival-based	Intimacy-based
• Experienced as urgent	Experienced as important
• See partner in transference	See partner as equal
• "Or else . . ."	Willing to feel disappointment
• Underlying shame	Underlying vulnerability
• Impossible to meet	Can readily be met
• Regressive	Expansive
• Rigid	Spontaneous, fluid

Triggers

Every living soul dances back and forth between state and process consciousness, between explicit and implicit memory. The idea of living completely in the now is not only a fantasy, but if it were possible would result in turning our daily existence into an unmitigated train wreck. Without explicit memory you would look at you partner each day and say, "Who are *you*?" You would never know whether an apple is something to take a bite out of or run from in abject terror. Life would be experienced as an incoherent psychedelic trip. Explicit memory imbues us with a sense of identity, of continuity, of familiarity.

Yet is also true that we have novel experiences; that we are continually oscillating between the identifiable and the uncertain. We travel from our history to our unfolding, between our reason and our intuition. When couples are bogged down in a seemingly intractable conflict, there is always this concoction of history and the present moment. What one perceives in the other is a product of assimilating the present with what one has already experienced. The result is not objective reality but a conflating of what one sees and what one remembers. No couple escapes the blending of then with now. What is called transference in the therapy room is even more active in the living room.

Triggers are those evocative behaviors or words from one partner that bring forth an emotional reaction in the other which seems out of proportion to the "crime." Because emotions are indelibly linked to not only our explicit memories, but more significantly to our implicit, body memories, we react to our partners with our own unique blend of life experiences and present realities. As Lewis, Amini, and Lannon describe it, ". . . a particular emotion revives all memories of its prior instantiations. Every feeling (after the first) is a multilayered experience, only partly reflecting the present, sensory world. When an emotional chord is struck, it stirs to life past memories of the same feeling." (24)

When one partner explodes with anger, bursts into tears, becomes highly critical, freezes the other out, or pulls back in fear from physical contact, it is likely a trigger response. The artistry of couple's work involves the delicate embrace of history and immediacy. The strength of one partner's reaction to his mate's inquiring, "Why did you get home so late?" is intimately bonded to his early life experience of being hovered over, invaded, anxiously smothered or otherwise prevented from independent movement. It is also tied up with how his mate asks the question and what unspoken feeling state lies embedded within her inquiry. His fiery retort of "Leave me alone!" is his triggered reaction, collapsing his history of being controlled with the in-the-moment energy exchange with his inquisitive (or accusative) partner. When she cannot "let go" and insists they must talk about it, you can be sure she is triggered by her past. Sometimes we like to say to couples, "If it can't wait until tomorrow, you can be sure it's about yesterday."

In our mentoring work we have found it extremely useful to provide couples with a simple explanation of this phenomenon. Borrowing from what is often called the Pareto Principle which suggests that there is an 80/20% breakdown that shows up in a variety of ways (for example, 20% of the people do 80% of the work), we suggest that triggers can be looked at through this lens. We employ this Pareto, or 80/20% principle as a straightforward way of helping people to see that the strength of one partner's trigger reaction to something the other says or does has much more to do with his history than what is happening in the moment. As we have stated, we offer couples very little in the way of new vocabulary. We have learned that new language too often results in clever new methods of avoiding the emotional truth. But, many couples we work with adopt this simple notion of 80/20% to better comprehend their disproportionate reactions. We often will hear partners reference this idea by saying "I know that's my 80% history speaking."

In working with couples' present-day struggles, there is obviously a powerful connection between the buried primary feelings, personal narratives about why things are the way they are and the in-the-moment conflict. It can be tremendously helpful for the couple to understand that the past is of much greater influence on the conflict than whatever the present day issue is. We have found that this awareness helps couples to both look more carefully at each one's own history and also to be more willing to take ownership for the piece that is truthful in the other's complaint.

The actual percentages (80/20) are contrived and have no statistical verity. (In Imago work there is a similar understanding which shifts the percentages to 90/10%). These numbers are utilized to drive home a very practical (and oft overlooked) point. **Your spouse may be overreacting but she's also right!** When

Sonia berates Lane for his lack of initiative and tells him to put down his guitar and get a better job, he cringes inside. By our asking her to look at what it triggers for her when he's playing the guitar, she can connect the dots to her ne're-do-well stepfather. She has a big charge around this dynamic and underneath her scolding demeanor (aggressive control pattern) she is frightened that her new family will be left to languish in semi-poverty just as she experienced as a little girl. But it's not all her history, some of what she is reacting to belongs to Lane. By investing him with "20%" of the responsibility for Sonia's reaction he can neither dump the entire blame on stepdad nor take it all upon his shoulders. When he is granted immunity from taking the entire burden for Sonia's reactions he is better able to acknowledge the elements of truth in what she says about him.

By recognizing the dual influences of both history and husband on her reactions to his behavior: 1.Sonia is better able to see Lane more accurately and therefore more compassionately and 2. He is more receptive to hearing her and can actually use her mirroring to see the ways he is truly avoiding his fears of change. Otherwise, her attack may spur a trigger response in him resulting in an entrainment of strong self-protective emotional reverberations. Breaking the cycle of mutually triggering responses is one of the great challenges in couples work.

Chapter Three

The Evolution of Relationship

The longer the two of us have lived together, the more apparent it has become that the committed relationship actually goes through many "marriages." Each marriage brings us to a higher level of self awareness, maturity, and intimacy. Within every relationship lies a latent potential for higher echelons of consciousness and deeper layers of intimacy with self and mate. The urge to evolve as a couple is evident in every relationship we have ever worked with. Even when a partnership seems hopelessly ensnared in a "spin cycle" of self-protective enactments of blame and avoidance, there remains a dormant longing to heal and grow.

There may seem to be an intense resistance to change in most relationships, but this is merely one aspect of a normal evolutionary cycle. Every one of us, no matter how secure our childhood was, is frightened by growth. Because growth involves breaking through the familiar and the conditioned into the uncertainty of the yet-to-be-experienced, we all naturally resist. Evolution involves the dissolution of progressive levels of self identity.

Committed relationship provides the ideal environment for each person to transform from a static identity to a fully alive, creative and spontaneous self. In our work we have seen couples who have immersed themselves in spiritual practices, meditation disciplines, intensive workshops, yoga, and various models of couple's therapy, but they still don't know how to come alive with each other. Our desire is to help them utilize the relationship as their vehicle of transformation. That is, to awaken to the richness of each enlivened moment which then opens the portal to creativity and self-leadership.

Nearly all problems couples present with can be traced back to this fear of change. Even when two people show up at your office declaring that something needs to change, it usually means, "I want you to modify my spouse so I don't have to change." Fierce arguments and icy chasms often are manufactured in order to avoid real growth. But through it all remains the undeniable impulse to emerge from the security of the familiar into the bright light of a new way of being.

Individuals are drawn together in commitment in order to fulfill life's great requirements. These are, to reclaim our capacity to feel that which we lost through the trials and tribulations of childhood; to open to the abundant pleasures of life in each moment; to know love as a full-bodied experience; and to allow love to be our launching pad into creative leadership.

Relationships are forged in order to discover or rediscover love. The infant who is lucky enough to have an attuned parent knows love. He knows the exquisite experience of two bodies in perfect synchrony, of complete and total surrender, of knowing beyond thought that he is connected, that he is not alone. As adults, this love can be embraced. It is within the reach of couples who, through the power of relationship, choose to face all that gets in love's way. The relationship offers the hope of healing the wounds of insecure attachment, and the enduring characterological effects of abandonment, control, betrayal, or danger. Though it is no minor undertaking, we are more than capable of rising beyond our habits of the heart and firmly entrenched neuropathways of the brain. Through relationship we have a second chance to become creatures of love.

When a couple tells us they have come because they have problems communicating, they are saying, "Help us find our way to love." Whatever the acknowledged problem, the unspoken longing is to drop into ardor's warm embrace. Therapists who adhere to clinical models which focus too exclusively on problem solving, miss the profound opportunity to help couples go where they truly want to go.

Love is not even the ultimate aspiration. Through love we can open to our creative and altruistic capacities. **That is, love allows us the freedom and invites the motivation to bring our gifts to the world**. Much of depression, despair and ennui are the results of living in misalignment with one's best qualities. When relationships are bogged down in self preservation, there is no space to evolve, no air to nourish each person's highest self. An exceptional relationship is one that strives toward creative leadership.

The EMM approach recognizes that relationships evolve. They begin in the high powered, neurochemically infused phase of enchantment. In EMM we call this the Eros Stage. It is followed, as sure as Sullivan follows Gilbert, by a lasting period of settling in, or "nesting." This is a time where relationships are driven by security and belongingness needs. We call this period which follows Eros the Security Stage. Subsequently, at some point in many relationships security cannot be maintained by the habits and control patterns the couple has established so they enter in a time of uncertainty and dissatisfaction with the status quo. We refer to this as the Transition Stage.

As a couple navigates through each evolutionary advance there is a natural shifting or rebalancing which needs to occur. Ultimately what the couple is challenged with during a period of transition is to transcend the previous stage and to enter into a new and expanded relationship. Robert Kegan [(20)] writes, "The hallmark of every rebalancing is that the past, which may during transition be repudiated, is not finally rejected but reappropriated." Thus, if a relationship fully confronts what is being asked of it from the challenging time of uncertainty and transition, they move toward a newer type of partnership that we have come to call the Exceptional Relationship. In this stage the couple transcends the immaturity of Eros and the limits of Security and enters into an open-ended and ever-evolving shared life experience which marries both Eros and Security.

Our work with couples supports this evolutionary unfolding. While some couples seek help to address a specific concern and may not wish to look any further, in our experience most couples want more. Even though they may not name it at the outset, many are longing to find something that they may have touched during the Eros Stage, or perhaps implicitly remember from childhood.

The remainder of this chapter is devoted to an exposition of these four stages of an evolving relationship and what it means to your work with couples.

The Eros Stage

In EMM we chose to call this first stage of relationship Eros, because the word captures the spirit of this magical time. Eros is not merely infatuation or romance, it catapults two people into non-ordinary states of consciousness. It is the elixir of life—love potion # 9. Under its spell we glimpse into the world of secure attachment, energetic freedom, interpersonal attunement, and a transpersonal experience of being complete. In Plato's words Eros, ". . . expresses itself in the sexual instinct but at higher levels impels the philosopher's passion for intellectual beauty and wisdom, and culminates in the mystical vision of the eternal, the ultimate source of all beauty." For Ken Wilber [(51)], Eros is "the drive that takes you beyond yourself."

"Falling in love" is the uniquely human proclivity toward deep connection and the (at least momentary) willingness to let go of protocol and inhabit our foolishness. We become soft, pliable, yet daring and outrageous. We will share a single bed, write sonnets, conjure up adoring appellations for one another, divulge our innermost secrets, feed each other, adorn ourselves with rose colored glasses as we gaze at the Venus or Adonis who stands before us, and laugh more deeply than we have in a year of Sundays. This is the stuff of Eros.

Neurochemical infusions of norepinephrine and dopamine catapult lovers into a passionate new world of wonder and enchantment. Research suggests that first loves leave such an indelible imprint upon the human heart that all subsequent relationships fall under its broad shadow. Additionally, our true first love, the undefended connection to mother or father, is also heralded when we open to an adult erotic connection. Eros approaches that fully embodied primal occurrence of unfettered emotional resonance that existed for many a child. No wonder the new lover is often believed to be a soul mate.

Partners in Eros encounter (or re-encounter) the experience of secure attachment. They feel the intersubjective sense of being known, they feel *felt*. And it is powerful. Though it will wane quickly enough, it's a potent and addictive experience to be sure. The rude awakening of the loss of Eros sends many a soul on a lifelong journey to recapture its compelling beauty.

It is the rare couple that bangs on the therapy door seeking help during the Eros Stage. More often, the partners are convinced they have discovered the secret to true love and know far more than any therapist could possibly know. And, in a sense, they are right. There is a knowing that emerges from breaking through the intellect. It is a surety that confounds the rational mind. The limbic resonance of two lovers and the entrainment of their energetic systems allow them access to the inner sanctums of the loving heart. All is right with the world.

When the two of us have occasion to work with a couple in Eros (typically in workshops) we are usually frustrated in our effort to be of any use to them. There is a fierce resistance to even touching on the tiny annoyances and vaguely troubling aspects of their perfect union. While Eros brings deep connection it does not liberate a couple from the confines of their control patterns. Indeed, part of the attraction is the neurologically triggered sense of familiarity. They are attracted to that which speaks to the brain's well-established neuropathways.

For example, Wendell is drawn magnetically to the demure female. His partner Kelly is taken by a man who can dazzle her with his grasp of information and his searing intellect. The control patterns each has developed are part of the fabric of attraction. Kelly uses her gentility to avoid her primary emotions while Wendell deftly rationalizes and justifies his own unacceptable feelings. That which attracted them in the beginning eventually becomes the source of annoyance and even disdain. This is because Kelly remains demure when they both need her power, and Wendell sticks to his reasoning when they could really use his vulnerability. We all are held back by the iterations of our programmed minds and our energetic constrictions. Eventually these relational styles or control patterns dominate the power of Eros, and it begins to recede.

Eros fades as time passes. Its departure coincides with a sea change in the nature of the now established relationship. The couple, without any conscious volition, segues into the second stage.

The Security Stage

If Eros is designed to awaken us to love's possibilities, the Security Stage provides a committed couple the tranquility of a safe haven. Where Eros is electric, the Security Stage is grounding. Eros is Mozart, Security is Yanni. This is a necessary development in the sustained relationship. Eros is so highly charged that it is untenable as a permanent state of being. As couples begin to entertain the notion of deeper commitment, there is a natural toning down of passion. While in the Eros Stage a couple's life beyond the relationship fades into triviality. The immediacy of the precious moment is all that matters. Couples are motivated by sexuality in harmony with heart. In the Security Stage dopamine and norepinephrine levels diminish and oxytocin elevates. This shifts the focus from passion to nesting, from groping to cuddling.

In the Security Stage there is more of a focus on the future. Once partners begin to seriously entertain the possibility of long term commitment there is more at stake. As they start to allow the other to become more significant they begin to feel more vulnerable. Letting somebody matter holds the divine paradox of allowing one to feel both safer and more vulnerable. We feel safe when we are not alone, we feel danger at the prospect of being abandoned. Thus in the Security Stage we nest and we fear being tossed from the nest by our beloved.

In this stage mates begin to return to more familiar patterns of relating. Quiet ones who came out of their shell in Eros return to quiescence. Boisterous ones who revealed a more tender side start becoming more controlling. Remember that what we are controlling through our control patterns are the feelings that were deemed too risky by our early environment and because we ourselves had not yet developed the capacity for self soothing. So instead we tell jokes to keep disquieting feelings at bay, or we find ways to put down our partner so as not to feel the vulnerable places of our own need.

In The EMM approach we conceive of a process where a child moves from a pure state of undefended love to the establishment of highly conforming behaviors that allow the child to live in her world. It looks like this:

1. The child (under benign circumstances) is born into a world where she is innocent and undefended. Here she immediately begins the process of attachment with a caregiver.
2. This highly charged experience of communion with another provides the child with the capacity to fully be and become, that is to both feel whole and to evolve.
3. At some point, the child becomes aware of the separation of caregiver and self. She begins for the first time to experience the sense of need for other. This deep reality of need is fundamental to our humanity, but for many of us it is rapidly suppressed.
4. Unmet need evokes the primary restorative emotions of anger, fear, and hurt. There is the universal experience of vigorous protest, when the caregiver is unavailable for the child to move through the discomfort of an unmet need. If the caregiver continues to be unavailable the child will eventually exhaust the protest and, feeling the pain of the loss of contact, collapse into a state of despair. Eventually the child reorganizes her inner world to adapt to the new reality of unmet needs. The primary restorative feelings are pushed down and replaced with habits of interacting that are designed to both adjust to a more sober relationship with the caregiver and to keep the strong emotions out of awareness. These behaviors are the control patterns.

One of the goals of the EMM approach is to, in a sense, reverse this process. That is, to help couples move through their ritualized habits of relating, which really take hold in this second stage, and to move back through a reconnection to primary emotions that are avoided in their interactions with one another. As couples begin to bring their anger, hurt and fear more to the forefront, a door is opened to both their historical needs as well as their mature need. This ability to touch the strength of our human need is so crucial to our humanity that it is impossible to fully open to love without it. You may become the most enlightened being on the planet through decades of meditation and inner exploration, but, in our estimation, you cannot fully feel love without knowing how deeply you need.

Entering fully into the felt awareness of need is incredibly vulnerable, and vigorously avoided. Couples in the Security Stage will find it most difficult to connect to mature need without first opening up to their primary feelings. What we have learned in our mentoring work is that it is often necessary to allow partners to embody their resistance to feeling hurt, fear or anger, and underneath, their need. The process of personal evolution always consists of a resistance to change. **This is a hallmark of the Security Stage, the couple narrowing their repertoire of interaction in hopes of protecting a fragile norm.** Each person simultaneously wanting the other to "improve" while creating rituals of engagement guaranteed to maintain the status quo. We often see this play out sexually, for instance, as one partner complains about the other's lack of sexuality while acting in ways to make the other feel anything but sexy.

The resistance to growth is best dealt with by acknowledging it as a reality. Instead of "resisting the resistance" we will have couples feel it, own it and express it—name it, claim it and aim it. So, for example, Libby is constantly after Theo to get him to do special things for her. She wants to be treated as she remembered her father treating her when she was five. Unfortunately, by age 6, dad withdrew his affection leaving her deeply wounded and rejected.

In one session we had her first embody her historical need. Standing and stomping, she was invited to shout: "I want you to treat me like a queen. It's your job to make me feel special!" This type of intervention begs the question from conventionally trained couples' therapists, "Why would you have a partner express such irrational demands?" All we are doing is offering a person space to express an energy that exists as an undercurrent in the shared energy field. Without saying it directly Libby is energetically shouting: "I need you to keep proving to me I am everything to you!" These early historical demands to receive something we either got and lost in childhood, or never had at all, weigh heavily on the present reality in a couple's interactions, and it nearly always feels liberating to express them with zest. While it may sound as if we are behaviorally programming Libby, nothing could be further from the truth. If we invite someone to try on a certain expression or statement it only shifts something in the shared energy field if it feels true to the individual. This is a process we call "catalyzing" which we will detail later.

Once Libby was able to openly express her implicit demands she discovered how much she did not want to feel the pain of her dad's rejection. For a little girl who was the apple of her hero's eye, the original pain was monumental. Yet in order to heal and grow she needed to surrender into the long denied hurt. Libby first needed to be supported in her resistance to the pain of her abandonment. The words that poured forth were, "I won't ever feel hurt again!"

By embodying both her historical need and her resistance to feeling, Libby could gradually begin to relax the constant pressure she felt which protected her from emotions which she believed she could not tolerate. What the two of us have learned is that people need to fully feel their resistance before they are ready to release it. The precise reason for this remains a mystery, but that does not make it any less true. It appears that, as people can express out loud their resistance to feeling (and move their bodies in ways that are consistent with what is being expressed), they are freed up to feel again that which was cut off so long ago.

In body-oriented therapy this process is referred to as "charge and discharge." Resistance is building a charge which eventually results in a surrendering into a more vulnerable space or discharge. Hence, a major task in the mentoring process for couples in the Security Stage is to give them plenty of room to feel their resistance to change.

It is essential to note here that none of us heal and grow in a vacuum. The evolutionary process occurs in an open energetic system which includes the therapist and the spouse. Robert Kegan, [20] discussing Piaget's developmental vision suggests that ". . . it does not place an energy system within us so much as it places us in a single energy system of all living things." Without the *felt* support of the larger energy field Libby could not, on her own, open to her struggle to reclaim her pain and her longing. Unless Theo was able to "be with" her as she brought forth her demands, her resistance, and finally her deep hurt, she could not have travelled there. Theo, for his part is much more available to hear and to open his heart to Libby, when he *gets* that it is not all about him. He then is more willing to take ownership for the ways he actually does reject her. The couple has effectively moved beyond their control pattern expressed through her nagging and his indifference.

People remain in the Security Stage often for decades precisely because change and growth is difficult and frightening. They come to therapy during this stage, to fix something specific—and most often that means their mate. So as therapist you are often asked to moderate their antipodal positions on whatever issue they are there to work on. Couples become transfixed between the very real but difficult to articulate longing for deeper connection and the formidable resistance to relinquishing "the devil they know." To abandon the control pattern is to move through blame, avoidance, and a stubborn definition of self. To break free of the bondage of one's well-defined self, one must feel emotions that are damned hard to tolerate and discover an embryonic new self that can only emerge from a heart that welcomes everything.

In the Security Stage there is either the unremitting use of aggressive control patterns: complaints, exasperated eye rolling, put downs, flaccid threats of divorce, litanies of prior transgressions, choruses of "if onlys," monumental efforts to find the next best therapy, and surgical use of insults. Or, there is a gamut of passive control patterns: getting lost in cyberspace, creative use of placating behaviors, preemptive apologies, damage control gift-giving, strategic employment of humor, and going through the motions with a thinly veiled disdain.

These passive and aggressive patterns are invoked with a genuine intent of either trying to make things better, or preventing a mess. Yet the undergirding is fear of feeling and resistance to change. As a parent guides the child to know and accept his feelings, so the therapist can support the couple in bringing more emotion to their lives. Getting to the primary emotions is a major accomplishment in couple's therapy. Most therapies tend to pathologize the expression of the protective energies of the control patterns. In EMM, we have found it highly beneficial to both contextualize and make space for the expression of what looks like unproductive reactions. **Blame, withdrawal, demand, even cruelty need not only to be placed in an appropriate context so that each partner understands why they do, think and react as they do, but also to be released from the energetic field of the relationship.**

For instance, in a mentoring session, we ask Gordon not just to talk about how he withdraws affection from Bonnie, but to embody it. We ask Bonnie to pursue Gordon seeking connection and affection. Gordon folds his arms, turns his back and walks away. By enacting this simple scenario they both begin to connect to emotions which were not accessible when they merely discussed the pattern.

For Gordon, who viewed his withdrawal as protection from being criticized by Bonnie, by embodying his response he suddenly realized that he also was "getting her back" for all the ways he felt rejected by her. For Bonnie, she began to feel a deeper sense of desperation when Gordon was cold, which led to her becoming more and more demanding. By making space for her *demanding* and his *withdrawing* they both could "drop deeper" in feeling states they were heretofore unaware of.

When couples remain ensnared in their control patterns, each partner will slowly build a **negative narrative** of the other. Negative narratives are highly noxious to the long term potential of the committed relationship. They consist of the internally accumulated assertions of a mate's most unflattering qualities which coalesce, over time, into a fixed perception. He begins to see her as a "whining, irrational, insecure, gold-digging brat." She views him as an "emotionless, arrogant, smarmy, buzz-kill." If the relationship deteriorates far enough, each begins to selectively ignore all the parts of the other that cannot be squared with the negative narrative. When the heart shuts down, the mind demands a justification. Instead of connecting to the hurt of a particular situation, it becomes easier to turn the other into a caricature. Maybe David Schnarch said it best; "It's easier to live with a pain in the ass than a pain in the heart." Negative narratives are anathema to seeing the Mystery in the other.

There comes a time in many relationships where the uneasy peace of the Security Stage begins to buckle under the weight of stagnation. Negative narratives, control patterns, and the often tenacious avoidance of constructive conflict engagement muzzles the vitality of the partnership. The contract to remain the same no longer satisfies one or both partners. The unmet longing for evolution, for fulfillment, begins to break through. Hold onto you hats when the couple enters the third stage of relationship evolution—Transition.

The Transition Stage

Rabbi Abraham Heschel once said that, "Only those who are lost will find the Promised Land." The Transition Stage as an evolutionary imperative might use this as its tagline. Security as the highest aspiration leads couples astray, wandering for 40 years in a desert of their own making. Embedded in their control patterns, each person slowly slips into repetitive behaviors and increasingly restrictive definitions of self and mate.

The two of us refer to this third stage as the ***crisis of transition***, for it threatens the very foundation of commitment. As a couple begins to feel the pull toward something greater than security, there is a seismic disruption in the status quo. The prospect of continuing along as they have for so many years causes one or both partners to awaken from their secure slumber.

In his landmark book The Evolving Self, [(20)] Kegan argues that every phase of evolution is characterized by a transition between one stage and the next. The transition period creates an emergency which only resolves when one emerges from an earlier stage into a new world that was heretofore unavailable to him. As Kegan says, "Any real resolution of the [transition] crisis must ultimately involve a new way of being in the world." This is precisely the case for a couple when the world they constructed in the Security Stage no longer works and seems to be collapsing around them,

Sometimes all hell breaks loose. One devoted spouse has an affair after 30 years, another one shares a long-concealed secret that could blow up the whole relationship. For instance, a man shares that he thinks he never really loved his wife, or she opens up about having rekindled a high school romance over the internet. Something seems to have gone seriously awry.

At other times the gradual erosion of passion, curiosity, vulnerability and playfulness catches up with at least one of the pair and she will come to the realization that she can no longer go on the way they have been. The quality of this realization is very different than the impotent complaint of a spouse in the Security Stage. The latter is usually tinged with blame. For a couple entering a transition crisis, they are confronted with a very real sense of spiritual discontent. In the fullness of this awareness they know that something crucial to their fulfillment is clearly missing.

The Transition Stage brings a relationship to the precipice of where it will need to go if it is to fulfill its potential. In our experience, couples who avoid the crisis of transition can never achieve what is possible. If the relationship is to thrive, a "breakthrough" experience is required. Each person will need to take risks to show up in newer ways. The blame and/or avoidance cycles which so characterize relationships embedded in security are supplanted by a trepidatious opening to the beckoning of the higher self. This is the self that is not satisfied with a relationship based on predictable habits of interaction no matter how functional they have become. This emerging self is willing to risk losing it all for the sake of truth. **In Transition, couples have three choices: one, to divorce; two, to look into the abyss and gingerly back off into the familiar world of their existing relationship; or three, to step into that very abyss and enter the free fall of the unknown and**

the novel. Couples that seek help during the Security Stage are usually looking to fix something that seems broken. In Transition they feel the calling toward something larger.

Harvey came to Corinne eighteen years into their relationship and declared, "I think I have a porn addiction." Corinne was shocked—somehow remaining unaware for years of Harvey's waning interest in sex. She passed it off as the natural progression in a long term relationship. But Harvey was not simply owning up to an unhealthy behavior, he was telling her that he could not go on adapting to a stilted relationship. He wanted to confront what was missing and was willing to risk it all.

He began to tell her what he had been ashamed to confess earlier. He shared his fantasies and his fears around bringing more of himself to her sexually. At first she judged him and told him to get help. She felt betrayed and mistrustful of him. Indeed, he had lied to her and this shook her to the core. Slowly however she began to acknowledge the ways she pushed away any efforts Harvey made over the years to bring more creativity and aliveness into their love life.

For his part, Harvey never clearly conveyed to Corinne his discontent. He just went underground. He brought his lusty, playful and aggressive parts to cyberspace. There he got to express wild and selfish energies. What he was looking for in his sex life was also what he wanted in every aspect of their relationship. He wanted to break through the conformity to a set of unspoken regulations that had come to define their relationship.

Corinne too wanted more. But she brushed aside the whisperings of an unfulfilled heart and settled for life as it seemed to be in all the relationships she was familiar with. She may have gone on this way forever and maybe not. Perhaps down the line her own need for self expression would have surfaced. Harvey's confession left that to conjecture. His admission of his secret world thrust the pair of them into a transition crisis.

In the early days of our couples work we may have referred Harvey to a 12 step program and Corinne to a program for spouses. The nexus of our work would surely have been about recovery and working with Corinne's feelings around betrayal. Maybe we would have addressed their family histories and how these contributed to their present struggle. From an evolutionary perspective we view what happened in a broader context. Harvey's porn compulsion can be seen as his effort to manage his feelings around a growing emptiness in their relationship and to bring life to his sexual needs. His control pattern involved retracting his energy from Corinne and bringing it to a safer, more manageable venue.

She too engaged in a passive control pattern of immersion into her own daily routines, ignoring the naked elephant trundling about the computer room. Neither of them wanted to address the affection (and erotic) vacuum that had sucked the life-force out of their marriage. What the two of us have learned is that for most couples Eros doesn't simply evaporate as a couple dons their matching bathrobes and sip the warm tea of security. Eros mutates and migrates from the relationship to work, family, hobbies, sports, perhaps affairs, and yes even addictions. Harvey looked forward to his virtual encounters with cyber-babes with an anticipation that was once directed solely at Corinne.

Harvey brought his addiction to light because he reached a point where he recognized that he was avoiding confronting the malaise in his marriage. Transition always involves bringing forth uncomfortable truths. These initial truths open the door to even more truth being shared and, if the couple is willing to stay with it, to a sense of liberation. Some of the security-busting truths we have heard include:

"I don't think I have ever had a strong sexual attraction to you."
"I hate what we have become."
"I'm not happy."
"I want to quit my job and devote myself to my art."
"I want us to have an open relationship."
"I don't want to spend the next twenty years like this."
"I don't feel my heart anymore."
"I think we hate each other."
"I don't know you anymore."
"I don't know myself anymore."

Statements such as these have the potential to move the relationship forward in a way that no therapeutic model or technique can match. Though Harvey did attend a 12 Step group, which served him well, his courage in acknowledging the oft ignored warnings of a dying relationship catapulted his marriage into uncharted territory. Both Corinne and he, tentatively at first, began to take more risks not just in their sexuality but in every aspect of their lives. This is the gift of the crisis of transition. For many it does not result in a storybook ending (actually for nobody) but for some, it unlocks and swings open the wrought iron gates of security and imprisonment.

In our EMM work with couples over the years we have come to realize that there are numerous opportunities for couples during the Security Stage to provoke mini-transition experiences. Couples do not need to wait 10, 20, or 30 years for a "big bang" occurrence to reinvent the universe of their relationship. They have numerous opportunities to step past their control patterns and to take the risks that evolution always requires.

In every session we have we are looking for the risk that seems to embody the growth edge for one or both partners. It may be for one to expose a wish or fantasy, for another to express cruelty, or fear, or a tenderness that feels shameful. Yet another may want to say no to things he never said no to before. All of these cause a tectonic shift in the shared energy field as well as the physical holding of energy within each partner. Additionally it supports the development of new limbic pathways resulting in greater plasticity of the brain.

As the relationship learns to tolerate more risk it enters the fourth stage.

The Exceptional Couple

When we developed the idea of an exceptional marriage it was clear to the two of us that we were not talking about some static state of "relationship enlightenment." In fact, the more we explored this possibility the more obvious it became that an exceptional relationship is an ever-evolving relationship. **In the exceptional relationship couples do not become enlightened, but**

emboldened. The primary characteristic of stage four is a higher vibration of energy. Couples are simply more alive and less risk averse. There is more of everything; More honesty, more laughter, more conflict, more eros, more passion, more chaos, more moments of pure love. Such couples are louder, messier, sillier, and wiser.

Paul Tillich [(46)] in The Courage to Be writes, "Life, willing to surpass itself, is the good life, and the good life is the courageous life. It is the life of the 'powerful soul' and the 'triumphant body' whose self enjoyment is virtue." The exceptional relationship is this life willing to surpass itself. It has nothing to do with completeness. We are never complete. This fourth stage is a celebration of our incompleteness as humans. Here resides our humility and our audacity. It is both humbling and audacious for each partner to live on their evolutionary edge. As David Whyte put it, "In the pursuit of marriage dignity is a dispensable luxury." Our leading edge is just that very next step that each person can take in any moment to break through the miasma of control patterns. It requires mindfulness and more. It is not just living in the moment, but opening to the next.

Brian writes of the leading edge in this poem:

The Edge

There are the temporal spaces
where we usually dwell
Past, Future, Present
Vying for prominence

The Past
Domain of smoky memories, clingy regrets, distant pleasures
The outback of our psyche.

The Future
Hovering artfully on the horizon
Saturated with imagination, giddy hopes,
disturbing flashes of our own demise.

The Present
Abode of immediacy, certainty, the power of now.
The solidity of knowing: "This is where I stand!"
The place, we are told by the wise ones,
where we belong.

And yet . . .
There is a fourth space still,
One that is easily dismissed
by the minds predilection toward knowing, toward believing.

A fourth space . . .
Will you come with me to the edge?
Will you join me on the precipice?
Are you ready to venture into the very next experience
where you both long and dread to go?
The edge is right here on the final wisp of your next exhalation.
The boundary between certainty and bewilderment,
between willingness and wonder,
between order and chaos,
between dogma and dilemma.
Will you cross over with me into that which aches to be expressed?
Into the liquid fire of your own irrationality?
Can you feel the pull, the calling, the siren sound
of your own birthing into your very next true self?
It is where you are most fully alive, vibrant, real.

The edge is beckoning
Inviting a reckoning
of past, future, and present enfolded into the precise next moment.
Come take my hand, discover your edge together with me.
Come with me into the light, into the darkness,
into the mess, into the joke, into the careening, carousing, cacophonous,
contemplative, contemptuous, complete new experience
that resides on the razor's edge of your emerging self.

The exceptional relationship is the home for self discovery. It is the launching pad for creative self expression. Motivated by what Roberto Assagioli [(1)] calls "divine homesickness," it is where couples re-discover Eros. But here the Eros has matured. Though the Security Stage is characterized by a shrinking repertoire of emotional expression, it also served to forge a deeper bond at least in those couples who later cross the threshold into the Exceptional Relationship. This attachment bond paired with re-awakening Eros results in the creation of a formidable environment for a very alive relationship. One of the major aims of the EMM approach is the merger of eros and security. This involves a shift away from fantasized attraction that is steeped in transference into an erotic attachment that emanates from the heart. In a sense, the four developmental stages: Eros, Security, Transition and The Exceptional Relationship can be summarized as an evolution from: *passion, to high security-low passion, into higher passion-low security, and finally high passion-high security.*

As couples learn to entrain their energies through expressing their emerging truths, limbic resonance seems to develop. The more a couple brings to each other the seemingly irrational reactions of their leading edge, the more security they cultivate. And the more security that is felt, the more open to deeper sharing of the vulnerable edgy experiences. Here, the shared energy field is liberated from the stranglehold of control patterns. The relationship comes to life.

We can see the movement from security to danger in Harvey and Corinne's relationship. For several months it was not clear to either of them that they would survive as a partnership. As Harvey aptly put it, "I know I created a shit storm." By allowing themselves to receive a great deal of support (which is vital to getting through a transition crisis) they eventually discovered each other in vibrant new ways. Each began to see the Mystery in the other. Corinne was surprised by how playful and assertive Harvey could be. He was moved by her penetrating curiosity and desire to explore herself in a variety of ways. She took up yoga and meditation. Together they began learning about Tantric sexuality. They came to delight in each other's unlimited potential. The philosopher Levinas suggests that the goal of true relationship is for each person to "infinitize" the other. By this he means that the other is always more than one's definition of her.

One couple came to work with us neck deep in a transition crisis. Over the 10 years of their marriage their control patterns were firmly established. Barb would have great plans for their future and nothing else mattered but that she create the picture-perfect family. This involved having four children, living in a very specific environment and having a dutiful husband who wanted exactly what she wanted. Justin went along with her vision and he became a satellite orbiting around her gravity field.

By the time they came to us the relationship was in real trouble. He was turned off to her and was clearly harboring great resentment for how she controlled him. His declaration of independence was to tell her he wanted a separation. Having always been the good boy, both growing up and in the marriage, his saying he wanted out was to a large extent out of character. While the two of us were aware that Justin's decision to leave was a transitional moment for him, we also recognized that it was an extension of his control pattern of withdrawal. Yet it was clear he needed to stand his ground. Barb was devastated, but notably when asked "Why?" she responded, "The family I had hoped for will never happen." Her distress was more a result of the loss of her vision than of Justin.

While it was clear that there was a true loving bond between them, he was shut down and she was angry and critical. She judged Justin for his lack of emotional responsiveness. She told him he was being "fake." Over the past five years he had taken up meditation and he believed it helped him to not judge himself the way she judged him. He told her, "This is who I am, I'll never be who you want." But Barb experienced him emotionally shutting down more and more as a consequence of his meditating. For her she realized that, beneath her judgments, she really did not want to be with a man who did not or could not share his emotions. She said that it felt too empty. When we pointed out to her that her critique of him was contributing to his pulling away she was able to acknowledge this.

To move beyond ending the relationship as just an extension of their control patterns (his withdrawal, her demands and criticisms) we asked Barb if she would be willing to take a risk. We invited the two of them to stand and face each other. Barb was offered the chance to say to Justin, "I release you." As we suggested to her, she was not releasing him from the marriage so much as from her judgments of him. We were asking her if she could open up to accepting his "otherness", to see him as much more that her image. She stood before him, body vibrating, tears streaming down her face, and said to him tenderly, "Justin, I release you to be who you are." These were not just programmed words, but a penetrating truth that rose up from her soul. One small tear trickled down his cheek as he walked the three steps that separated them and embraced her.

At this time we do not know if they will separate or keep going as a couple, but her courageous capacity to accept his otherness to, as Levinas said, infinitize him, shifted them both in a fundamental way. This is an elemental aspect of an exceptional relationship—to embrace the other for who he is, even if it means that you do not choose to be with him.

The childhood historical need is for compensation from some past injury, or for a partner to be the "perfect mate" as defined by one's early experiences. As couples live more in stage four, they are nourished more by the experience of intersubjectivity. That is, the authentic need in the present moment is to be known. The human capacity to share experience, to *feel* together, goes to our very core. Laughing is a clear example of such intersubjectivity. Exceptional couples laugh more, express more anger, cry together, and show up for each other when worry and anxiety overtakes one or the other.

Such high volume intersubjective knowing is captured beautifully in the following exchange at the end of a session. This is a couple we worked with over for 18 months and the woman Pria was responding to her partner Joel's deepening acceptance of her. Pria, eyes sparkling and moving excitedly in her chair looks at Joel and sings out, "I feel so much love for you.

It just feels so vulnerable to love you this much. It's like if you ever left me I would have to hunt you down and kill you." Joel, breaking into a huge grin responds with equal sincerity, "That's the nicest thing you've ever said to me." The sharing of this wild energy is a sure sign of a couple that can tolerate emotions wide and strong.

Such sentiments as expressed by Joel and Pria speak to an embodied and passion—saturated brand of love. In our work, we are aware of the difference between personal, high-vibration love, and the more global kind. There is the love that meditation elicits, one that grows out of dropping into a theta brainwave state of peaceful awareness, an openness to all that is. It is a comprehension of the temporality of human emotional fluctuation, a detachment from the drama of life. And this is beautiful and powerful.

Then there is the love that emerges out of the lived expression of the human emotional realities. This love is felt through the heat of shared feeling states. As anger, fear, hurt, need, remorse, and other emotions are embraced, felt, and physically released, we experience the kind of love that fills our heart so our chest feels like it will burst. This love explodes throughout our body as a vibrant sense of deep human connection, as empathic resonance, as limbic merging. We are profoundly moved by the presence and Mystery of another who has journeyed with us through the treacherous terrain of our emotional landscape. This Mystery—the yet to be discovered places within every one of us—can open us to the radical recognition of our partner's uniqueness and separateness. Simultaneously it embraces the larger pool of consciousness we both bathe in together.

To Levinas, [31] "The soul is the other in me." And, "The other is always more than the I bargains for, more than the I wants, more than the I can handle." The openness to the unmanageability of the other is part and parcel to the exceptional relationship. The I that can handle the totality and Mystery of my partner is an I that is itself evolving. When we cease trying to get our partner to be as we think she should be, when we can allow her need for the thermostat to be set at a different temperature than we think is "normal," when we are not so threatened by her unfolding talents, we begin to transcend the fragile I. We become fellow travelers on the magical Mystery tour.

For a couple to get to a place where they can travel on this bus, there needs to be a commitment to growth. In EMM we tend to view commitment as the willingness to stay in the truth of whatever comes. This is more a commitment to process than to person. But we choose to do it with another who enlists along with us. The pathway to an exceptional relationship involves three distinct phases in the mentoring approach. *These three are:*

1. Healing
2. Pleasure
3. Creative Leadership

Let's take a closer look at each.

Healing

As we noted earlier, some couples will come to you solely to solve a particular problem. It is not part of their agenda to open up a Pandora's box of unmetabolized experiences from their past. Behaviorally focused treatments will often meet their needs. But to move toward what is possible in a committed relationship it is almost always necessary to venture into the origins of their present struggles. While couples therapy today is generally not viewed as the best environment to heal one's past, in the EMM approach we believe that it can often be the ideal milieu.

By healing, we are referring to assisting either partner in bringing forth the disavowed emotions from earlier in life and having them witnessed and held in the moment by both the mentors and the committed partner. Healing involves making the connection between what is being enacted in the relationship in the here and now, and the primary emotions which were locked down at a young age.

Most couples whom the two of us work with need to reclaim long disowned emotions in order to evolve. To borrow a term from Michael Washburn, we may call this "regression in service of transcendence." Insight alone about what occurred in the past offers very little in helping a couple to break free of the iterations of their control patterns. Wilhelm Reich emphasized this point when he described the nature of character analysis "(It) works with high-pitched realities and not with shadows of memories from the past. A memory may or may not develop in the process of emotional upheaval. It is of no therapeutic importance whether it does or not."

In Reich's day there was no awareness of the difference between implicit and explicit memories, so he was referring to explicit recall. In EMM, as partners are encouraged to embody present-day emotions arising between them, there is often an organic opening into a deeper level of the same emotion. This opening is the implicit, or body memory coming to life. If one is hurt by something the other said, and cannot get beyond it, chances are good that a body memory has been triggered.

Healing then, happens when a person can build a bridge between present enactments and past injuries, and is not simply what happened to them, but how they learned to metabolize the energy. Carly and Spencer have been married for 11 years. Each had been previously married. They came to us because she was sure he was in love with another woman. She was constantly interrogating him about a particular relationship with a co-worker. He was exasperated and adamantly insisted he had not cheated on her. But the more he protested, the more mistrustful and controlling she became. We learned from her in the second session that she had experienced tragic losses a few years before they met. Several close relatives including a son from her first marriage had died over a short period of time.

Carly lived through that period in a state of shock, and eventually just moved on with her life without ever entering into the profound depths of her painful emotions. As she and Spencer moved out of the Eros Stage she gradually began to experience him as slipping away. Her control pattern was to stay on top of the situation so she would not be shocked down the road if he left her. She was controlling against having to open up the wellspring of grief that dwelled deep within her implicit memory.

Our work with them shifted to supporting Carly in making the connection between how she felt about the prospect of being rejected and abandoned by Spencer, and her earlier losses. Initially she wanted to keep the focus on him. It was only when we could all agree that Spencer was never going to admit to doing what she accused him of andt that he was committed to her, that she could turn to her own pain.

First through her recounting her experiences of loss, particularly that of her son, and later through working with her body, she was able to bring out powerful long-held emotions. She screamed, sobbed, cursed out God, and thrashed her body about on a mattress. Simon encouraged her and cried with her both in his heartache for her and in relief that what had been held between them for so long was finally being released. As we will detail later, we use various body-centered interventions and equipment to support this "regressive" healing work.

Subsequently, Carly's energy shifted from hypervigilant attention to Spencer's every move to a more vulnerable expression of how fearful she was of losing him. It was only then that Simon acknowledged that when things were bad between them that he *had* felt attraction to his co-worker, though he never acted on it. He was fearful of admitting it because he did not want to lose Carly. As is often the case in the shared energy field, subtle energies are often picked up on and then get translated and distorted through one's narrative. Carly's narrative that "everyone I love leaves" took over once she sensed that Spencer's affections were drifting away from her. His passive control pattern of withdrawing, denial, and playing the rescuer only served to heighten the anxiety and terror Carly held deep inside.

He learned early in life that the only way he could receive affection was to be the good guy and caregiver. Until Carly did her healing work Simon did not feel safe enough to reveal anything but 100% faithfulness. It is fairly common that when one partner makes the connection between present enactments and historical wounding, the other begins to heal as well. His energy entrains with hers much as infants in a nursery learn to cry in unison.

Most often the wounding that results in the formulation of control patterns results from early life breaches of attachment and characterological reactions to danger, abandonment, control and betrayal. But in Carly's case the trauma of the overwhelming *adult* experience of loss created similar wounding. Just as the child is overwhelmed by the power of the parents, adult trauma can be equally flooding and therefore damaging to the entire system. The results are boldly displayed in the enactments of control patterns in the committed relationship.

Either partner may be the first to loosen the grip of control patterns, and it is then often followed by the other relaxing his hold. With Spencer and Carly it could have played out differently. Spencer's own history revealed the character wounding of manipulation and betrayal. He was used as a child to meet the emotional needs of both his parents. He learned early that if he was the shining star he would receive approval. Spencer was initially drawn to Carly when she was in desperate straits after her losses. The control pattern he so assiduously employed was to overwhelm her with caretaking so that she would never be disappointed in him.

It is possible that in our mentoring work, we could have pursued his wounding and helped him touch the fears of inadequacy that haunted him constantly. But the path of least resistance in this instance seemed to be through Carly's wounding. Spencer held such a deep mistrust that she would stand by him if he was less than perfect that it would have been a huge risk for him to admit to any negative feelings toward her.

So healing involves using the present dynamic being expressed in the shared energy field of the relationship and then going back in time to when the protective reactions were first used to stop the bleeding of unacceptable emotions. Healing does not occur from simply remembering events. Often there are no specific, concrete memories from childhood to draw upon to make sense of present-day behaviors. Most of the time it was the fabric of everyday life that created an inhospitable atmosphere for the expression of primary affect. As partners can, in effect, travel through time and recover what they lost (access to primary emotions) they begin to loosen the grip of the control patterns. Affect tolerance, or the ability to stay grounded in present consciousness as strong emotions course through the body, is the fundamental requisite for healing.

Healing manifests as an opening to an undefended sense of love as partners begin to reclaim their feeling selves. The undefended, wide open love a child feels toward a parent and indeed toward life itself, recoils against the forces of conditionality. That is, as a child learns about approval and disapproval she withdraws from the free spontaneous flow of pure love. Her responses to the world become more calculated. Healing occurs as the adult moves backward from control patterns, through an awareness of all the resistances to encountering her primary feelings, toward the embodied connection to these powerful affective energies, into a contact with the authentic experience of need, and ultimately to the open channel of pure love. As she surrenders to grief, awakens to fierce rage, opens to ancient terrors, she makes room for the pure love that resides inside the eye of the hurricane.

When one partner goes through such a healing transformation and love breaks through, the therapy room becomes a sacred ground where mercy seems to fill the air. We often will invite the partner who went through the healing experience to "follow love's impulse." We encourage this because, even when one is wide open with a loving heart, there are still the voices that say, "It's not safe to show too much." The invitation to follow love's impulse helps the person to release the last holdings of control and trust that love, fully expressed, will be tolerated. For the wounding occurs not only from the contraction of primary emotions, but from the rejection of the wide open heart as well. For Carly, following love's impulse was simple. She turned toward Spencer and said, "I love you so much, it hurts."

Pleasure

Human beings are supremely equipped to feel pleasure. Tragically, in long term relationships too many couples learn to compete in a fierce contest for who has the least pleasure. In our own relationship we began to notice over time all the ways we would each complain about our days. Our goal was to prove to each other how hard we worked and how little fun our respective lives were. It felt risky to acknowledge the pleasure of life, particularly when it seemed the other was grinding it out. To have pleasure was to risk resentment and disapproval. We developed, in effect, a "misery collusion."

We learned that we were not alone in this relationship pastime. Many couples create lives of "quiet desperation" because to live in pleasure is to risk opprobrium. In a culture that values productivity over pleasure it is small wonder that we choose to spend more time "kvetching" than "kvelling." There is a certain degree of vulnerability attached to the acknowledgement of pleasure. Yet our capacity to experience pleasure is considerably larger than most of us realize.

The far-reaching impact of enculturation conditions and shapes the brain to attend more to gaining approval and acceptance than dwelling in pleasure. The quest to be valued supersedes the longing to feel fully alive. Yet pleasure is always right there to be savored. The seat of pleasure is in relationship. To be in pleasure is to be alive and to be alive is to be in relationship.

The power of relationship is powerfully illustrated in an intriguing experiment. Heart cells separated in a petri dish will continue beating for a short period of time and then fibrillate and die. But as Joseph Chilton Pearce describes it, "We could take two live heart cells, keep them separated on a slide, and, when fibrillation began, bring them closer together. At some magical point of spatial proximity they would stop fibrillating and resume their regular pulsating in synchrony with each other—a microscopic heart." [(33)] These tiny heart cells sprung back to life when they entered each other's sphere of influence. This entrainment of energy is the source of pleasure.

Life fully experienced is pleasurable. The contraction from life, through numbing ourselves and resisting the flow of energy and process consciousness leaves us devoid of pleasure. The great paradox of life is that pleasure involves pain. To enter into the stream of life we will invariably feel the ache of unmet needs, loss, insult and threat. If we allow our organic reactions to these inevitabilities, we increase our experience of pleasure. When we try and hold tight to a moment in paradise we relinquish the exhilaration of flow. Couples in an exceptional relationship will more often opt for uncertainty over predictability and this ups the pleasure quotient significantly.

As we will discuss in the next chapter, part of what makes a relationship exceptional is the ability to move through painful interactions to not only repair but to grow from the conflict. **Security is not based on freedom from pain but on the willingness to learn from the differences that will continue to arise in long term partnerships**. Pleasure springs up out of the couple's trust in the power of discord. When we attempt to build security out of peace and harmony alone it is a papier-mâché edifice that cannot hold up when the winds of discordance blow.

The healing of attachment breaches comes about not from each person becoming the other's complete parent, but in each inviting the full and frank expression of emotional reactions that inhibit intimacy. Pleasure emerges from two parallel processes. First, the deep sense of intimacy (secure attachment) that emerges from the awareness of being received, even in the negative reactions to the other. Second, the sense of agency and therefore autonomy that results from taking responsibility for one's own growth, what Kegan calls our "evolutionary renegotiation."

When our partner welcomes our unsavory reactions we begin to trust that we can be ourselves in the relationship. When they refuse to take care of us, when they no longer attempt to meet our historical needs, we are held accountable for our own evolution. The more this occurs, the more pleasure we feel.

The long term committed relationship is for most people the one and only place to move this deeply into oneself. **Partners that can stand heart to heart, lie skin to skin, and breathe fully together in the vulnerability of their mature need for each other know pleasure.**

In the Eros Stage there is the wild pleasure of love's re-awakening. But this is an immature love that mimics the child's sense of being fully embraced. In eros the new lover takes unparalleled delight in the awareness that "I am cherished." This unripened love must transform for a more evolved pleasure to take hold. The pleasure in the exceptional relationship goes beyond secure attachment and includes the transcendent experience of living on the edge of one's emerging self.

The dance between our historical needs and living more fully in the present is continual. The pleasure that comes from being met even when one is mired in history is liberating. Mark and Kate were married for 7 years. They had moved well beyond the Eros Stage and were slowly sinking into control patterns which were robbing the relationship of its previous vitality. Mark played the role of hero, making lots of money and never openly asking for anything from Kate. But he would often explode with criticism about Kate's not taking care of the house or "improving" herself. He held a negative narrative that she was just using him and did not really want to "show up" for him emotionally.

In one particular instance, Mark was coming up on an important event in his life which was cause for celebration. Kate said to him in a mentoring session, "I want to throw you a party." This offer immediately threw Mark into a deep mistrust about whether she was offering this from the generosity of her heart. He believed that he would have a price to pay for her largesse. He was afraid that he would be disappointed. He declared that Kate had "a history of not holding up her end of the bargain." This started to trigger in Kate a reactive defense of all the ways she has shown up for him. We asked her instead if she would be willing to simply repeat to him, "I want to do this for you." Mark was invited to bring out all his mistrust and protestations. His words came gushing forth: "I don't believe you!" "You'll let me down!" "You'll make me pay!" "You don't really want to do it.!" Kate kept repeating, "Mark, I want to do this for you. I want to throw you this party."

Slowly Mark began to soften. It was apparent that he was inhabiting a young place, or "part" of himself. With innocence and vulnerability he began to ask "Really?" "Are you telling the truth?" Kate kept going. Mark began to cry, but then suddenly went back to "I can't trust you." We then had him hide behind a cushion and peek out whenever he felt the urge to make contact. He moved back and forth playing out his inner struggle between need and mistrust. Finally he came out from behind the cushion and stood before Kate shaking and telling her how scared he was to let her care for him. The pleasure that was growing in their shared energy field was palpable.

Because Mark was embedded in his mistrust of Kate, he had to see her through the lens of his negative narrative. For her part, she was convinced of her own narrative that Mark is incapable of letting her care for him. As she stayed with the place in her that wanted to give to him, she dropped (at least for the moment) the part of her that could get hopeless and withdrawn. As they transcended these control patterns, love and pleasure erupted.

As couples open to the energy that becomes available when they release the control patterns, sexuality evolves as well. For many couples sex falls prey to the stifling influence of firmly established control patterns. Sometimes, if a couple is fortunate, sex is a refuge from the arid interactions which begin to take hold in other areas of their lives. David Schnarch suggests that there are three categories of sexual relationship, "the sexually dysfunctional, the sexually functional, and the blessed few." As he puts it, "Some individuals would rather be frustrated with a tolerable level of deprivation than cope with the vulnerability of valuing, and the hunger of longing."

In our estimation, the pleasure quotient in sex rises not from incorporating new tantric techniques or learning how to have multiple orgasms, these are secondary options. Pleasure in sex grows as partners bring more of themselves out into the open as they take their clothes off. This is what we have come to call exceptional sex. It is, we believe not just accessible to the "blessed few." We will return to this later in a more detailed discussion of sexuality in a committed relationship.

Creative leadership

In the EMM approach, we view the exceptional marriage as one that exists in the context of a larger reality. The purpose or possibility available through the crucible of commitment is for each partner to become more wholly human and more open to full self expression. As we addressed earlier, the drive toward full self expression is fundamental to our nature. Even in the earliest hominids there remains evidence of the indomitable spirit of creative expression. Cave etchings speak to an urge that surpasses mere functionality.

Each one of us is reaching, reaching, reaching for more of who we are. We want more of that healing, more of that pleasure. The human drive toward growth leads us to our deepest impulses to share. We are born in relationship, evolve through relationship and are fulfilled by our relationship to the community of humankind. Our higher, more expansive impulses toward empathy and altruism open to us when we emotionally awaken. The exceptional marriage cultivates love, and love compels us to bring out to the world the gifts of our own creative leadership.

In the mentoring work the two of us offer couples, we hold the broadest vision of each person manifesting his and her human potential. An exceptional relationship is one where each partner becomes a leader, a creative force. The partnership supports the ongoing unfolding of both individual's higher selves. The organic next phase is to bring forth these gifts to a world in desperate need. In some way, big or small, every couple can use the healing that happens between them as a springboard to helping others. This is love's grand purpose.

Couples are often consumed in the daily demands of making it in the world. The pleasures of wonder, curiosity, and intimacy get replaced by the lesser gratifications of distraction and indulgence. Not that there is anything wrong with watching football or eating a fluffy croissant, but when these become the primary outlet for some semblance of enjoyment, life-force gets gridlocked.

As mates in commitment learn to open to life through emotional and creative expression there is a growing inclination to reach out to the world beyond the immediate dyad. The most obvious arena for creative leadership is in the sacred obligation of child-rearing. For those couples who traverse that path, there is abundant opportunity to bring forth creative leadership. However, this is a subject for another time.

Beyond the family, after children are raised or when a couple is childless, we invite them to explore what they have to offer, both individually and together. The openness to creative leadership results from each person taking delight in the other's gifts. During the Security Stage, there is more fear of a partner's success and thus an unconscious tendency for each to diminish the other. This inclination to keep the other small is born out of a misguided attempt to create security. As couples move through transition and start exploring what it is like to grow together, more and more of their respective gifts, or core qualities emerge from what Michelle James calls "the fertile unknown." So many couples we work with remain disconnected from these core qualities and, as a result, fail to bring these gifts to life. This is, in our estimation, a prime purpose of an exceptional relationship.

Chapter Four

Fighting the Good Fight

One thing every couples therapist knows—be prepared for battle. Whether it's the incendiary, scorched earth repartee of actively and unabashedly angry combatants, or the covert, guerilla style, implied and disguised violence of genteel opponents, the battle *will* wage. In the EMM approach conflict is essential to an evolving relationship. Sam Keen suggests, "A passionate life is a continuing dialogue between self and other. And all real dialogue according to philosopher Karl Jaspers, is a 'loving combat.' To become who we are we must learn to wrestle. Push-pull. Yes-no. Love must be muscular."

There is really not a day that will go by in the life of a couple where conflict (spoken or not) is absent. Little tensions, out of sync desires, diverging responsibilities, all add up to pregnant periods of discord. Most often these fly by barely noticed. From time to time they may flare up into an exchange of harsh words and critical comments. Blame is the ultimate weapon when conflict arises. When spouses butt heads there is sure to be a healthy dose of blame and judgment.

Many couples seek help because they say they don't know how to communicate. This generally means that when differences arise one of three possibilities occur; they engage in unresolvable bouts of arguing, or one partner is perpetually nagging while the other is withdrawing, or they both go blank and close off to each other. In all three instances, the couple is ill-prepared to move through difficult emotion al realities.

In our work we have come to reject the notion of conflict resolution. By focusing on the resolution, or outcome of conflict, there is a bias against entering into the heat of battle. But by going *into* a conflict couples have an opportunity to truly expand and evolve. The two of us prefer to use the term "conflict engagement" to describe what path to take when there's trouble brewing in paradise. In conflict engagement the emphasis shifts from outcome to process. We work with couples to help them, not only build their tolerance for strong emotions, but to discover the deeper truths and potentialities woven into the fight.

When conflict arises it triggers all kinds of biochemical and autonomic responses which usually serve to heighten the struggle. A couple who is fighting about money for instance, enter into sympathetic arousal to defend and protect much more personal and tender spaces within. The threat is less about available cash then about such things as competence, control, honor, need, regard, abandonment and love. Each person drops into fight or flight to protect these more vulnerable realities. Neither partner can really hear the other from the expanse between their respective foxholes.

In this chapter we will explore the form and function of conflict as a positive force in the committed relationship. We will look at conflict as a biological imperative, as the doorway into true intimacy, as a basic component of the evolutionary process, and as a challenge to you, the therapist.

First let's lay out what we consider to be the essential principles of conflict.

Basic Principles of Conflict

1. Most conflict is inherently valuable.
2. Conflict serves a biological function of allowing individuals to charge and discharge built up energy.
3. Conflict is part and parcel of mature interaction. Couples need to exert their influence on each other by expressing their differing ideas, values, intentions, or emotional reactions.

4. Good conflict is "improvisational." It does not follow a predetermined script and is often messy and scary before it leads to deeper connection.
5. Erotic energy is often embedded in conflict. When power greets power, sexuality erupts.
6. Differences between spouses lead to stimulation, which then leads to growth.
7. Creative self-expression is dependent on conflict.
8. Honest conflict charges our energy and opens the way to more tender emotional expression.
9. Physical violence is not part of conflict. (It's actually conflict avoidance.)
10. Control pattern-based conflicts are used to protect against our more vulnerable feelings. They never get beyond self-justifying and accusation.
11. Couples will sometimes remain in blaming conflict until each partner can admit to their desire to hurt the other. There is a revenge factor in many of our conflicts, and it needs to be acknowledged to be released.
12. Most conflict has little to do with issues and much more to do with finding intimacy through the pathway of autonomy. In other words, we need to first be able to speak up for ourselves before we can open up to our partners.
13. Lack of honest conflict is the great destroyer of many marriages.
14. Conflict between spouses is most often a reflection of each partner's internal conflicts.
15. Honest conflict typically leads to a deepening awareness of disowned aspects within oneself.
16. Good conflict often results in an "ah-ha" moment for one or both partners as they drop the veils of tightly held myths, or they release down into a restorative feeling.

Conflict erupts when tension mounts. At certain times, in our sessions, it is more important to let the fight escalate than to intervene in order to restore harmony. **It is often the anxiety of the therapist that leads to an intervention designed to halt the conflict.** These interventions are often premature and can abort a very vital interchange. The reality is that most couples act differently toward each other in the therapy room than they do on their own turf. Granting them the leeway (up to a point) to have it out with each other can be of great value to your work with them. In some instances by allowing a battle to take place the couple will actually feel safer. But this depends on if the fight progresses beyond blaming.

Once a conflict begins to be enacted in the session, the couple quickly forgets that we are there and real-life interchanges take over. We value this not only because it allows us to see how they emotionally respond to each other, but sometimes the tension just needs to be discharged. We are, after all, dealing with two human beings who are trying their best to be decent to each other most of the time. But the body that holds back frustration, hurt, fear and disappointment is gradually building up an intensity or charge. So many fights, we have learned, are really excuses for letting off pent up energy.

There have been sessions too numerous to remember where the two of us have tried valiantly to get each party to hear what the other is "really" trying to say beneath their anger. One of us might ask a partner, "Can you hear that she is really hurt when you do that?" To which he replies, "I try my best, but apparently it's not good enough!" Then one of us would turn to her and ask, "Do you know that he feels like whatever he does it will never be enough for you?" To which she retorts, "I don't get why he can't just admit his mistake!"

Under such conditions, we have learned, it is often more helpful to the couple for us to encourage them to bring it all out. We are aware there is vulnerability that each person is protecting, but sometimes the energy needs to get bigger first. Instead of trying to bypass the anger that is clearly in the room we would prefer to give it a container in which it can be fully and safely expressed. We know there is substantial controversy surrounding this issue of expressing anger, but to us there is no doubt it has its place. **It has been our experience that when the therapy room does not allow for the energy of the conflict to be expressed as it is in the kitchen, authenticity suffers.** The couple tends to adapt to the perceived therapeutic expectations which they hear as, "You should be able to avoid these unproductive fights if you would just learn to follow our suggestions. If you can go to what is underneath your anger, or see what you are really trying to say, than this messiness could be avoided."

The idea that conflict can or should always be avoided is more harmful than helpful to two human beings trying hard to forge a life together. Yes, it is crucial for each of them to learn to access emotions that the conflict is protecting. But, as a child sometimes needs to protest (the breaches to attachment and the injuries to his emerging self) so too adults in relationship will remonstrate when provoked. To get them to acknowledge vulnerability when alarm bells are sounding is not only too much to ask, but a bypassing of the inborn need to protest.

There is almost always a palpable tension when we meet with a couple for the first time. Each person is afraid—frightened on two fronts. First, that they will be exposed in front of strangers, professional strangers at that. They will be portrayed by the partner in ways that will cause the professionals to dislike them. All of their inadequacies and foibles will be under scrutiny—sexual difficulties, trouble expressing emotions, not making enough money, always criticizing, spending too much on QVC, never being happy, being too needy and so on. This exposure of one's shortcomings is truly a frightening prospect.

Second, the fear of abandonment runs very deep. Coming for therapy is an acknowledgement that something is awfully wrong and maybe unfixable. So, often, each person is fearful that therapy is the doorway to the demise of the relationship. These fears set in motion a process of self protection which involves both parties activating sympathetic arousal in the autonomic nervous system. The resulting situation reveals itself as two people defending themselves in highly patterned and characteristic ways.

Conflict, under such conditions, shows up in a well-choreographed display of passive and/or aggressive control patterns. Such conflict is like a controlled burn. It allows for a certain amount of energy to move without resulting in a conflagration. This kind of discord, erupting from each person's own style of fight or flight (aggressive or passive control patterns) rarely moves past self protection. It plays out as some variation of "I'm right and you're wrong." Others may go to "I'm wrong, you're right" as an outward mea culpa, but tucked beneath the words is an unspoken criticism of the other.

In a relationship characterized by an aggressive/aggressive exchange, there is endless quarreling and bickering, occasionally erupting into a messy or even violent fight. These battles can result in days of anguish for one or both parties. In an aggressive/passive pattern one party is continually trying to get the other to "improve" while the passive partner typically becomes more withholding and builds up silent disdain. In the passive/passive exchange, there is a growing deadness in the shared energy field. Each person tends to remain more in cognitive, state consciousness. One may minimize while the other expresses a level of despair, but there is very little energetic charge in either.

Tracy and Heidi displayed this passive/passive pattern. After 16 years, Tracy was saying that she needed more space, that she wasn't sure if they were right for each other. Heidi was the adapter, always trying to accommodate Tracy. Over the years she tried to meet Tracy's expectations in order to "make her happy." Neither of them got angry or outwardly critical. Tracy simply grew colder over the years and Heidi withheld more and more of her desires. Their sex had long since stopped and neither seemed to give it much importance. Much of our work with this couple involved supporting them to express what they did not like about the other with greater intensity. One way we accomplished this, for instance, was to have each of them complete the sentence, "I don't like it when . . ." By bringing the negative out into open, the atmosphere between them became less stifling.

For two people who each came from highly critical families, it was difficult for either of them to begin to see the value in anger and conflict. When sparks began to fly however, it opened the door for healing to occur. It is not that the two of us try to create a fight where none exists, we are simply giving them permission to go where they were not sure it was safe to go.

Whatever their style, most couples need to learn how to fight and to understand that fighting is essential to a vibrant and alive exceptional relationship. Conflict is the portal to healing and transformation. The first function of fighting is to honor the biological reality of the fight or flight response. To try and get two people who are threatened by each other to understand what is happening beneath the level of threat is most often, not only near impossible, but an avoidance of a very valuable experience.

Conflict, then, is frequently necessary to break through the backlog of unexpressed emotions. In EMM, we recognize that there is always a dynamic tension between the push for autonomy and the pull of intimacy. In this perpetual life struggle the child must first learn to say "No!" before she can freely say "Yes." Emotions on the anger end of the spectrum are what may be called "autonomy-enhancing" emotions. Often, only when there is adequate space for these to be expressed can one open up to "intimacy-enhancing" feelings. We will explore this in detail later.

Intimacy often occurs only after each individual is able to experience separateness. "Make-up sex" for instance, is likely a function of the release that occurs when two people allow themselves to, in essence, thump their chests, snarl, growl, claim their territory and feel good about having protected the province of their own selfhood. Then they can move from fight or flight into an erotic openness. Often what couples open to is not sexual in nature but rather, their primary emotions—such as hurt, or an acknowledgment of the fear that fueled the conflict.

Because fear is at the base of much of the conflict that couples express in a mentoring session, they need the mentors to provide a safe container for the release of highly charged emotions. It is often the case that a couple is arguing about what seems to them to be an important topic (money, kids, the holidays, extended family) yet the essence of their fight is some variation of "I'm right and you are not going to change my mind." Often we will suggest to them to continue arguing, but to bring to its basic level. So we may have them shout back and forth such phrases as: *"My way!" "You're wrong!" "I'll never give in!" "Admit I'm right!"*

There are numerous variations of such phrases that speak to the basic power struggle and, when utilized at the appropriate time, can result in a couple releasing the hold of their respective entrenched positions. Sometimes pleasure erupts in the shared energy field and both partners really get into the absurdity of the struggle. In our experience not every session has to end up with both sides being more tender and understanding. Sometimes there is great pleasure in standing in one's autonomy and allowing a partner to do likewise. In fact, we believe there needs to be more of this. Just as a two-year-old is compelled to express his "no" fully, partners also need to embody their sense of agency and individuality. Therapeutic interventions that seek compromise in a power struggle miss the developmental import of two people "having it out with each other." **What we have witnessed is that when each person feels connected to his or her own authority or personal leadership, solutions magically emerge**. What seemed like a monumental problem dissolves into triviality. No behavioral compromises required.

It is a significant component of the healing process when two people get to express with full energy parts of themselves that have long been denied. In attachment work such as that espoused by Susan Johnson's Emotionally Focused couples work, there is support for each person to discover the vulnerable place beneath the protest. This is, of course, vitally important. Additionally, we have found that it is just as crucial to have each partner embody the simple protestations that lie at the base of the conflict.

As a case in point, Paula and Ralph came to us in an embittered struggle. She complained that he was always denying responsibility for things she swore he said. He was distressed by the way she challenged him about what he said and how she questioned his memory. They could go at the debate with tremendous vigor. He would say, for example, "I said it would take three days for the car to be fixed" and she would retort, "No you didn't." You said it would take five days!"

Our task was to help them discover what they were protecting so fiercely. We learned that Ralph had a mother who was constantly yelling and berating him, while Paula's parents both would deny obvious truths, telling her she was wrong and causing her to doubt herself. So when she was told by Ralph that her recollection was incorrect she felt a powerful need to protect her own sense of reality. She would come back at him with an intensity which mirrored his mothers yelling.

We helped them distill their reactions down to simple, and potent statements. For him it was, "Stop yelling at me!" For her it was, "I'm not crazy!" We made space for each of them in turn to fully embody these statements with all the force of their energy, while the other stepped aside and observed. Each then began to feel a release and opened space for self compassion as well as empathy for the other. We believe it is essential for partners to have space to fully feel their self-protective emotions. Our task with them is to help them to make the conflict what it is really about and to open to the energy that never had room for full expression. This is where healing begins. We want to help them break the energetic entanglement that results from fighting about the wrong thing (as when Ralph and Paula quarrel over how many days) and to bring it to true energetic release, to help them really stand up for themselves.

From an evolutionary perspective, each partner is perpetually grappling with the tension between protecting his or her self-identity and the "urge to emerge" into a more expansive and inclusive selfhood. There is an "evolutionary renegotiation" that needs to take place as each person is challenged to grow beyond narrow self definitions. Pain and fear often show up as a resistance to this motion of life. Every one of us hangs tight to the way we see ourselves, our partners, and the world.

Our consciousness evolves through the confrontations that are endemic to commitment. But we resist these opportunities when we are unwilling or afraid to take in new information that sometimes can only come to us through the reflected energy of an intimate other. For Lily, an evolutionary renegotiation took place when she made it past five years with Wayne. In all her previous relationships she dated men who were kind but passive. With Wayne, however, she was met by a man who was not intimidated by her. As a result, Lily began to discover a frightened "little girl" aspect of herself. She resisted this for quite a while, but in order to move forward with Wayne she ultimately began to embrace and love the qualities of the "little girl," which included a tenderness she never knew she had. She had to let go of her previous self-definition as a woman who could always dominate men, and expand it to include other aspects of her humanity.

In our view, the relationship is a form of natural therapy. The mentor's role is to assist the couple in developing the basic skills involved in taking the energy that is available between them and using it to transcend the present embeddedness. Each partner can, through the energy of conflict, help the other to open up to new realities, deeper connection to disowned emotions, and higher levels of self awareness. Through conflict the relationship can serve to guide each partner to play out the organic tensions between autonomy and intimacy, inclusion and distinction, agency and need.

When one partner says to the other "You're not my therapist!" she is really saying, "Stop removing yourself from what is happening between us." A good therapist, in our estimation, does not remove himself from what is happening in the moment. He is emotionally involved. Partners are in the very best position to create an environment where each can use his or her own reactions to support the other's growth. This usually fails to happen because couples do not know how to take a conflict beyond their control patterns and into the emotions that lay beneath.

There is gold buried in our partner's blaming statements. Though our first reaction is to protect ourselves, eventually we can come around to accepting the kernel of truth, the "20%" responsibility in our beloved's critique of us. When a spouse can embrace that which has merit in his partner's blame-throwing, and not take on the "80%" that doesn't belong to him, he opens up to an evolutionary renegotiation. Conversely, when a couple keeps the conflict centered squarely in a perpetual reenactment of their control patterns, the environment remains hostile to growth. Though the couple appears to be insisting upon change, there is an implied contract to maintain the status quo, so that nothing novel or dangerous can emerge.

In working with couples who are blaming each other, the mentor needs to make enough room for the blaming statements to inform her of some important truth. When Jessica accuses Saul of being selfish she is actually on to something that he needs to look at in his life. While the word selfish is really nothing more than character slander, some of Saul's behaviors can rightfully be called into question. His weekend golf ritual cuts deeply into the available time they have together. While branding him as selfish is more designed to hurt than help, it can be valuable to Saul to hear how much his decisions impact Jessica. In this regard, blame is often the initial doorway into change.

The natural therapy of commitment, at its best, can allow partners to push forward the evolutionary impulse. Your partner can be the transmitter of deep knowledge and emotional liberation because she feels you in a different way than *you* feel you. Together you can give birth to something new. But this requires a willingness to tolerate differences and to have the humility to witness openly the impact of your own limitations in the way they affect your closest loved one.

Conflict engagement requires both humility and authority. Humility is the pathway to compassion, as I come to see myself as I am in any given moment. The word humility derives from hummus or ground. To be truly humble I must be grounded in who I am, and open to who I may become. Authority requires me to tell the truth to my partner even when I am not sure how she will react. It is the pathway to true equality. Each partner in a conflict tends to see the other as a threat. That is, each gives the other tremendous power. In this sense, conflict challenges both of them to "speak truth to power." Conflict engagement, then, offers both parties the sublime opportunity to move from self protection to a personal evolution into humility and authority.

There are two levels of conflict that generally play out in the committed relationship. First is the patterned exchange of energy which reveals itself as arguing over some particular issue. A couple in therapy will take turns each making their position on a given subject clear. They are half talking to each other and half persuading the therapist of the rightness of their respective positions. These conflicts are motivated by self protection and are enacted through each partner's control patterns. The specific styles of each relationship (aggressive-aggressive, aggressive-passive, passive-passive) will play out over and over again. There is a certain "energetic charge" that is maintained in this conflictual tango. In other words there is an attempt in the conflict to keep some measure of connection going. However, it is leading nowhere and is gradually crushing whatever emotional freedom that is remaining.

Couples mired in this first level of conflict live in what Scharmer refers to as an "autistic system." He tells us that in an autistic relationship "what a system picks up from its environment or outside world is limited to the frames, concepts, and structures it already has. Nothing new gets in . . . The system is autistic in the sense that whatever impulse is trying to penetrate the boundary between the outside (the world) and the inside (the system), it will always trigger the same kind of response: a . . . snap response that is programmed or hardwired into the system through patterns of the past." [(40)]

For a therapist to intervene when a couple is locked into their patterned interactions can be quite challenging. It can be very difficult to get a word in "edgewise." The self protective charge that is fueling the couple's exchanges is never easy to break into. Let's take Leticia and Gary for instance. In a recent mentoring session, Gary brings up that he hates Christmas because he thinks Leticia goes overboard and gets stressed out. She pounces back that Gary never makes any effort to create a meaningful holiday and is over-focused on work. The two of us attempt to intervene by slowing them down and asking them to pay attention to what is happening inside. Marcia says, "Gary, what does it feel like when Leticia says you never make any effort." Before Marcia even finishes Gary is retorting, "I think it's ridiculous how much you spend for gifts." Brian invites him again to become aware of what is going on inside even as he accuses her of overspending. But Leticia is all over him for his accusation. The closed autistic system will not allow for anything to penetrate. Sympathetic reactivity is high and the felt sense of danger precludes any shifting inward.

Often it becomes necessary to find a way to either "amplify" or "cut the energy" in these types of autistic exchanges. We will be detailing this later, but with Gary and Leticia, we ultimately had them first ***simplify*** and then ***amplify*** the conflict. Leticia was encouraged to say "You work too much!" Gary got to express himself by saying "You spend too much!" Subsequently, as some of the intensity was released, we cut the energy and turned our attention to one of them at a time and asked the other just to remain present but not to speak. Then each was able to drop below the sympathetic reaction and discover what we call the "sensitivity trigger."

The sensitivity trigger is the "Ouch" response to something a partner says or does which relates to something from one's own past. For Gary, it turns out he has an "ouch" because he hears Leticia saying "You are never enough." This evokes painful experiences from childhood where he was constantly compared to his sisters. For Leticia her sensitivity trigger was that she never felt seen for all the positive things she did. This mirrored her own childhood hurt over being rejected for being overweight and others ignoring all her good qualities.

The second level of conflict occurs when couples move beyond their habituated style of discord and a heated exchange erupts. Here is where curse words fly and ugly utterances pour forth. Tempers rise and cruelty has its moment in the sun. Each person moves from trying to defend their respective sense of self and acquiesces to the urge to unload hurt upon the other. For some the aftershock of such hostilities leaves them reeling for weeks. For such couples these fights can just never be allowed to occur. For others still, they can happen with some degree of regularity.

In our mentoring work it is our contention that this second level of conflict can serve an important function in the shared energy field. The challenge of two separate individuals each trying their best to live in harmony will lead, on occasion, to a natural eruption of pent up energy. Just as a child can throw a tantrum when her frustration reaches a boiling point, so too adult emotions need to spill over from time to time.

Anger manifests in several different ways. First, it most often shows up as blame. This is what we see in couples when they are in first level conflict. Second, is what can be called "self-affirming anger," which is a positive and clear form of saying "no" to anything that a partner may experience as wrong or injurious. We'll come back to this in Chapter Seven.

A third form of anger erupts from what in Core Energetics is referred to as the "lower self." This is usually a disowned aspect or part of each one of us which is capable of cruelty and destructiveness. Arnold Mindell [(28)] refers to this as the "terrorist" residing in each one of us. It is connected to the normal human desire for revenge. When a spouse calls his partner "useless" or "lazy" or "fucked up in the head," he is operating from this inner place of cruelty and is motivated by revenge. He wants her to feel as he believes she has made him feel. Paradoxically at the heart of even his most mean-spirited verbal attacks lies a desire to have his partner know him better. Cruelty emerges when one feels victimized. An "out of control" barrage of hurtful comments pours forth.

These second level conflicts can be dangerous. When one or the other partner loses control of anger there is the potential for physical violence. For many, harsh language also leaves a lasting wound and the words are taken deeply to heart. It is obviously crucial for the relationship therapist to know the couple well enough to ascertain their capacity for such conflict. As we stated at the beginning of this chapter, physical violence is really an avoidance of conflict. It is designed to cut off the painful experience of another's negativity being directed at the person perpetrating the physical attack. The cruel irony is that all perpetrators of physical violence perceive themselves as victims.

But in society's sincere efforts to curtail domestic violence, the pendulum sometimes swings too far. **In EMM we have come to recognize that even in really strong relationships there is the occasional "meltdown."** Every now and then many couples blow up at each other. Because they care for each other, the potential for an eruption of strong emotions exists. Just as a child screams "I hate you!" at a parent she loves so much, all of us feel the wrath of shattered ardor. As Marcia likes to remind couples, "There is no such thing as wrathful indifference."

For two people to honor and attend to their own rhythms there is a necessary struggle that arises. No two of us walk through life with the same pace, tempo, energy, aspirations, needs or desires. Assimilation of our diverse natures involves inevitable conflict. This conflict is the alchemic process of change and transformation. So when therapy does not give adequate space for these disquieting passions, evolution suffers.

The life cycle of a second level conflict includes a number of important stages. In the attachment literature we learn that when there is a breach of attachment a child goes through several distinct phases. First, there is *protest*. Here the child's energy and responsiveness is alive, vital and undefended. She expresses herself outwardly and forcefully in order to effect a response from the caregiver. But it is a mistake to think that the protest is enacted by the infant just to get a response from the caregiver. Protest also serves the very vital function of cultivating the child's sense of agency. She protests when something is not right and she cannot fix it on her own. She possesses in that moment a sense of innocent entitlement that allows her to call out for assistance. There is no shame, no etiquette, no subversion in her protest. It is clear and pure. The infant who is protesting is claiming her spirit, her spunk. She is not only demanding attention, she is saying "I am here!"

Eventually when protest proves ineffective, when the child is not met in his fullness he will sink into *despair*. This is characterized by a devitalized energetic system and what appears to be a learned helplessness. The sense of agency is lost and the child exhibits what can be described as an energetic collapse. The infant despairs the futility of exerting control over his environment. His soul contracts and he tries to cope with a new reality, one in which he feels at the whim of a universe which does not bestow on him the status of CEO. The little one's aura shines a little less brightly.

The third phase is *detachment*. Here, the child adjusts herself to a reality in which she cannot effect responsiveness. She develops an adaptive style of remote attachment. Life goes on and she learns to bury her need. In detachment there is an accommodation to the new world of life outside her control. While this accommodation carries a certain tragic sadness because of the diminishment of spontaneity and life-force, it also creates internal shifts which can be the harbinger of adult capacities for emotional tolerance, vulnerability and adult need.

We see some of this occurring behind the scenes of a second level conflict drama. But in an adult committed relationship it's even more complicated. When we use the term conflict engagement, we are suggesting that couples learn to go through fights as a way to grow. We have identified the following stages of second level conflict:

1. Enactment of Control Patterns—bickering, blaming, or avoiding.
2. The Chaos Phase
3. Retreat
4. Second Awareness
5. Repair and Self Ownership
6. Emergence

Let's explore each of these stages.

Enactment of Control Patterns

This first stage is really the level one conflict of self-preservation. Each party has settled into his or her own style of dealing with differences. Sometimes these, what mentor Judy Gotleib describes as "niggling exchanges" serve to keep some level of energy moving between partners. They can rise and fall in intensity but generally never lead to any kind of breakthrough or illumination. At their best, the level one squabbles can be an effort to evoke more energy but when this happens, the result is typically a second level conflict. Most often they lead nowhere and help to maintain a closed system where each partner remains embedded in a fixed reality.

The Chaos Phase

Second level conflicts are characterized by an out-of-control chaotic expulsion of held down energy. Political correctness goes the way of the Dodo. There are fissures in the control patterns, especially for those who tend to employ passive ones. The "nice guy" morphs into Mr. Hyde and "demure lady" brings out her Black Widow side. The fight escalates beyond self-preservation to scorched-earth.

In the chaos phase parts can show up that have been absent for decades or have never before been met. There are far more couples than will ever show up in data on domestic violence who have, at some point, shoved or restrained each other. For those who are, as Arnold Mindell [(28)] says: *die Rachsucht*, or 'addicted to fury" there is a bigger problem. But for most couples, the chaos conflict is a tipping point. It can lead to either a fearful retreat into even more deeply entrenched control patterns, or it can open up the couple to something higher and actually lead the way toward an exceptional relationship. In the chaos phase there is an eruption of taboo sentiments ("Go fuck yourself!" "You asshole!" "I fucking hate you!" "Drop dead!") There is also an escalation in energy, and sometimes an impolite disclosure of long held dissatisfactions ("I hate the way you wear your hair!" "You're a lousy kisser!" "Do something about your weight!") These exchanges are, to be sure, injurious, and yet they can often lead to significant breakthroughs both in the shared energy field as well as within each partner's own evolution.

When there is a breakdown of structure things do get messy. It also creates an opening for more vitality and spontaneity. Even though there may be a lower-self cruelty motivating the harsh exchanges, there is also a desire to free up the stultifying energy that the control patterns create. In our view, if a relationship cannot survive messiness it remains limited in its potential.

Retreat

It is often necessary when couples engage in the messiness of the chaos phase for each person to pull back for a period of time. This can vary from person to person, from couple to couple. Occasionally the retreat phase can last just a few minutes while partners collect themselves, so to speak, before they can drop down into more "intimacy-enhancing" emotional states. Sometimes it can take a day or two or three. Retreat involves a pulling back into oneself, allowing the fight-or-flight energy to subside and a taking stock of one's emotional state. In retreat, couples can follow one of two paths. First, they simply brush aside the chaotic event, maybe offer a perfunctory apology and "move on." Second, if each person truly becomes more mindful of what s/he is feeling beneath the rage, there is the possibility of something beautiful unfolding.

Second Awareness

When one or both people can begin to notice what else is occurring besides the hostility, they can begin the process of moving from autonomy-enhancing charged up energy toward more vulnerable intimacy-enhancing emotional connection. This second awareness requires the individual to ask herself, "What else is going on in me?" As she settles down from the adrenaline-infused chaos phase she can be with herself and notice what is occurring somatically and consciously. The capacity and willingness to do this is essential to the evolutionary process.

Repair and Self Ownership

When partners attempt to reconnect after a knock-down-drag-out fight it is a delicate and precious interlude. Both are apt to feel multiple emotions, ranging from numbness to shame, from hurt to remorse. How a couple negotiates the repair and self ownership stage is, to put it mildly, pivotal to the relationship's development. In this stage each party has the opportunity to take responsibility for what they said or did that was harmful to the other. Repair happens both when one takes responsibility for his negativity and destructiveness, and when he is willing to hear what his partner has to share about her experience. Repair requires empathy, or entrainment with one another's energy and experience.

Emergence

In the EMM approach we place great emphasis on what the level-two conflict has to teach each party. For all the pain and consternation to be worthwhile, there is a need to make connections between what happened in the fight and what new awarenesses it offers to each person. In Evan and Thomas' situation, they had a huge and messy fight about sex. Evan controlled the amount of sex that occurred because he didn't want it as much as Thomas. All sort of accusations and epithets were tossed about during the chaos phase. Thomas accused Evan of cheating and Evan accused Thomas of being abusive. As they worked their way down through the stages, the relationship emerged into a new level of existence. Thomas not only saw how controlling and threatening he could be (repair and self ownership) but he learned how vulnerable he felt asking for intimacy. He came to see how he equated sexual responsiveness with an acceptance of who he is (emergence). He felt deep pain about all his past rejections by heterosexual men who used him sexually. For his part Evan acknowledged how he sometimes turned to the internet and took his sexual energy away from Thomas (repair and self ownership). He also became more deeply aware of the profound affect his older brother's abuse had on him (emergence). They took these emotional awarenesses back into the bedroom and began to have a more complete and heartfelt sexual relationship (emergence.)

When we take the **emergency** of level two conflicts all the way to a growth in self awareness and an expansion of our emotional responsiveness we **emerge** on a higher evolutionary plane. In John O'Donohue's words, "When you open your heart to discovery, you will be called to step outside the comfort barriers within which you have fortified your life. You will be called to risk old views and thoughts and to step off the circle of routine and image." . . . your soul loves the danger of growth." (30) Conflict can be dangerous—it can also be the stimulus of growth.

Chapter Five

From Reactive to Embodied

The pathway to an exceptional relationship runs directly through the human body. Intimacy is conversation on a cellular level. Two people grow together by touch. We all want to be touched—physically, emotionally, inspirationally. We meet each other not through neocortical exchanges of abstract information, but through limbic resonance of shared experience; through tingling sensations running up the spine as a loved one draws near; through erect and moistened genitals; through the wild undulations of a shared belly laugh; through an engorging lump in the throat as appreciation and gratitude threaten to overtake us. We are most alive when we succumb to the unpredictable vicissitudes of our own life force.

Here's a poem by Marcia:

The Untouched Body

She needs the great serpent
To tighten around her body
Not so she dies
So that she can feel.
In the absence of presence
Where is an infant to go?
Lost for many years
Until the undulating body
kneaded by hands
Needed in turn.

Coiling and wrapping
In a plethora of pulsation and passion
Penetrating skin and sinew
To the spine,
And then the soul
Forever together
In a tangled dance of renewal.

Relationship is, at its very best this "tangled dance of renewal" where partners entwine in myriad shapes and vibrations. Couples in the tangled dance vacillate between greater form and greater fluidity, at one moment flexing the muscles of individuation and in the next, tissue softening into union. The embodied relationship embraces not just the consciousness of a self aware mind, but the electricity of beings who are open to the fluid movement of shared energy.

David Wallin has identified three approaches toward experience that people tend to abide by. He says, "I find it very useful clinically (as well as personally) to think in terms of three primary stances toward experience: We can simply be *embedded* in experience, we can have a *mentalizing* or *reflective* stance toward experience, or we can be *mindful.*" (italics his) [(48)]

In the EMM approach we have found Wallin's formulation to be extremely useful as it applies to a couple's interactions with each other. In our work we add a fourth possibility which we call *embodiment*. When couples seek support, our goal is to help them move or evolve through these four gradients of awareness and interaction.

One of the great misconceptions surrounding emotionally expressive interventions in individual, couples, or group work, results from the confusion between embeddedness and embodiment. The litany of criticisms against the open expression of feelings is voluminous. It has been vilified as honesty dumping, emotional diarrhea, verbal abuse, whining, and unbridled self-expression. Relationship specialist Terrence Real tells us: "Psychotherapy has been a major aider and abettor of what I have come to call the barf-bag approach to intimacy . . . Here's the real deal on venting. When you are hurt or angry, spewing is not being authentic; it's being a brat." [36]

The chastising is so pervasive it has left many who practice somatic and emotionally expressive work cowering in seclusion. Again, though these (ironically virulent) reactions are largely based on the failure to distinguish between reactivity and embodiment. It is our hope in this chapter to make this distinction more lucid. For we certainly agree that reactivity alone solves nothing and can be harmful. But embodiment grants us our full humanity.

Arnold Mindell argues that there is a western bias against emotional expressiveness. "Consciousness," he says, "has become synonymous with reduced affect." [28] Regularly, in our relationship mentoring we bear witness to couples who have succumbed to the cultural norm of reduced affect. It is, perhaps, one of the greatest reasons why relationships fail. Mindell goes on to say, "Eurocentric concepts such as 'acting out' imply that emotional expressiveness (the very core of many cultures) is pathological. Such concepts are merely cultural biases, not truths."

When we talk about helping couples come alive, it has everything to do with using the energy that exists in the shared energy field to become more expressive. As we will see shortly, embodiment takes us from being embedded in our fixed reality, through a growing capacity to reflect and bear witness to parts of ourselves that are needing attention, and ultimately to an emerging competency in "conscious emotional expression."

To summarize, we call the four gradients of awareness and expression:

1. Reactivity
2. Reflectivity
3. Mindful
4. Embodied

Let's review each of them.

Reactivity

What Wallin refers to as *embeddeness* we will call *reactivity,* as it relates to a committed couple. Wallin states, "Much of the time, without being aware of it, many of our patients are too embedded in problematic experience—too identified with what they believe and feel—to be able to envision alternative views of that experience . . . When embedded in experience, it's as if we *are* the experience as long as the experience lasts." (italics his) [48]

In couples therapy the dyad is often ensnared in a reactive stance. Partners are embedded in their fixed sense of reality and all other possibilities recede into oblivion. When reactivity rules, neither person is able to see outside the box of her/his own making. Colored by narrative and accented by implicit triggers, neither can envision a separate reality. How each person *feels* is indistinguishable from a wider truth. There is no separation between reaction and reality. In reactive mode neither party can step back and breathe in a wider perspective, an alternative point of view.

To make matters even more challenging to the couples' therapist, reactive partners not only are unable to see beyond their reactivity, they can't even identify what they feel. Reactivity is the offspring of fight or flight response. The stakes in the committed relationship are very high. Both partners can become extremely threatened by each other's perceived attacks. Immersed in sympathetic nervous reactivity there is no space for either partner to step back and witness what feelings might be present. All the focus is on defending oneself. When the therapist asks, "Can you tell me what you're feeling right now." the reactive person most often responds with comments like "I'm just trying to show that her version of the story is incorrect." Or. "I feel like he simply won't ever take responsibility."

On occasion if the therapist queries about a specific emotion there might be an affirmative response: "Are you feeling hurt by what he said?" "Yes, it's just not right for him to talk to me that way." While tangentially acknowledging the feeling, she instantly brings it back to what is going on with him. It is often a monumental challenge to crack the cycle of reactivity.

As we discussed in the prior chapter, when partners are triggered by each other and they enter into a blame-and-defend cycle it is often helpful to either *simplify* and *amplify* the energy, or to find a way to break into the reactive energetic exchange. By breaking in, we mean literally infringing on the reactive sparring. So, for instance, in a mentoring session we will sometimes physically reposition ourselves between the pair so that the energy gets re-directed toward us.

When a couple is in a reactive stance toward each other, the system is closed and, though energy exchange can become high-pitched, there is no real movement toward deeper understanding, emotional awareness or self ownership. Where there is no sense of safety, there is no room for growth. The threats to one's autonomy, or one's sense of connectedness, causes distress, and makes it nearly impossible for either person to actually listen to the other. Everything is heard through the filter of personalization. When a spouse takes personally the reactions of his partner he is nearly always going to want to protect himself. As a result, he cannot truly hear beyond what he perceives is a personal attack. He can't hear that she may have a need, or that the intensity of her reactions comes from her own history (remember 80%—20%).

If you recall from the Chapter One discussion of the shared energy field, couples are not simply reacting to each other, they are each shaping the quality of the others response. Partners in a reactive cycle tend to see the each other's reactivity as isolated and separate from how each is coming across. So a partner might say "I asked him for a favor and he blew up at me." The spouse who says this appears incredulous at her mates "overreaction." But there is an amalgam of shared energy that comes into play which is completely overlooked by the offended mate. In this case, she approaches asking him for a favor with a hardened edge because she suspects he will say no. He doesn't hear it as a request, but a demand with an ". . . or else" energy cleaved to the words. He responds with resistance because he perceives she is manipulating him, which he holds as part of a narrative he has about her. Thus each is not merely reacting but is shaping and being shaped by an ever-mounting history of interchanges. This is the nature of shared energy—it is forever molding each partner's responsiveness when they remain unaware of how they are being influenced by one another.

When reactivity has taken hold it is a mistake for the couple's therapist to assume that either party can truly listen to the other. The capacity for empathy is low and the brain and neurological system operates in service of protection, not honest expression. Daniel Seigel writes, "(The) state of hyperarousal leads, neurologically, to the inhibition of higher perceptions and thoughts in favor of the dominance of more basic somatic and sensory input. In this situation, we don't think; we feel something intensely and act impulsively. What this means is that an individual who enters a state outside the window of tolerance is potentially in a 'lower mode' of processing. In which reflexive responses to bodily states and primary sensory input are more likely to dominate processing." [44]

What Siegel calls the "window of tolerance" is the human capacity to manage strong emotions. Beyond a certain level the human nervous system contracts back into a highly defended posture in order to protect the organism's integrity. Couples engaged in a reactive cycle have stepped beyond the window of tolerance and are only minimally capable of reason and detachment from defensive interactions. When you are working with a couple embedded in reactivity very specific interventions are called for. We'll address these momentarily.

The characterological posture each person brings into the relationship can also fuel the embeddedness in reactivity. Those who were raised in a dangerous world are more likely to see threat in everything. Much like with disorganized attachment the individual who was what Stephen Johnson [15] called "The Hated Child," can get paralyzed and dissociated in the reactive exchanges. She cannot tolerate her partner's intense energy and is extremely cued into every inflection in his voice and nuance in his deportment. She cannot tolerate too much distance nor too much closeness. Her reactivity may send her spinning into dissociation or swelling with fury, every mole-hill an Everest.

The spouse who, as a child, was emotionally deprived, is very reactive to his partner's rejections. He sees rejection often where there is none and withers in response. His reactivity is more likely to be expressed through passive control patterns and involves a measure of despair over not having the power to influence his partner. There is likely to be a great deal of withholding energy in his reactive stance. His reactive withholding starves his partner of affirmation, sensuality, laughter, and spontaneity. He doesn't believe she will be there and silently excoriates her every time she isn't.

The partner who suffered from a domineering and invasive childhood environment will be triggered into reactivity by a mate whom she perceives as controlling. She too is apt to employ more passive control patterns. It will be difficult for her to distinguish between her internal state of chronic self-protection, resistance and pent-up tension, and the external reality of what her partner is actually doing. His attempts at connection may be experienced by her as domination. As a child she felt smothered, oppressed, and stifled in her attempts to individuate. With her spouse, her reactivity reveals itself as victimized complaining and a seething resentment. She gives in to him and holds it against him with no small amount of negative pleasure—the righteous satisfaction of one who always sacrifices. Her partner cannot win.

Finally, the individual who was betrayed and manipulated as a defining quality of his childhood will react with mistrust and accusations toward his spouse. The shattering recognition that his caregivers used him as a prop, prized him only for what he could do for them, or seduced him sexually, froze him in perpetual suspicion. It is not just that he can no longer trust others, that is bad enough, but he can't even trust his own instincts, his innocence betrayed. Generally he will use more aggressive control patterns and will not be able to let down his guard. Because trust is such a sacred and delicate bond in a relationship, the child who was betrayed and taken advantage of will remain in a state of hyper-caution even as an adult. When he believes she is lying, out to get him, or tricking him, his autonomic nervous system fires into high arousal.

Melinda and Tracy worked with us for over a year. Tracy was out of work for nearly two years and had a great deal of difficulty maintaining any regular employment, though he was well educated. Melinda was a professional woman who worked hard and supported the household. She was bitter toward Tracy and regularly talked (unconvincingly) about leaving him. He was raised by a mother who was extremely controlling and over-protective of him. Though he looked and acted depressed he actually seemed to have an abundance of energy that was held back. His character stance was to react to Melinda with passive resistance. For her part, Melinda grew up in a family where nobody showed up for her. Money was always tight and neither parent was emotionally tuned into her. She exhibited a character stance of a deprived and abandoned child.

She held a belief that she would always have to do it all, and reacted to Tracy with bitterness and disgust. In their reactive exchanges she would complain and he would accuse her of being insensitive to his depression and try to prove to her how hard he was working at getting a job. In our work we helped them to move past the reactive exchanges by *amplifying* and *simplifying* the conflict and also by breaking the energetic reactive spiral. Breaking the reactive spiral involved shifting the focus away from their present conflict and toward their character wounding. In one session, Tracy was invited to express anger toward Melinda's parents for abandoning her, while she stood near him. He directed protective anger by pounding on foam and declaring "How dare you leave her all alone! You should have taken care of her!" This served to allow him to step up in his power, and for her to relax her vigilance. We call this "expression by proxy" and we will discuss it in more detail later.

At a separate time we supported them to amplify and simplify by having him express the place in him that said, "I won't be controlled by you." Melinda was given the space to shout out, "Help me, I can't do it all alone!" Here, the energy was directed toward each other and because of the previous work where Tracy defended Melinda energetically through the "expression by proxy" it was safer for both of them to amplify the reactivity. By simplifying the statements it clarified what the demands and immature needs were. Instead of remaining locked into a power struggle they both felt relief. Simplifying is a crucial tool in assisting couples to go straight to the heart of what each is attempting to convey. As Alexander Solzhenstsyn once pronounced, "Everything you add to the truth subtracts from the truth."

As a couples' therapist, breaking the stranglehold of reactivity as played out through each person's control patterns is a heroic undertaking. To put it bluntly, this is where the couple needs you to step up. The sympathetic nervous stimulation toward fight or flight is hard to drop when the threat is sitting or standing two feet away. In these moments the couple is looking for a "stronger and wiser other" to establish a flexible balance between secure connection and intrepid exploration. The reactive duo wants and needs your energy to be "bigger" than their reactivity.

The couple does not know how to break the reactive cycle and though they hang to it tenaciously they want to know you are not daunted by their struggle, because *they* are! Your passivity in the face of their monumental struggle for autonomy and integrity reinforces the internal sense of despair that co-exists with their outer protestations. To "cut the energy" or to help the couple amplify and simplify involves what Wallin calls "the improvisation of relational moves." The creative aspect of EMM means to move back and forth with the couple in a mutual exploration of pathways to releasing the reactive spiral. The significance of doing this is hard to overestimate.

Cutting the energy of reactivity requires emotional fortitude, a willingness to engage in trial-and-error, and a fair amount of risk taking. To be able to come between the highly charged exchanges requires of the therapist compassion and strength. It is too easy for you as therapist to get reactive and controlling yourself. There are many ways to break through the embeddedness of reactivity and you have to discover your own personal style. Chances are you will need to do some growing yourself as you take this on. The two of us have been challenged to find parts within ourselves that can avoid getting swept up in trying to fix them, shut them up, or simply let them go on and on.

When it comes to breaking the energy, anything is possible with different couples at different times. Some examples from our experience include:

- Simply telling the partners to "stop" when they have been going at each other heatedly and fruitlessly. This needs to be done from a place of authority not from frustration or overwhelm. You can explain to them that you stopped them because the combative nature of their interaction is just the beginning of the story and you want to help them find the rest. Exhibiting first the strength to stop them can create a sense of safety which then allows you to compassionately direct them to what primary feeling they may be protecting. Your strength is a vital ingredient in the creation of a safe environment to help them drop below fight or flight.
- Getting them to stop will sometimes lead to physical intervention. One of us may, for instance, hold a partner's hand, helping him to stay in contact. Often, having them stand allows for movement and gesturing which supports a full fight-or-flight release. We may ask one to look us in the eyes, breathe, and bring all her attention toward the one of us she is standing with. On occasion, if the room has become really electric with reactive charge we may go more radical and drape our body over a spouse's shoulder and help "ground" him as his energy spins off in a whirlwind of self protective undulations—all the while verbally reassuring and supporting.
- Frequently it is necessary to re-direct their energies away from each other. This can be done by bringing your attention to one partner and helping that person make the connection between the present reaction or trigger and any similar experiences from his past. This is not just an intellectual exercise, but a way for them to feel how much they have been affected by similar conflicts in their history. You are helping them to validate the intensity of his reaction. This can then be done with the other partner as well.

- Often we will take this a step further and break the energy by devoting most of a particular session to one person. In other words we will, in essence, provide an individual session for one person while the other is observing and perhaps even playing a role. For example, Elly and Simone can easily fall into arguing about sex. He accuses her of totally controlling their sex life and she attacks him for being boorishly insensitive. Intervening at these times was no small undertaking. Invariably they would ignore us and go right back to sniping at each other over who was more to blame for their almost non-existent sex life. On one occasion we asked them both if we could use the session to focus on Elly and her experiences around sexuality. (We already knew that her first sexual encounter was with an older cousin who convinced her to provide him with oral sex.) By supporting her in going back to that experience and reclaiming her primary restorative feeling of anger, she could express what she was holding for so many years. She could amplify and simplify her basic reaction. The words that came to her that she never got to say were, "You can't have me!" So, with Simone witnessing we invited her to direct the strength of those words toward her cousin. She screamed over and over "You can't have me! Until it became "I'll never let you in!" Simone was moved by this and gently approached her. He stood near her and said "I don't want to hurt you." This softened Elly and she cautiously moved to make contact with him. By devoting the session to her (it could just as easily have been him) the reactive exchange broke and both could allow more vulnerability to emerge.
- Another possibility is to help each spouse to connect to what is happening in their bodies. Have them bring "second attention" to what is occurring in their eyes, neck, stomach, jaw, chest, pelvis, etc. Ask them how it feels in their bodies to be trying to convince the other—to really attend to what is happening on levels other than the narrative. As we will discuss shortly this is bringing mindfulness, or presence to the conflictual moment.

- Cutting the energy can also involve having each partner identify internal "parts" that they are protecting or using as protection. They can name these parts (scared kid, warrior woman, critical parent, cave dweller, etc.)
- Have them draw pictures of the conflict, or how they see the other.
- Get them to engage in sandplay,—which involves providing them with miniature props and sand trays. This can help them to step back from the reactivity and explore it consciously through play.
- Have them switch roles.
- Let all of you switch roles so that each can observe and "feel into" another's experience. This means *you* becoming one of them and one of the couple taking on the role of the therapist. Whenever the two of us have switched roles with a couple it awakens something in them to observe, with a bit of distance, the intensity of their own shared energy.

By working to break the energy of the reactive cycle we are helping the partnership to step back and create space to identify what is happening rather than being submerged in it. As a couple can become more cognitive and can bring language to the charged emotions they gain a certain power to control the flow of energy better.

Reflectivity

The joke goes: The words that strike fear into the heart of a man are those uttered by his spouse: "*We need to talk.*" The amazing neocortical capacity to reflect upon experience opens the doors to an entirely unique way of perceiving the world. This is a bold evolutionary thrust into a glittery new universe of abstractions, logic, symbols, linearity, assumptions, recollections, narratives, and for some folks endless dialogue about "what you meant when you said blah, blah, blah."

Couples who are able to step beyond the enveloping bonds of reactivity achieve liberation. This is an emancipation from the confinement of life spent in self-preservation consciousness. To be able to talk ***about*** experience is to open enough distance between you and your impulse to defend-and-attack and to notice other realms of possibility. How remarkable an achievement! When a couple can relax their autonomic ping pong match, they open space for dialogue. In this new expansiveness they can actually learn something from their interactions.

Reflecting is a mythic leap into reason. It provides couples with the tools and skills to step outside the moment and cogitate on what just happened. It permits the pair to add context and comprehension to otherwise chaotic and high-pitched exchanges of energy. It also introduces to the partnership the idea of causality. In this new environment things get explained. Explanations offer comfort and solace to the bewildered couple who can make no sense of what is happening between them when reactivity rules. The acquisition of meaning offers us a greater sense of control when existence itself fails to do so. **A couple who can rationally discuss what is happening and crown the discussion with meaning have brought order to the feral world of unchecked fight-or-flight ferocity.**

Helping couples learn to discuss matters has been the topic of countless self help books and courses. This is an essential undertaking and a crucial developmental leap. Insight-oriented psychotherapy operates on the premise that knowing one's story can free one from unconscious repetition and enactments of historical patterns. When Cyndi could tell her partner June that she gets critical and controlling because she saw her father do that to her mother, she is, in theory, better equipped to choose a different option. That is, to move past her control pattern. She can have a deeper compassion for a behavior she does not like in herself and she can experience greater empathy for the impact it has on June. This is so because she has moved some distance from the control pattern and because, by placing it in a larger context, she provides meaning and sensibility to what looks like an offensive and destructive behavior.

Cognitive reflection can thus support an entry into a couple's emotional universe. The conceptual weaving together of history with present-day control patterns allows partners to see each other in a wider contextual framework. To know that your partner's tendency to energetically vacate the room during sex is called dissociation and that it stems from an abusive childhood illuminates what had previously been both unfathomable and painful. It can help morph anger into concern or guilt into relief. It allows for the metamorphosis of **implicit** memories that are only felt as inchoate bodily experiences into **explicit** recognition of negative childhood experiences. This is the power of naming.

For instance, we worked with a couple Judith and Roy who had been together for only about a year. They both had been involved in a polyamorous lifestyle and were struggling over whether to choose monogamy. Judith wanted to keep polyamory as an option but Roy hoped to remain monogamous with her. As we learned about her history she was able to connect some dots between her childhood and her present choices regarding sexuality. Judith was abruptly abandoned by her father when she was four years old. At this age she idealized him and felt an undefended love for this godlike man.

Judith quickly learned to accommodate to her dad's loss by getting tough. She constructed a façade of control and an absence of need for the man. In her 40's she met Roy through a community they both were part of and they soon entered a phase of intense eros. But as they began to emerge from eros and consider a future together, the debate over polyamory ensued.

By making a connection between her father's abandonment and her desire to have sexual contact outside of her relationship with Roy, she began to get in touch with how much fear she still held over the possibility of yet again "falling in love" and being deserted. She simply could not let a man matter too much. As she described it, she needed to keep other men available "in the bullpen" in case it didn't work out with Roy. Thus, by being able to describe her story she could reconnect to a primary restorative emotion (fear) and begin to consider what was truly right for her. (Note, we are not suggesting that all inclinations toward polyamory or other alternative relationship styles are the direct result of some early-life experience. In this case however, Judith herself made the connection.)

Another couple we work with illustrates how often the seemingly mundane is evoked by the historically profound. Carmen and her new lover Michael were moving toward deeper commitment. They were seriously considering moving in together. She was very vocal about her desire for Michael to move into her apartment and he could not understand why she was so resistant to finding a new place closer to where he worked. In soon came to light that Carmen, who was an immigrant to this country, had a reason for her reluctance to move. At age 11 the violence in El Salvador resulted in her whole family undergoing a forced expatriation from her native land. Under very trying conditions they had to flee and were left without a home or a country for several years. As she conveyed her story she could make contact with a voice in her which said "I will never be forced to move again." She took Michael's strong desire to find a new home for them as pressure and it immediately resulted in her intense resistance. The awareness of this link helped them both to approach the subject with greater understanding. Another therapist had attempted to help them negotiate a compromise around living arrangements. In doing so she missed the gold lying inside the conflict.

The climate that is conducive to reflection is one of safety. Until the partner is not seen as threat and indeed until the therapist is experienced as capable of holding a safe container, caution reigns supreme, and self-preservation consciousness rules the day. As we have emphasized above, to get a couple to reflect upon what is occurring between them when they are in the heat of battle is a monumental therapeutic undertaking. The partners need to feel secure enough to know that they can allow reason to surface. It is the job of the therapist to steward the couple through the transition from reactivity to reflectivity.

Ken Wilber [(53)] makes the distinction between *translational* and *transformative* experiences. When a couple can reflect on what is happening they are able to translate incoherent subjective experiences into a shared language. But reflecting has its limits. While it helped Teddy to hear from a professional that he may be suffering from mild Asperger's for instance, it did not result in any major change in the deep shame that he would feel when he did something "inappropriate." For him to translate his social ineptness and his propensity to miss cues from his wife into a medical condition was a great relief. But more must occur for him to transform his strong sense of humiliation into compassion. This will include his ability to become mindful of and to embody his interior subjective world. Translation is Wilber's way of describing the ability to reflect. It is necessary but insufficient to the ongoing process of personal transformation. Evolution requires more that cognitive comprehension. Additionally, reflection alone is not merely insufficient, it has its drawbacks.

A couple enters your therapy room and each partner spends twenty minutes explaining what had occurred between them the previous week. You ask one of them how he feels when he relates to you that their weekend at the bed & breakfast was a major disappointment. He replies, "I feel that she has trouble letting go. I think she is a lot like her mother in that way." She chimes in, "I feel like you have this thing about my mother, I know that you wanted more sex but I feel that you are being unrealistic. We have sex more than most couples I know." He then goes on to describe the history of their sex life with very little affect. When a partner analyzes his mate without looking inward first, we consider this a form of "psycho-slander." While insights from one partner toward another can ultimately be supportive, it is often done in the spirit of deflecting personal responsibility.

With this couple, each person is embedded in her or his story. The story itself becomes a control pattern which keeps both of them from coming in contact with emotional truths. The story, in effect, takes each partner further away from the present reality and their respective subjective experiences. Each person is operating from state consciousness and is not prepared to cross the threshold into process consciousness. The potential for transformation is encrypted in their shared energy field. The more each person can experience in real time what is happening in the flow of their subjective experience, the more they can evolve. Attachment wounds can heal when energies entrain. Staying in the story nullifies this potential.

Daniel Siegel informs us, "Patterns established early in life have a major impact on functioning, but the individual's experiences continue to influence the internal model of attachment. This suggests that new relationship experiences have the potential to move individuals toward a more secure state of mind with respect to attachment. Intervention studies support the idea that a relationship-based treatment focus can enable proper development to occur." [(44)] Couples rely on reflectivity when they do not know how to enter the flow of the shared energy field. But as they begin to develop this capacity, they can actually move from self preservation consciousness borne of insecure attachment and become more fully self expressive.

This is a major objective in the EMM approach. We believe it is not just the therapist who can help each person heal by entering into a "relationship-based treatment focus" but the partners can heal each other by learning to entrain their energies and nurture limbic resonance. When they are fixated in a reflective style of communication they may develop intellectual understanding but not the profound sense of security which can only arise from the entrained experience of "feeling felt." It is our contention that the committed relationship is a remarkable environment to heal attachment wounds, to break free of the bonds of character enactments and in opening the shared energy field to a transcendent "higher self" expression of power, creativity, gratitude, undefended love and inspiration.

Typically when one partner is expostulating, the other is either tuning out or internally prepping her retort. One or the other will say, "I'm just trying to make my point." Occasionally it will be a point well taken, but by the head, not the heart. Couples who remain in a reflective stance with each other are generally flat and static in their interactions. There is little chance of being open to intuition and the flow of emergent energies. They are neither in the moment nor open to the inspiration of the irrational in their shared energy. Furthermore, such couples will struggle to make sense of their interactions through cause-and-effect logic. "I use the internet because you are never available." "I nag because you would never do anything if I didn't stay on top of you." "If I knew you were really attracted to me I wouldn't be so insecure."

One way we challenge the reflection tendency in couples is through an exercise we often use in workshops. Based on the principle of "no first cause" we will ask partners to first fill in the sentence "If you were more (less) _______, I would be more (less) _________." Thus, using the above example one might say, "If you were more available sexually, I would use the internet less frequently." We then ask them to complete the sentence, "If I were to use the internet less, even if you were not more available, I would feel ______."

The answers are often illuminating and can get the person in touch with a primary feeling. For instance we might hear responses such as:

"If I were to use the internet less, even if you were not more available, I would feel:

- Resentful
- Insecure
- Afraid to show my need
- Anxiety
- Better
- Like I would have to be more assertive with you
- Like I would have to face my own sexual inadequacies
- I couldn't blame our sexual problems on you
- Deprived

By breaking the cause-and-effect narrative, each partner is confronted with what else is present when the story changes. The "no first cause" exercise gives them the opportunity to anticipate what might emerge if either one changed her or his half of the equation. **Linearity and causality result in the adoption of a narrative which places oneself in the role of responder to the other, not as the creator of one's own life experience.** From this consciousness each is determined to wait for the other to change first. The best way for the relationship to transcend this pattern is for each person (or at least one of them) to step beyond the limits of reflectivity and into the here-and-now experience of mindfulness.

Before we leave the subject of reflective interacting however, it is worth exploring with some detail the control pattern of **withholding**. In many relationships one or both partners tend to withhold energy from the other. What does this mean? **Withholding can be described as a complex array of energetic, cognitive and behavioral processes which result in a suppression of spontaneous responses ranging from love and delight, to need, anger or fear.** The withholding individual tends to modulate affect and inhabit the world of intellect as a way to stay within Siegel's "window of tolerance."

Whereas a highly reactive person is exhibiting sympathetic arousal and "comes on like gangbusters," the withholder outwardly looks to be displaying parasympathetic activation. But internally he tends toward a subjective experience of emptiness, collapse, and being "cut off" from his feelings. Not only is he withholding from his partner, but he has in effect, been neurologically conditioned to deny himself access to his own full emotional repertoire.

In attachment terms, the dismissive parent creates an environment where it is necessary for the child to learn to withhold any outward expression of need, fear, anger and sadness. Children, as early as the second year of life, have already learned to mask their feelings and hide expressions they sense will not result in attunement. This style is re-enacted in the committed relationship. While there is in Core Energetics terminology, an energetic "collapse" (a learned helplessness), there is often sympathetic arousal not overtly expressed.

Typically the withholder will acknowledge that she does not open up because she believes she will not be responded to positively. Her narrative is often that the other in either incapable or unwilling to respond affirmatively to her emotional expression. This was often exactly the case with her primary caregiver. But in her present relationship the 80/20% principle holds sway. She may indeed point to instances where her mate "let her down," but the strength of her impulse to withhold can be traced to her formative experience.

The withholder may only see that his withholding is caused by a failure in his partner and he is therefore merely protecting himself. However, withholding can be motivated by other internal and external realities. A spouse can withhold for these motivations as well:

- Shame avoidance—"If I show you how much I need I'll be humiliated."
- Cultural conditioning—some cultures are simply more expressive than others.
- Hostility and cruelty—there is often a silent "Fuck you!" in the withholding of energy.
- Fear of giving up the "superior" position in the relationship. By withholding, one partner keeps the other seeking affection, contact and approval.
- Dissociation—truly being "cut off" from the awareness of one's subjective experience.
- Flooding—being aware of multiple emotions moving simultaneously and not knowing how to integrate them or distinguish them.

The brilliance of naming "parts," as exemplified in Richard Schwartz's Internal Family Systems model, [(43)] is to organize and codify interior states in a way that can be shared with a partner. To be able to say, for instance, "A part of me is attracted to you, but another part is afraid of rejection" can be remarkably effective in bringing the withholder out of the shadows. This is utilizing the uniquely human capacity to mentalize or reflect constructively and compassionately.

Though it is limited, the reflective approach to confronting life transcends the reactive. To name is to bring order to chaos, continuity to broken pieces of experience, meaning to madness. Using symbols, logic, and concepts opens our world immeasurably. The couple who can communicate about internal parts can share on a deeper level. In mentoring we use the power of reflection to provide tools to assist couples in the sacred task of mutual evolution. As we discussed earlier, several concepts specific to the EMM approach have proved particularly valuable to couples we work with. They bear repeating.

- For partners to understand the difference between early imprinted needs and present adult needs helps them distinguish demand from request and to recognize how they see each other in transference.

- The 80/20% principle helps couples to separate what is the truth of one's personal responsibility and what is historical. We have found that it can even help at times to break the reactive cycle.
- The idea of "No first cause" helps partners to move away from the belief that each is only responding to the other and that therefore the other must change first.
- Understanding "triggers" allows each person to link his strong reaction to an historical antecedent. He gets to see that what evokes the strongest reactions to his partner is a doorway in to self-awareness, and ultimately to "right-size" his reactions to his mate.
- To be able to identify that their habitual styles of interacting are designed to protect each of them from strong emotions which were not supported in childhood is often illuminating for couples. We frequently hear couples we have worked with refer to their "control patterns" when discussing how they are stuck. It helps them to see the connection between passive and aggressive behavioral patterns and the emotions that are being protected.
- Finally, many couples benefit by being able to name basic feeling states. The concept of "primary restorative feelings" helps them to communicate more directly and actually opens each person to a more direct connection to undefended emotional truths. It also helps them to comprehend the necessary function of restorative emotions.

Ultimately, a relationship needs more than the capacity for reflection. To move beyond reflectivity, couples need to be supported in relying on other potentialities that are often still lying dormant. One way to do this is by taking the couple out of left hemisphere reliance and open them up to the other half of communication, namely sensate, energetic, and non-verbal forms. As Siegel tells us, ". . . the left hemisphere is the center of the cognitive machinery that attempts to explain events and therefore, in (Michael) Gazzaniga's view, is the primary motive to narrative thinking." He goes on, "The right hemisphere . . .

also appears to be more capable than the left hemisphere of regulating states of bodily arousal. This suggests that whatever factors directly impinge on right-hemisphere processing, such as bodily input or non-verbal emotional expressions in the voices, body signals, and facial reactions of others, may have a direct impact on a person's own emotional state before the involvement of a linguistically based consciousness, or a rational, linear analysis of an ongoing experience." [(44)]

In our work we rarely ever let a couple remain seated for an entire session. We find that to do so encourages a fixation in the reflective stance. Getting them to move their bodies, to begin attending to what is happening in the here-and-now, and to engage in a variety of non-analytic forms of communication (shared breathing, sound, music, dance, wrestling, simple phrases, poetry, fantasy play, etc.) is an essential aspect of the EMM approach.

Mindful

Tich Nhat Hanh once said, "The miracle is not to walk on water. The miracle is to walk on the green earth in this present moment." It is miraculous, to be sure, when a couple learns to stand in the naked truth of the present moment. When two souls emerge from the shadows of their own self deceptions and move gracefully with the ever-fluctuating, fervently unpredictable surge of life-energy, wondrous possibilities spring forth.

The mindfulness movement in psychotherapy has been nothing short of revolutionary. It marries Eastern and Western sensibilities in a profoundly effective and compassionate collaboration. **To introduce a mindful approach to your couples work is to radically alter the rules of engagement. It is as if one is meeting her partner for the first time. Here, the relationship unfolds in real time.** It manifests as an empty cup waiting to be filled by the Great Mystery of life's unfolding nature. To be mindful is to have absolute permission to show up as you are—fully adorned in your own idiosyncracies. To be mindful is, in a very real sense, to be humble.

As we apply mindfulness to the committed relationship we are asking couples to behold each other in the immediacy of the enlivened moment. We want to help them unclutter the transmission and reception of vital life energies. We want them to keep meeting each other for the first time, to fall in love over and over again. To be mindful in relationship is to enter the intersubjective space of connection beyond words and beneath reactive posturing. Mindfulness extends us past both objective and subjective knowledge. As Christian de Quincy suggests, "Whereas the ultimate ideal of objective knowledge is control, and the ultimate ideal of subjective knowledge is peace, the ultimate ideal of intersubjective knowledge is relationship—and dare I say it, love." (6)

Mindfulness *is* the experience not the explanation. As a rule, we need less internal dialogue and more simple grounded awareness. Just as the child needs the stable sense of presence that an attuned parent provides as the foundation of secure attachment, the ability to witness oneself non-judgmentally is an imperative for the adult consciousness. In this way, a mindful stance is akin to self-parenting, to both behold and be held, as the witness-self can provide unwavering acceptance of all internal states. The ability to practice mindfulness is intrinsically healing as it can gradually provide access to previously split off internal states. The witness self holds a steady ground for various energies to come to light.

In the following chapter we will be going into greater depth on this subject of mindfulness as it applies to the core interventions of the EMM approach. We prefer the term "presencing" to mindfulness as it speaks to a wider aptitude and suggests to us the spirit of approaching a state of being fully in each moment cognitively, emotionally, energetically and mutually. Presencing suggests awareness in mind and grounding in body. For two people to be present together is even a greater challenge than for either alone to enter a mindful space of awareness. The shared energy field brings more complexity to each moment.

Rinaldo and Stephanie have been in a committed relationship for 11 years. Both were previously married and had children from those marriages. Rinaldo is an accomplished artist and has lived a highly creative and "edgy" life, using psychedelics and engaging in various sexual exploits. Stephanie is very creative in her own right, but lived a somewhat more sedate life before meeting Rinaldo.

They both work very hard in trying to forge a life together. It was obvious to us that they loved each other and, in spite of many differences in the way they approached life, were determined to grow together. Rinaldo had an aptitude for talking. He can, in a ten minute monologue, shoot off on any number of tributaries, each with its own pearls of wisdom and genuine insight. However, listening to and trying to keep up with his narrative expositions often feels like herding cats. The problem was, any time we attempted to slow him down he bristled over "being controlled." Particularly when Stephanie would react to him it could result in his angrily shutting down and her snapping at him impatiently.

Much of his early life he had to be the "good boy" who took care of his mother. From an attachment perspective he had an extremely dismissive mother who never really received him. She had her *ideas* of him, but was never just with him as he was. He also was forever falling short of his father's expectations. His father was a successful businessman and tried to push Rinaldo in that direction, completely ignoring his obvious artistic abilities. Like many creative kids in school, Rinaldo found himself at the bottom of the pecking order, below the athletes and the intellects.

Stephanie grew up with a physically abusive father and married a violent man with whom she lived for 15 years. Whenever she feels intense energy coming from a man, she tends to withdraw and get sullen. After periods of being withdrawn she will snap at Rinaldo and become critical. He is hypersensitive to her moods and vacillates between trying desperately to be the good boy and attacking her for wanting to stifle him.

In one particular session Stephanie was talking about her frustration over having to share her car with Rinaldo for the past several months because his car had died and it was going to take a few more months before he could afford a new one. He responded by saying he understood how she felt trapped and then went on a long verbal journey (reflecting) about all the ways *he* felt trapped. He reminded her how different he is from her husband and then onto the way they both leave messes in the car and then onto yet another tangent. Even though embedded in his story there are meaningful little awarenesses, Stephanie begins to energetically disappear. We watch as she drifts off into her own world. Following Rinaldo proves to be exhausting even for us. At a certain point one of us asks him if he has noticed that Stephanie went away. It is apparent that he gets upset with this and only tries harder to express himself with even more words. We stop him (with some effort) and tell him that we too have a difficult time staying with him.

One of us suggests to him that his flight of insights and ideas are part of his creativity, but perhaps also stems from his difficulty just *being* with Stephanie, much like his mother could not behold him. We ask them both to stand and face each other and for Rinaldo to let go of his words and see what is there. Immediately his anxiety rises. The void that exists when no words are spoken seems too much for him to manage. He moves toward her apologetically attempting again to make contact with words and a forced embrace. We stop him and again ask him to stand and face her with no words. As they stand silently we notice that he takes her in for the first time. She begins to cry, softly at first, then comes deep, soulful wailing as she opens up to the pain of all the times she was unseen. Together they stand, two invisible children stepping out of the shadows. Rinaldo struggles with competing impulses to be the good boy who tries to make mommy feel better, and just being present. We encourage him to simply stay with all of it.

Presencing with a partner can be profoundly healing and ultimately illuminating. Past, present and an unfolding future encapsulated in the span of a few moments. It is truly amazing how infrequently couples just live in the moment with each other. For many partners it never happens. As we will discuss in the next chapter, presencing is vital to the EMM approach and one of its core interventions. **To stay with the flow of process consciousness, to let go of the narrative, leads to a close encounter of the best kind**. It is a wildly, ferociously, dynamically intimate connection. It is most often avoided because people are afraid of what may show up. The enlivened moment contains everything, from our wounding to our glory. Making space for all that is the stuff of presencing.

The compulsion to be more that who we are, the pernicious overreliance on having answers and solutions, the adoption of control patterns to carefully avoid potent feeling states, and the confusion between our imprinted childhood needs and the fully human primal need to be felt by another all mitigate against presencing. Conversely, entering into a mindful awareness of the moment liberates us from enacting our past unconsciously. If a partner is unaware, for instance, of his mistrust of his mate's motives he may perpetually have "one foot out the door."

Eve and Jordan are just such a couple. He married Eve at age 49 (she was 40). It was a first marriage for both of them. Jordan always suspected women would take advantage of him and right from the outset he entered his relationship with Eve cautiously and suspiciously. Now two years into the relationship he is convinced that Eve only cares about what she can get from him materially. He recites a number of examples of how she only cares about what he does for her.

The two of us see that while there is some validity to his claim (she did want a big diamond and a large wedding) Jordan is so caught in his negative narrative that he cannot see all the ways she truly cares for him. He confuses his feelings of mistrust for an absolute conviction that she is untrustworthy when it comes to wanting what's best for him. That is, without presencing he cannot step back enough from the drama and actually experience his mistrust. Instead he enacts a control pattern of accusation and emotional withdrawal. He can feel in his body an energy that says "I won't let you in." No matter how she tries to convince him she loves him, he cannot relax his guard.

Presencing always requires slowing things down. When Jordan is able to rest into his present experience he begins to feel a frozen block in his throat and chest. He becomes aware of how he is fiercely protecting against all the ways he's been hurt before. Eve becomes more aware of her sense of helplessness, of how she can never get through to Jordan. He is able to tell her that his mistrust runs very deep and he doesn't know if he can get past it. She feels the pain of their impasse as well as a relief that he is acknowledging that it is not all about her. They agree that, although things are difficult between them, they both want to continue working on it. As we continue our work with them we will, no doubt, help him to embody what he holds inside those frozen places in his throat and chest. Meanwhile, rather than enacting his mistrust by continuously pointing out to Eve what he dislikes, he has taken ownership of his fear of opening up to trust.

Stern writes, "The present moment that I am after is the moment of subjective experience as it is occurring—not as it is later reshaped by words." [45] **Helping couples enter into the experience of the present moment will always involve you, as therapist, doing the same.** In our work with Rinaldo and Stephanie, it was when we could allow ourselves to slow down and notice how we, as well as Stephanie, were lost in Rinaldo's words. The over-reliance on reflectivity removes us from the subjective experience of connection that results from presencing. When we are trapped in chasing the content we miss the abundant opportunity available in the moment.

Often presencing will bring about a profound opening to authentic contact, but even presencing has it limits. To be attuned to one's in-the-moment experience is to have sufficient separation to see that which previously was invisible. This is an imperceptibility borne of immersion. As the neonate cannot make a distinction between self and other, without sufficient detachment we too are fully entangled in our subjectivity. We **are** our feelings. We **are** our story. So detachment is crucial to awareness and presencing. Yet it alone can sometimes leave us arid and disconnected from the vitality of our embodied experiences. As Charlotte Bronte wrote in Jane Eyre, "It is vain to say that human beings ought to be satisfied with tranquility: they must have action: and they will make it if they cannot find it."

Embodied

It is fair to say that the *sine qua non* of the EMM approach is to support couples in embodying their shared experiences.

Embodiment is not embeddedness in emotional reactivity. It is not analyzing. It is not simply being aware of the moment. It transcends all of these. **In a very real sense, embodiment is the coupling of our primitive nature with our higher-self capacity to simultaneously bear witness**. The boundary between attachment and detachment dissolves when one embodies experience.

In The Happiness Hypothesis Jonathan Haidt writes: "I once heard a talk by the philosopher Robert Solomon, who directly challenged the philosophy of non-attachment as an affront to human nature. The life of cerebral reflection and emotional indifference . . . advocated by many Greek and Roman philosophers and that of calm nonstriving advocated by Buddha are lives designed to avoid passion, and a life without passion is not a human life. Yes, attachments bring pain, but they also bring our greatest joys, and there is value in the very variation that the philosophers are trying to avoid." [(13)]

The embodied expression of emotions that were long ago exiled is a miraculous thing to behold. In EMM we welcome the power and intensity of held back energies and see first-hand the healing and liberation it evokes. We hold with great reverence the opening to historically forbidden emotional truths as they emerge between partners who long to truly see each other. It is one thing to tell a partner "I get angry at you when you don't listen to my requests", and quite another to consciously expose the potent rage that is wedded to a long history of disregard.

In a recent situation with a couple who were on the verge of breaking up, this is precisely what needed to happen. Maureen and Douglas came to us in a very precarious place. He felt he was being constantly criticized by her for actions that to him did not warrant such hostility on her part. She felt that he never listened to her and kept doing things she had asked him repeatedly to stop. They were entrenched in a reactive interchange that Douglas described as a war where "both of our armies, navies, tanks, and nuclear weapons come out."

In the third session we chose to work with Maureen's reactivity. As we connected her anger at Douglas to her "80%" history, she revealed that her mother displayed utter disregard for her personal boundaries. Her mother would ignore Maureen's request to not walk in on her in the bathroom, or in any circumstance where Maureen wanted her privacy. In a variety of ways Maureen's mom would invade her privacy, even to the extreme of walking in on her during a sexual encounter with her boyfriend and refusing to leave.

Maureen's reactivity to Douglas when she felt discounted and assaulted by his energy, was overwhelming to him. In this particular session, we asked if she would be willing to bring the full force of her reactions to her mother, in a way that she never could actually do with mom. Lying on a mat, we invited her to kick, punch and scream at her mom for disregarding her. As she began moving her energy, a torrent of words also poured forth. She screamed: "Get out of my skin!" "Get away from me!" "I will kill you if you come any closer!" "This is my body, not yours!" After the wave of rage moved through her, she curled up in a fetal position. Feeling a pit of nausea in her stomach she said to her mother, "You make me sick." She clutched her abdomen and the tears began to flow. All the while we encouraged her to allow the feelings to come and to know that there was a larger space in her that could remain watchful of what was emerging.

Douglas looked on with a mixture of emotions. Though he was frightened by the strength of Maureen's feelings, he also could, for the first time, appreciate why she responded to him so intensely. As she released some of the rage and pain, she began to loosen her guard with Douglas and was able to tell him how frightened she gets when he doesn't listen to her. She spoke these words from an entirely different emotional space than the one she had occupied only 15 minutes earlier. By embodying her fury she was able to touch upon how deeply her need to protect her boundaries really was.

Rarely in life do we get the chance to express our full emotional truths. Yet we bring into our committed relationships highly charged aspects of our interior world which we regularly squelch out of fear, self judgment, or suppression of life-force. In the EMM approach there is plenty of space for each person to move with lively energies that are constrained in every other arena of their lives. Sessions are characterized by fluid movement among various emotional realities. Spouses vacillate between calm discussion and raucous exchanges; between grousing and deep mourning; between icy withdrawal and outrageous flirtation; between trembling in fright and quaking with laughter; between rage and remorse.

Embodiment of whatever needs to come through us allows for greater and greater opening to our expansiveness and access to our longing and our be-longing. Emotions run high in long term relationships yet unfortunately even in therapeutic environments there is little support for their physical expression. The couples we work with are encouraged to discover what lies inside the external patterns of interaction. They are welcomed in all of the seemingly inglorious places which dwell not too far from the reach of their consciousness. They begin to discover that great wisdom resides within their anger, fear and hurt. They come to realize that the pathway to profound connection is often through the body's urgent need to express itself.

One of the limits of mindfulness is that, for many, when anxiety is high, sitting and being with it never seems to result in a "dropping beneath," "letting go," or "transcendence" of the emotion. It is often not possible for individuals to remain in a space of watching their frantic feelings. Instead, they give up and go back to some distracting activity, or mood altering medication to regain a sense of control. In embodying, we make room for the over-charged person (which is a regular occurrence in couples therapy) to express the frantic energy through the body—to discharge energetically something that feels way too big to passively observe. **By embodying, we help individuals and the couple to trust the flow of energy as it moves and informs the organism**. In our experience it is through this willingness to participate in the movement of energy that greater consciousness arises. We come to see self and other more clearly after we honor the movement of boisterous and rambunctious energies.

While conventional methodologies tend to support a certain degree of emotional release, particularly of sadness and grief, we would like to offer a justification for a fuller embodiment of the spectrum of human emotions.

Some reasons to help couples embody:

- Embodiment acknowledges and honors the integration of mind, body, and spirit as indistinct aspects of our humanity. Since these distinctions are artifacts of the neocortical mind, in the real world physical expression is organic. It needs adequate space in the therapeutic domain. Flailing of arms, raising of voices, stomping, burying one's head in shame, are all just as important as any insight in an EMM session.
- Embodiment helps spouses to release characterological tensions in the body which interfere with the ability to entrain with each other. A person who has developed characterological protections against betrayal, for instance, holds chronic tension in the form of hyperarousal and hypervigilance which result from deep mistrust. His mistrust is far more than a mental suspicion. Embodiment gives this person space to feel just how strongly he resists letting down his guard.
- It allows one to gain confidence that intense or taboo feeling states are not going to overwhelm one's coping capacities. People are often afraid that if they permit certain emotions to arise they will be overcome by them. Embodiment helps them to realize that they are larger than their most powerful emotions.
- Embodiment also allows an individual to see that her feelings are not too much for her partner to handle. Since many of us, as children, began to suspect that the caregivers could not tolerate our intensity, we learned to "protect" them from the full force of our emotions. Most of us were implicitly encouraged to reign in not only our primary restorative feelings, but our joy, passion, sexuality and innocent curiosity. We then do the same with our committed partners. As a spouse learns to embody more of these energies it creates greater freedom and safety in

the relationship. Conversely, when we learn to conform to what we believe is expected of us we gradually build resentment and create more and more distance from our partners.

- Embodiment opens up space for the release of non-verbal and pre-rational implicit states. Because it is often these implicit states that are showing up in the couple's interactions, and they are not readily accessed through our normal modes of communication, embodiment is an essential alternative form of "communication."
- Similarly, it opens space for the expression of "trans-rational" states. As a partner moves through her protections and her primary restorative emotions there is often an emergence of deep empathy, compassion, gratitude, love and nurturance. Unless the conditions support the open expression of the higher emotions, they are often downplayed or shunned. To embody is to make room for these trans-rational qualities.
- It supports an increased sense of agency. Remember that children from insecure attachment environments will respond first with protest, then despair and ultimately detachment. Such individuals have learned to accommodate to a lack of attunement with others. They have lost their ability to engage in protest. In our mentoring work we have learned to encourage partners to reclaim the natural impulse to protest. Often, in doing so, they create an opening to also feel the grief and despair that coexists on the far end of their protestations.
- Embodiment brings partners closer. As one and/or the other moves through strong feelings, there is often a "dropping down" into more vulnerable and tender places. The boundaries soften and each person becomes more available to the other when the tension of holding back is released.
- It allows for an integration of disowned parts. Following the Internal Family Systems precept that we each are made up of various sub-personalities, embodiment makes space for these exiled "selves" to be fully expressed. In doing so

the individual is no longer unconsciously enacting these parts within the relationship, nor is he projecting them onto his partner.

- It creates sensory, respiratory, circulatory and nervous system integration as well. When one is allowed to not only notice and label an energy moving internally, but to release it into the room and in front of a mate, there is a synthesis among all of these systems. When these are in harmony the organism relaxes and the barriers between self and other thaw.
- Embodiment supports the individual in separating from the childhood needs which get transferred onto the spouse. By embodying the secret demands left over from childhood, we have seen partners experience a deep sense of relief and often discover great delight in the exposure of these "elephants in the living room."
- The need of the child (and the adult) to protest is not just one designed to elicit a response from a caregiver (or partner), it is also critical to the individual's "spirit." That is, even when the protest is not met with an affirmative response, the individual still feels better, more alive, from having expressed herself. Without the protest, which embodying supports, she can sink into the state of despair characterized by learned helplessness. In this state she is energetically collapsed, and lives from a narrative that says, "No matter what I do it won't make a difference." Thus protest is our antidote to learned helplessness and prevents us from adopting the same defeated posture to all of life's travails.

Just as presencing emanates from the attuned parent, witness consciousness, or god-self, embodying acquaints us with the vibrant child-self, the wisdom of the body, or what we may call the intuitive non-rational self. Both are vital to healing, evolving and deepening connection to ones partner.

What we know from neurobiology is that neurons in the brain and muscle cells share one quality which distinguishes them from all other cells in the body. They both are what can be described as "excitable." That is, they "light up" when an external stimulus causes the body to respond affectively. By embodying we are simply responding to this muscular excitability. Something wants to move! In committed relationships there is so much neural and muscular activity that to ignore the call to action is akin to stifling the baby's cry. Brain and body, awareness and aliveness—these cannot be divided.

Sometimes, it is true, a subtle energetic response is enough. There is not always a need for the body to express itself in a big way. Yet is equally true that there are often key moments in an individual's experience where the entire organism is begging for space to express itself. Particularly in committed relationships, where the stakes are frequently very high, embodied expression is so desperately needed.

When a spouse criticizes his partner we hear comments like, "It touched a raw nerve" or, "It was like a punch in the gut." It is not simply that one's mind takes issue with what was said, but that one's entire being responds to what the two of us call *sensitivity triggers*. These sensitivity triggers are experienced as a cringe or an "ouch" within one's body. The "ouch" a spouse feels when criticized by her partner nearly always relates back to childhood criticisms. It is our connection to our primary feelings, which means it almost always goes unattended. Most couples miss the "ouch" and go directly to the control patterns which define their relationship. The energy bypass results in repeatedly missed opportunities.

For example, Charlotte expressed her criticism of Lenny for "never doing enough for Christmas." Each year she anticipated he was going to buy her just the gifts she really desired and to "go overboard" for her. Lenny hated Christmas season because he believed that Charlotte would get so frantic and stressed out by doing too much. He looked at her as wasting time, energy, and money and ultimately making the season unpleasant.

Lurking not too far behind these judgments of each other there were very clear sensitivity triggers. For Charlotte, her entire body would recoil when Lenny accused her of wasting time and money. She cringed because she felt so unappreciated and indeed unseen for what value she brought to the family. As an overweight child she often felt that her generous qualities went unnoticed and all anyone saw was a fat kid who had no redeeming value.

For Lenny, his trigger resulted from Charlotte's judgment of him being so wrapped up in himself that he was thoughtless and uncaring. He grew up in a highly competitive family where he was regularly criticized for not "getting it right." So every year he would grow terribly anxious over the prospect of Christmas shopping. Charlotte had often expressed her disappointment over his choice of gifts and he came to hate the whole experience.

By helping them to actually feel the somatic response to one another's judgments, each of them were able to first enjoy more self compassion and then to experience more empathy for the other's emotional reality. Until they could let themselves feel the "ouch" they had been stuck in a reactive cycle over this issue for 15 years, in effect ruining every Christmas! By creating access to the very palpable hurts both Charlotte and Lenny experienced, they were able to connect to the "trans-rational" state of compassion and empathy.

As the two of us have emphasized throughout this book humans are creatures of relationship. All of us hunger to be spontaneous and playful with each other. We are less interested in figuring things out than we are in being touched. What we have gradually forgotten, both as individuals and as a species, is that the body already is awakened. Each one of us is magnificently attuned to the forces of nature which move around and through us. When we are in love we are illuminated. When we are heart-broken we are perfectly aligned with our highest nature. When we laugh together we are in harmony with the moment. Nothing more needs to happen when we are experiencing an embodied moment. We are one with ourselves and with our lover.

Chapter Six

The Four Levels of Engagement

What does it really take to be of service to a couple in need? What do you as a therapist really have to offer? The couple typically initiates contact by phone and one of them, often the one who is most overtly distressed, tries to describe what has gone wrong in ways s/he hopes makes sense to you. It could be sex problems, or bad communication, or an affair. Perhaps they have three children and don't even know if they like each other anymore. But they are reaching out in pain, or numbness and no small amount of vulnerability.

You are the expert. You're supposed to know what to do to help them overcome that which has caused them to seek you out. They are relying on you to provide something which is extraordinarily difficult to describe. Doctors give medicine. Chiropractors give adjustments. Marriage counselors give . . . advice?

If you are at all self aware you will probably sometimes feel like a fraud. "Who am I to help this couple? Look at all the warts and blemishes in my own relationship." Or, maybe you're not even in a relationship! You know that what they are bringing is not far afield from your own difficulties past and present in close relationships. On occasion you may even leave a session thinking that the couple has it more together than you do. Or they say something that touches a vulnerable, unhealed spot in your personal interactions with a loved one.

If you are committed to doing this work, to be with couples in their most intimate struggles, then it is wise to be prepared to meet yourself in new and often challenging ways. **After all, the art, the skill, of couples work involves suffering**. To enter into the soul of the struggle is to suffer with, to clash with, and to melt into the sinewy reality of unadulterated intimacy. If you want your couple to really confront the struggle then you're all in it together. It is an immersion experience.

There is an inosculating quality to the relationship between therapist and couple. Unless you are willing to join them in their gallant effort to grow then you can only be of so much value. Mentors in the EMM approach learn to bring their whole selves, their beingness to this sacred invitation the couple offers. The mentor uses her own embodied awareness to entrain with them as they desperately look for a way back to truth and a way forward into even newer truths.

To be of service is not to have answers, but to be curious, to be affected, and to be willing to plunder the unknown regions of instinctual domains. Of course, this runs counter to prevailing thinking on the subject. The quest for verifiable and replicable techniques has left us with a short list of tools to deal with a short list of problems. While this is good as far as it goes, we are still left with untold suffering for too many couples.

With the EMM approach, we seek to open an improvisational interchange where the couple and the mentor(s) keep moving back and forth until the wisdom of the shared energy field does its own magic. This magic arises from each person's core impulse to heal, to feel pleasure and love, and to give back. As we mentioned, these are the qualities that we seek to promote in the evocation of an Exceptional Marriage.

The creative source is the shared wisdom of life-force that exists in the room in every moment of every session. The mentor's job is to tap into it. To do this we utilize four levels of engagement with the couple. In this chapter our desire is to acquaint you with how to incorporate these levels of engagement into your work and to begin to get a deeper understanding of the profound possibilities that exist for couples when they begin to disembark from the revolving door of control patterns and crack open the "evolving door" of embodiment.

The four levels of engagement are as follows:

- Presencing
- Leading by following
- Bridging
- Catalyzing

But before we go into a detailed explanation of these, we wish to take a few moments to introduce the concept of ***metaskills***. The idea of metaskills was formulated by Amy Mindell [(25)] and refers to a set of traits which a therapist must possess in order to be effective. We have borrowed the term and have adapted it in a slightly variant version to support the EMM work with couples. Essentially, what we are suggesting by metaskills is that couples can learn how to transform the struggles, flash points, and habitual styles of interaction by developing aspects within their basic nature.

Metaskills inhabit the world of non-linear reality. They are not an accumulation of aptitudes that are added to an existing information base. For example learning your first language is a metaskill, as is learning to walk. In contrast, learning negotiation skills, conflict resolution, active listening, sexual techniques or communication skills are for the most part "add-on" knowledge that requires specific information. Metaskills involve our primal capacity to sense, intuit, and flow with what is emerging in any given exchange between partners. They typically are an emanation of the collective wisdom available in the shared energy field. To put it simply, metaskills are aptitudes we all already possess albeit in undeveloped form. Unlike some of the other skills mentioned above, they require no rehearsal.

One of the tasks of mentoring is to assist partners in committed relationships to activate the following metaskills. Remembering that these skills do not have to be acquired, only elicited, the mentor can invite both partners to discover what is already innate to their humanity.

Such metaskills include:

1. Yielding to the flow of process consciousness. This means staying connected to what is occurring moment

by moment and sensing the difference between what is narrative (state consciousness) and what is present in the enlivened moment (process consciousness).

2. Becoming more open and aware of disowned parts (aspects of who you are, such as cruelty, greed, vengeance, fear, need, sexuality and others).
3. Being aware of how you are affected by what your partner is bringing to you whether it is complaints, criticisms, needs, demands, compliments, desire or anything else.
4. Learning to embody your various energies that will show up as emotions, sensations, thoughts, memories, or impulses. This means, not only mindful noticing, but also the capacity to allow these energies to move through you even as you remain centered in a deeper core consciousness.
5. Embracing your "edge." This means surrendering to the non-rational intuitions which call to you from your creative source. This involves paying attention to images, undefined feelings, irritabilities, inspirations and other irrational pieces of consciousness that can move through your field of awareness very quickly and are often dismissed as unimportant. Trust this emerging energy as a signal of your deep knowing and your evolving self.
6. Embracing your curiosity. This means cultivating the innocence of not knowing. Todd Kashdan in his book <u>Curious?</u> writes: ". . . we found that curious people treat their partners as vast unknown territories to be explored, asking lots of questions, as they continually penetrate deeper into new terrain." [(17)]
7. Opening to a greater awareness of all the judgments you hold toward self and partner. This involves a movement (which is never fully realized) toward a radical acceptance of your partner's "otherness."
8. Attuning to the moment when an emotion has run its natural course and entering the organic flow into the next emerging feeling state. This means, for example, knowing when the energy of your anger has been expended and

a movement into pain or sorrow is wanting to occur. In EMM we refer to this as the "sacred shift."

9. Discovering and holding the intention to get to the full truth. This requires that even in the face of strong negative emotions within, you can find a deeper intent toward love and understanding.
10. Learning to trust and make room for your higher core qualities of compassion, gratitude, humility, altruism, and creativity.

These metaskills, we believe, are inherent to our humanness. They involve both a reclaiming of what we once possessed (innocence, open flow of emotion, curiosity) and a willingness to open to our "larger selves" where we learn to appreciate the "unthought known" and the guidance of the shared energy field.

As we move through the remainder of this chapter keep in mind that the four levels of engagement we will be discussing are all predicated on supporting couples in the advancement of their metaskills. When couples arrive for mentoring, our firm belief is that each person's impulses toward growth, connection, and truth are ultimately greater than the protections they have established over the years. We have come to understand that the strength of the control patterns is in direct proportion to the level of wounding which one or both partners endured. Indeed, one of the most significant aspects of an individual's wounding is how it resulted in a separation from these metaskills. When one was terrorized, ignored, invaded, or betrayed the sad consequence is most often a loss of connection to the spontaneous, intuitive, and trusting aspects of our beingness—a tragic occurrence indeed.

Let us now return to the four levels of engagement as a central feature of the EMM approach. We will begin with *Presencing* and follow in order with*; Leading by Following*, *Catalyzing*, and *Bridging*. Often in a given session with a couple the order tends to unfold in this way, but it can play out in a variety of ways. Following an agenda is anathema to the EMM approach. Therefore mentors learn to acquiesce to the wisdom of the moment in the employment of any of these forms of engagement.

Presencing

Over time couples in a committed relationship tend to see each other more and more through the looking glass of narrative. Each views the other in increasingly narrow ways. "He's a good father, inhibited lover, loyal partner, and not particularly successful wage earner." Within the confines of these descriptors everything else gets marginalized. There are times when he's not such a great dad, when his secret sexual fantasy world might knock her socks off, when there are limits to his loyalty, and perhaps his best or most marketable qualities have remained untapped because of necessary sacrifices that he made. Narratives have a way of causing near-sightedness.

In any moment there is opportunity for each partner to see the other anew. When narratives dominate the landscape of the present moment, couples are living from their history. The "learned helplessness" that exists between partners routinely results in them missing the obvious. In Martin Seligman's famous learned helplessness experiments, dogs who were given electric shocks could initially escape by jumping a barrier in the cage. Then, however, shocks were administered on both sides of the barrier. The dogs soon learned to give up. Even when an escape route was again made available, the dogs remained lethargic and unaware. It is much the same for couples trapped in narrative who fail to see the escape route from the cage of their control patterns. The simple process of presencing can open up new vistas of possibility in an otherwise stagnant relationship.

Presencing, in Scharmer's view is a term used to denote an action which involves both sensing and the choice to remain in the moment. He tells us: "Presencing, the blending of sensing and presence, means to connect with the Source of the highest future possibility and to bring it into the now. In that state we step into our real being, who we really are, our authentic self."

This way of being in the moment, not as simply a passive experience, but as a participation in an ever unfolding mystery, is a vital aspect of our mentoring work. Eckhart Tolle writes: "In a sense the state of presence could be compared to waiting. This is not the usual bored or restless kind of waiting that is a denial of the present . . . It is not a waiting in which your attention is focused on some point in the future and the present is perceived as an undesirable obstacle that prevents you from having what you want. This is a qualitatively different kind of waiting, one that requires your total alertness. Something could happen at any moment, and if you are not absolutely awake, absolutely still, you will miss it." (47)

To drop below narrative requires this ability to stay connected to one's own experience even as it is not neatly packaged. For a spouse to say "I don't know why but my heart is beating faster" is to presence sans narrative. Mindell tells us, "I suggest that presence is a *pre-sense. Pre* means 'before' and *sense* means 'feeling' or 'perceiving' something. A *presence* is something you can almost feel before you can describe it as a feeling." (italics his) (26)

The clear truth is that couples who come for therapy are rarely present with what they are experiencing. In our work with couples we begin most sessions with some kind of attunement, which is designed primarily to help each partner become more present. We arrange their chairs so they are mostly facing each other, angled only slightly toward us. Sometimes we'll have them close their eyes and notice what is occurring within. We may ask them to pay attention to any thoughts, emotions, sensations, memories, or images which pass through their field of consciousness. Often we will then suggest, with eyes still closed, that they each begin to bring their partner into their awareness and to notice how that affects what is happening inside. Then we invite them to open their eyes and see each other.

Before we go into any story we encourage them to stay with what is occurring within and between them in that very moment. Often the whole session will flow from what emerges. Our aim at the beginning is, of course, to cultivate the experiencing of presencing, of being fully with the flow of energy as it is felt in real time. It is amazing how often couples say that they never are just still and attentive with each other.

By starting in this fashion we are setting the stage for them to be with each other in a very different way than they are familiar with. We are helping them to begin to pay more notice to the flow of information speaking to them from the neck down. That is, to create more space for emotion, intuition and energy to converse with them. Not infrequently, one or both will notice that when they bring their partner into their field of awareness they experience tension, or tightness in the chest, belly, throat or elsewhere. This is a significant moment, for it confronts them with the truth of how guarded they have become in each other's presence.

By tuning into how the awareness of each other actually results in palpable body responses, they can embark on a radically new way of communicating. As ridiculously simple as it seems, the introduction of body awareness into the communication equation brings with it the potential for a sea change in the couple's interactive dynamics.

In general, most spouses, when asked to look at each other are only aware of what they see in the other. *"I notice he looks bored," "I'm aware that she wants me to speak first," "I see that look where he frowns and turns his eyes away. I know he's disapproving."* While these may all be important awarenesses, they function to keep the focus on the other. This invariably results in each person missing what is most primary, namely what is happening within him/herself.

The attentiveness to other at the expense of cutting off from one's own subjective interior, is at the heart of the trouble many couples grapple with. A partner will delude herself into thinking that she is only responding to what the other is putting out. When this happens, the control patterns erupt and an interminable struggle to "get my partner to see what I see" ensues. So much of the challenge in this work is to shift each person's attention from other to self as a baseline. Sometimes by asking a simple question—"How does it affect you, when you see him looking bored?"—it is possible to change the flow of the interaction. Sometimes it is not so easy.

In a recent session with a couple we had only seen a few times we encountered how challenging it can be to create presencing. Frank and Maureen, two professionals in their mid-thirties, came to us on the suggestion of a friend. They have been married five years and have fallen into very entrenched control patterns with each other. Frank engages in a largely passive control pattern by isolating and refusing to share when Maureen questions him about where he is going. When he feels too "pressured" by her he will occasionally resort to cursing and name calling. By the time we began working with them his mantra was "I'm done!" or "I've had it!" When we ask him to look at Maureen all he can see is her neediness and insecurity. He is tuned out to his own inner reactions.

Maureen has a more active control pattern where she will indeed interrogate and debate with Frank. She will challenge his version of conversations they had and push to convince him that his memory of an event is faulty. Her energy gets very animated and intense when she thinks he's portraying her inaccurately. She debates with him over the details of a story he is recounting. He then looks to us and says, "You see I can't get a word in edge-wise!" It appears to us that the more frustrated, disdainful, and contracted he becomes, the more anxious and intense she gets, and vice versa.

At a particular juncture, when Maureen is questioning Frank intensely, Marcia takes her chair and moves it next to Maureen's. At first Maureen looks startled. Marcia asks if she can put her hand on Maureen's shoulder. Still looking fearful she says yes. Almost instantly she begins to cry. Now looking both sad and scared Maureen grabs a tissue and starts dabbing her eyes. She begins to insist "I'm OK, I'm fine, I'll be alright," all the while casting furtive glances at Frank.

It was very clear that when Marcia approached her with compassion her armor cracked momentarily and she dropped beneath her fierce "interrogator" energy. As we have stated earlier, the strength of the control pattern is proportional to the wounding it is protecting. Marcia's connection, exemplified by placing her hand on Maureen's shoulder, led to an energetic penetration of the control pattern. For a brief moment Maureen could sense that Marcia *saw* her frightened and pained self which lay cowering behind her tough exterior.

The fleeting exposure of her vulnerable self was quickly supplanted by her repeated assurances that she was fine. Later she would tell us that she was concerned that Frank would be critical of her tears, which indeed holds some truth. But the graphic contrast between her tears and her insistence she was OK carried the mark of an early, childlike response to someone who was rejecting of her vulnerability. The ghost of a parent or some other significant person haunted her whenever she cracked the veneer of her control pattern. It was as if she were saying "See I'm OK, please don't reject me." Maureen exhibited all the characteristics of one who grew up with ambivalent attachment. Frank mirrored perfectly to her the caregiver who was there in one moment and gone the next.

During the session, when we attempt to bring her back to her inner experience, her anxiety rises and she can only turn her focus toward Frank. "He hates it when I get upset" she keeps telling us. Frank does exhibit impatience with her emotions. He tells us, "She always gets emotional and then tries to make it all about me." When we ask him to express what is happening inside, how he is feeling as Maureen shows distress, he can only say, "I'm sick of it, I've had enough" Both of them are locked into an intense reactive cycle. They have real trouble understanding what we are asking when we invite them to see what they are experiencing in the moment within themselves.

As we discussed in the previous chapter, breaking the reactive cycle often requires tremendous effort on the part of the mentor. To bring a couple such as Frank and Maureen into a space of presencing may take a number of sessions to accomplish. When the threat level feels high, it is not easy for any of us to bring our awareness inward. We are biologically primed to place our focus on the threat, which manifests to us in the form of our partner. Presencing requires a willingness to relax our hyper-focus on our partner and to slow down enough to feel the subtle signals our bodies are trying to send us.

Sometimes it is so difficult for two spouses to drop their reactivity and feel what is occurring inside that it requires us to name what they might be experiencing. For instance, one of us may say, "It looks like you may be feeling some shame when she criticizes you." Or, "Are you aware of any anger as you describe to us his affair?" When people have not had much exposure to their inner world of emotions they need us to help them begin the process of giving life to their interior, subjective experiences.

Just as you may assist a five year old by saying "Are you feeling mad at mommy?" so too with the adults who come to you for help.

Presencing involves primarily the ability to actually feel what is occurring subjectively, and secondarily the capacity to give it a description. For many who seek our help, there is a learning curve in this regard. As one gradually begins to get in touch with long ignored interior states, the world begins to change. If Maureen could learn to let herself cry and be informed by her tears rather than quickly squelching them, her whole stance toward Frank would change. If she could begin to sit with her emotions and not try to override them, she would ultimately begin to release her fear-driven impulses to debate and convince. Because somewhere, long ago, she was not received in the expression of her emotional life, she abandoned these parts of herself. Before she can even make space for the sadness, she will need to enter a loving presence with her formidable anxiety.

To be able to simply say to Frank, "I get scared when you tell me you're done. I'm afraid that you think it's all my fault and so I don't know what else to do but try to convince you otherwise." This might be the simple truth she would notice if she could slow down, turn inward and remain present with what is emerging in her. The gift of presencing is to become more whole, more alive, and more innocent. When David Schnarch talks about *self-validated intimacy* he is referring to one's ability to be intimate with one's own truth, one's own disavowed parts. To share these truths with your life-mate is to stand in presence. For Maureen this will come when she can distinguish the frightened child whose parent was unpredictably available, from the reality of herself as a competent and capable women. More mirroring by us will be essential.

John O'Donohue has said: "Presence is alive. You sense and feel presence; it comes toward you and engages you. Presence is the whole atmosphere of a person or thing. The human body longs for presence. The very structure and shape of the body makes it a living sanctuary of presence." [(30)] **Conversely, narrative is a corpse. It is mummified presence, existing not of this moment, but of a bygone reality**. While it may carry useful and important particles of truth, its existence contaminates the moment and devitalizes the exchange between intimate partners.

Couples tend to dwell in the narrative as they describe what is going on in their relationship. Knowing the story of the relationship and each person's own past is, of course, of great importance. In the EMM approach we attempt to weave story with an ongoing recognition of the present moment. Simple interventions by the mentor breathe life into a narrative. For example, when a husband is telling how he felt left out when their first child was born, the mentor may draw his attention to how he is tugging at his shirt tail and ask him to describe what that gesture is saying. Or, the mentor may suggest he look at his wife so that he can see that she is exhibiting tenderness as he talks. Often when the story is being told the partner is lost in the reverie and is very distant from the vitality of the moment.

In couples work we are attempting to help spouses to enter what Daniel Stern calls the "intersubjective matrix." [45] We can describe this matrix as a place where the interior of one person enters the interior of the other. While this is always going on beneath the level of conscious awareness, a major task in couples work is to bring the intersubjective matrix to the fore. The unrealized truth in relationships is just how deeply each partner can feel what is occurring between the two of them. They know each other in ways far beyond the knowing that come from habits and patterns of interacting that have coalesced over the time they have been together. This other kind of knowing emerges from the shared energy field which is, at all times, signaling each person of its existence. Most of us have simply redirected our attention to limited bites of information which serve to reinforce our narratives. As we begin to learn to presence we become wiser, more empathic, and ultimately more self-responsible.

Because most of us have learned not to speak unless we were absolutely sure of what we were going to say, we become increasingly more adept at tuning out all the implicit, non-rational messages. In EMM we encourage each partner to make space for these intuitive, not fully formed snippets of awareness. One basic way we encourage this is by being relentlessly inquisitive about micro-movements of energy each person exhibits. To us everything a person does has meaning. If a man starts blinking more rapidly we'll ask him to notice and invite him to make sense of it. When one woman begins to talk about the lack of sex with her lover, her voice gets tight and higher pitched. As she brings awareness to it she detects there is anger that she is choking off from expression.

Another way we support partners in presencing is to give them permission to express themselves without knowing the reasons behind a response they may be having. For instance, Tracy often fails to express himself because he says "I don't know what I'm feeling." This frustrates his partner Ronnie who thinks that Tracy is just refusing to share. But Tracy genuinely has difficulty naming his inner experience. We encourage him to allow his responses to Ronnie to be very basic. For many people like Tracy it helps to simply say the words "I don't like . . ." without having to give a rationale, or to name a specific emotion. To say "It hurts me when . . ." or "I'm afraid because . . ." can be experienced as awkward, contrived, too vulnerable, or not quite accurate. But to simply say "I don't like that you just finished my sentence" can change the course of Tracy's relationship. He doesn't have to know precisely what he feels or why he feels that way to express an important truth.

Presencing helps us to know these simple realities. To name just what you are aware of is enough. Often we will have partners look at each other and just state whatever each is aware of as it arises. They can go back and forth with the ever-fluctuating movement of energy as it makes itself known to them. It is amazing to note how difficult it is for a couple to stay present with whatever is emerging in them. There is generally a drifting away from this "process consciousness" back into narrative or 'state consciousness." Yet, just five minutes of mutual presencing can lead to increased self awareness and heightened intimacy.

The most common problems couples have staying with the flow of present experiences are of two types. First, most people tend to keep the focus on the other, so we may hear responses such as: "Right now I'm aware of how pretty you look," or "I am noticing that you seem uncomfortable." Each time this happens we ask that person to bring it back to himself and state what he is aware of within *himself* as he sees his partner's pretty face. This needs to be reinforced many times, as the "default" awareness of most people is what they notice about the other.

In this example of a man being aware of his mate's pretty face, by bringing the attention back inward new vistas of consciousness may unfold. He may become aware for instance, that he likes her smile, but that he also is afraid to say anything critical. He may be aware of a part of himself that is trying to control her by telling her how pretty she is, in effect sending a meta-communication which says "Let's be nice to each other." Or, he may simply enjoy seeing her face, but needs to become more aware of how this "lands" in his body. That is, where does this pleasure reside in him?

The second common problem involves a conflating of the present moment with history. So an individual might say to her partner, "I'm aware that I have been feeling upset with you all week" or "I'm in touch with feeling disappointed over the fact that we didn't make love on Saturday like we said we would." This last statement speaks to just how difficult it can be to separate history from the present moment in a committed relationship. It could be that, in the moment, the wife *is* still feeling disappointment, or more likely, she had felt disappointed earlier and is simply using this present experience to address it. But in the moment something else may be activated. In the present it might be that she looks at her partner and, seeing him, is reminded of how she had felt disappointed over the weekend, or that in this precise moment she is aware that she is blaming him for not initiating sex. In any case, her task in presencing is not to go back in time but to continue to stay with what is between them now. So it may be that she notices that she tightens up when she shares with him her feelings about the previous Saturday. The mentor's task is to keep her connected with what flows from this sharing.

Even though we want couples to learn to drop into the flow of immediate experience, the present will always be inextricably connected to each person's history. Shortly we will be discussing what we call "bridging" which involves a conscious merging of one's history with its manifestation in the present. But it is enormously valuable for couples to learn to trust this flow of information that is available to them in real time, now.

The tendency for all of us is to see both ourselves and our partners as patterns of behavior rather than complex, fluid and ultimately mysterious uncategorizable beings. So we describe ourselves and each other in terminology that spans across time. "I am clumsy"; "She is irrational"; "He's always complaining"; "She's never on time." These are the ways our narratives keep us from staying with our direct experience. Helping couples to practice presencing is the antidote to this tendency to judge, predict and pigeonhole.

It is equally important for the mentor to be presencing right along with the couple. At the outset of our sessions we are attuning together with the couple. Our greatest tool is our ability to "feel into" the moment and use what we sense to communicate with the couple. While we want them to focus primarily on each other, we are sensing what is happening in the shared energy field and paying particular attention to what is occurring beneath the control patterns. If we get "triggered" by the couple we are responsible for connecting to what is going on within us. Classically this means confronting our own countertransference. If you can see countertransference as the conflating of history with the moment, it is incumbent upon you as therapist to come back to your immediate experience and use it to guide you.

So, for example, if you find yourself frustrated by a couple's reactive cycle it may be triggering how you felt around your parents. You may move unconsciously into your own control pattern and try to reason with them, or to press them to listen to each other. Perhaps you unwittingly begin to side with one of them as you did with your folks. Presencing for you would involve coming back into your immediate subjective experience and most likely connecting to a primary feeling. Maybe you are angry, or scared, and consequently feel pressure to calm things down. By entering into your own flow, you will be open to other possibilities than that of enacting your own control pattern. Instead of trying to get the couple to change (the enactment of your control pattern), you are better able to assist them in slowing down (modeling presencing).

Because what you are feeling is both connected to your history and is part of the present shared energy field, it is often useful to take what you are aware of through your own presencing and offer it to the couple. So you might say to them, "I'm aware of how hopeless this must feel," or "I'm guessing that this must be incredibly frustrating to be going around and around like this." Every subjective experience you have is both an aspect of your own history and a holographic slice of the shared energy field. If you are feeling frustrated, overwhelmed, lost, or anxious, chances are good that this is floating out there in the shared energy field.

Presencing is the first of the four levels of engagement which characterize the EMM approach. The essentials of presencing and its place in EMM can by summarized as follows:

- Presencing supports couples in accessing their metaskills. By focusing on the richness of here and now experiences, each person can tap into his/her organic wisdom. The skills necessary for an evolving relationship are already available, though they may be dormant, in each partner's core consciousness.
- Presencing involves listening to the body as a primary conveyer of emotional information. The limbic brain, the heart, the muscles and even the intestines all participate in the exchange of energy between intimate partners. Neurons inhabit both heart and digestive tract as they do the brain. Often, when partners attend to the signals from their internal organs and muscles, they discover a newfound source of wisdom.
- In couples work, the goal is mutual presencing. In mutual presencing each partner is developing a keener awareness both of what they sense in the other and how they are responding, in the moment, to that sense. Arnold Mindell refers to a phenomenon he calls "quantum flirting." The essence of quantum flirting is that what one person is drawn to notice in another is a product of reciprocal energetic communication. When a woman notices that her spouse is playing with his lip while she is revealing

something vulnerable, his lip-playing is a kind of flirt which draws her attention. She may have not noticed, or tuned into something else, but her attention to this behavior has meaning for both. Presencing allows partners to begin entering the flow of shared energy as it reveals itself in quantum flirts.

- By helping two people attune to each other we set the conditions for mutual presencing. Attuning involves shifting away from the dialogical, discursive mind and into greater awareness of subtle vibrations which are generally overlooked when words dominate. These vibrations (which can be experienced as flashes of intuition, physical sensations, changes in emotional states, or slight movements toward dissociative splits or energetic "flooding") emanate from the shared energy field and are often the most critical moments is a particular session. Thus in every EMM session the mentor will take time to help the couple attune.
- Presencing makes space for greater access to implicit memories. Much of what is occurring in a couple's shared energy field is an emanation of past experiences which are felt by an individual as very real and in the moment. By opening to a wider recognition of what is happening in the now, partners can begin to tie together (bridging) the historical antecedents with the present manifestation of something that has become problematic. In one particular session, Travis was telling his spouse Corinne how unhappy he was with his job. Suddenly he stopped and said, "I think Corinne is getting annoyed at me." We asked him to notice what in Corinne led him to this conclusion and also to tune into what happens to him when he senses her annoyance. By doing this, Travis became aware of how sensitive he is to subtle cues he picks up from Corinne (quantum flirts), and, by feeling how he responds, he could bridge the present to its origins. He felt a clutching in his throat which he understood to mean "Stop talking." Long ago he had learned not to express unhappiness in his family because nobody wanted to

hear it. The clutching in his throat is his implicit memory. By presencing this entire sequence Travis could not only bring some coherency to it, but he could also choose to try options other than shutting up.

- Presencing can help a couple move beyond the "autistic relationship" where everything becomes ritualized and there is no space for novelty. By presencing, a couple can begin to look beneath the control patterns which have come to characterize the relationship. Partners can access the wisdom of the collective consciousness, or the mind-at-large. Both partners enter "shaman mind" so to speak, where each is informed by the world beyond their skin. In this regard, presencing invites a "*jamais vu*" experience where a partner may have a sort of cosmic sense that what was once familiar is now feeling altogether novel. That is, he sees a common moment with an entirely new awareness.
- Presencing builds trust in aspects of one's humanity other than the intellect. For most of us we have come to over-rely on our analytical thinking and have separated from sources of wisdom which actually are more essential to intimate connection. This building of trust in one's embodied, non-rational aspects is vital to the attainment of an exceptional marriage

Leading By Following

Most experienced therapists are adept at observing a client's non-verbal signals. By pointing them out, the therapist hopes to open the client's awareness to things she may be trying to reveal which were long ago excommunicated from consciousness. A slumping of the shoulders or a vacant look seizing control of a client's eyes are each vital sources of information which have fallen prey to internal shunning. The therapist who notices, gives the client a precious gift. The undetected slump, or the missed vacant look, strum the familiar chords of insecure attachment, loneliness and ersatz connection. **We each become what others choose to see. That which was missed in us by those who**

mattered we soon ignore within ourselves. The therapist who sees the client in ways she does not see herself is helping her to become whole.

The premise of leading by following is to create a dance between the EM mentor and the couple. One of the fundamental tools of effective improvisation is to say "Yes" to everything that shows up. Leading by following is the improvisational affirming of life force as it expresses itself in the non-verbal, energetic atmosphere of any particular session. Part of what we are attempting to do with couples is to support a welcoming atmosphere in which each partner learns to open up to something new. (Much of what is described as resistance in therapy is a clinging to the familiar and a protection against moving too far and too fast from what one believes to be true and safe.)

Leading by following is about taking the energy and running with it. What is showing up in a couple's session is the material you have to work with. Leading by following begins by "entering into" the expression of energy one or the other spouse is displaying. We once witnessed, for example, a barely perceptible shaking of the head by one partner as his mate described her struggles in getting pregnant. By bringing awareness to his nearly indiscernible head movement, a wellspring of emotion sprang forth. As it so happened, this couple had endured three rounds of in vitro fertilization to no avail. The wife was determined to push on and the husband dutifully was going along. When we asked him about his head shaking he described how difficult it had been for him to continue the IVF. He described how their sex life had been reduced to a clinical function and how he was now having trouble getting aroused.

The practice of leading by following with this man involved us first bringing attention to a somatic event (head shake), then, after he described his struggles, we encouraged him to enter more fully into the movement. As he began to more vigorously shake, we asked if there were words. He starting saying, softly at first, and then with mounting volume and force—"Enough!" As he allowed himself to express his discontent and indeed his exasperation for the first time, his partner became upset. She tried to cajole him and tell him that she needed him to be "on board" and that unless they were positive, she would never get pregnant. We asked her if she could make space for his distress and suggested that his held back emotions were actually bringing greater tension to the situation than his freedom to express what he had learned to politely hold back. As we encouraged him to continue he opened up about how he felt like he was losing her and that it was no longer worth it to him to keep trying in this way to have a baby.

This led to several sessions focused on both of their needs and fears. The movement into this space was predicated on taking what was available (his silent "no") and following it to its full organic expression. Over time this actually allowed the wife to enter her grief, which she had been fiercely resisting, about the prospect of not being a biological mother. His "no" led the way to the pain she so fiercely resisted. Leading by following in this instance meant trusting what was emerging non-verbally and following it to its natural destination.

Stanislof Grof, MD, calls this type of attention to the movement of energy the "watercourse way." Like the flow of water, energy seeks to move and find its direction. It travels around, over, and sometimes through obstacles. Grof writes, "Instead of focusing on a predetermined fixed goal, we try to sense which way things are moving and how we best fit into them. This is the strategy used in martial arts and surfing." (12) We would add to this that it's a good strategy for the "marital arts" of couples work.

For you, as therapist, to lead by following means that you react to the energetic expression, which is being bypassed by both partners, and then invite that energy into the room. It is frequently useful to look at the partner who is listening while his mate is talking. The listening partner is often having very powerful responses which are outside of immediate conscious awareness and yet available for more overt expression with just a bit of encouragement. At other times, the speaking partner will be communicating on multiple levels and your task is to bring attention to a piece that she is overlooking.

We follow when we respond to the energy that is asking to be noticed—the quantum flirts. We lead when we offer encouragement for a particular movement, emotion, sound, or frozen place to step forward. As with the compliant husband just mentioned, leadership was exercised when he was encouraged to amplify his head movement and to give it words.

In another situation, the two of us were working with a couple who were in distress resulting from the husband's recent relapse into prescription drug abuse. In one of our meetings the wife, Myrna, was grilling her husband, Josh, over whether he had once again taken painkillers. As she was challenging him he would become more hostile and less disclosing. It was impossible for us to be able to discern the truth about whether he had taken painkillers again. At one point we asked Myrna what she was experiencing in that moment (presencing). She replied that she was frustrated. Her general countenance, however, suggested something much more that frustration. We reflected back to her that her eyes were widened and that she was sitting on the edge of her chair. We also noted that her hands were gripping her knees.

When we encouraged her to amplify these non-verbal expressions she felt panic starting to rise in her chest. Her breath grew shallow and tight and her hands became clammy. One of us asked her what her widened eyes were saying. She immediately responded, "Watch out, don't get fooled." As Josh witnessed Myrna's reaction it triggered a cascade of responses in him. But before we turned our attention to him, we stayed with what was unfolding in Myrna.

Brian went over and sat beside her and instead of trying to calm her down supported her in letting the panicky energy speak. She started to feel anger rise up as she stood up and began to move about the room. Brian asked her what she needed to do and she replied "I need to scream." We both encouraged her to do so while Marcia moved closer to Josh and asked him to hang in with what was happening. Myrna balled up her fists and commenced screaming, "I don't believe you! Tell me the truth, Goddammit!"

The energy in the room became very high-pitched. Marcia continued to support Josh while Myrna had her tirade. She began to express fear that she couldn't trust Josh and then she recalled that her dad had lied to her family repeatedly about his gambling, until the family eventually had to sell their home. She said several times she could no longer tell if Josh was lying or not, all the while pacing the floor. Anytime he looked tired to her, Myrna surmised he was on painkillers. She started to feel the panic rise up like a post-traumatic stress response. The felt sense was that her world was about to come crashing down.

Josh, meanwhile, had sunken deep into his chair and was staring off into some faraway space. Marcia attempted to make eye contact but it was as if he was staring through her. She said to him, "Where have you gone?" Her words touched off in him a response that had enormous charge behind it. He directed his reaction to Myrna: "You don't care about me. You don't know how exhausting my work is. All you care about is your needs!" Marcia asked him to stay with those words "You don't care about me" and to feel the strength behind them. Josh began to "leave" again and Marcia asked him if he could remain aware of where he was going.

By now Myrna had brought her full attention to Josh, even as she was still highly charged herself. Josh grew quieter and started to describe a childhood relationship with an older boy that developed over a five year period, beginning when he was twelve. Josh was sexually abused by the sixteen year old who plied him with cocaine and convinced him to engage in sexual activity.

As this memory unfolded, both Myrna and Josh drew closer together. Josh was entering into the felt experience of being used and seduced by the sixteen year old. He described the feeling when he realized he was being taken advantage of as a "punch in the gut." Marcia asked him to "feel into" the punch in the gut. Josh placed both hands over his solar plexus and doubled over and the words that came out were: "it hurts so much."

Myrna was crying at this point and she came over to Josh and took his hand. Brian asked her what was behind the impulse to make connection. Myrna replied that she had become aware of how she had turned Josh into her father and how she had in some way wanted him just to meet her needs. She said that her heart broke to hear his pain and that she had never seen her dad's pain.

Josh began to feel his remorse for how he refused to let in how much Myrna truly did care for him. He saw the fear behind her mistrust. Additionally, Josh began to see his addiction in a new light. He became aware of how attention from someone, cocaine, and sexuality all had occupied the same space for him as a twelve year old. He also saw how hard he was trying to avoid the deep pain which revealed itself as a punch in the gut.

As they both began to make contact to the historical wounding that manifested as the control patterns each had cultivated to keep the emotions at bay, they could begin to make authentic contact. Myrna's need to micromanage Josh so that she did not have to face the dread she encountered as a child began to gradually dissipate. Josh's sporadic substance abuse kept occurring for another year as he struggled to come to grips with the pain of betrayal. Slowly he began to build trust that Myrna was not just using him and he could bring more of his inner world to her.

There are several aspects of this particular session that we would like to highlight. When we shifted the session from the story and brought attention to Myrna we were inviting her back into the experience of the moment. She described herself as feeling frustrated. This seemed to both of us to be inconsistent with how she appeared to us. Presencing, in this case, involved confronting the difference between the client's self description and the energy she was putting out. It helped her to have mirrored back to her how she was coming across.

Leading by following, in this instance, took the form of suggesting she amplify the expression of energy that was showing up in her body language. The moment she became self aware and began to intensify what she was exhibiting, she felt panic. Leading by following thus meant going with the flow of energy that was already filling up the room and bringing consciousness to it. This took Myrna into an emotional state she was trying desperately to avoid. Throughout her relationship she exerted enormous energy to keep the panic at bay. To avoid the panic, in her mind, was to make sure she was not being fooled by Josh. If she could just stay on top of Josh's relapses she could avoid catastrophe. This was, of course, an effort she was not fully conscious of. As she became more aware of how her panic was calling the shots she could easily bridge the experience to her childhood. In doing so, there was a real opportunity for healing to take place.

At that particular juncture another example of leading by following occurred. Brian, instead of helping Myrna to manage the anxiety and keep it in check, invited her to move *with* the strong energy that was coursing through her body. Her own inner wisdom informed her that she needed to scream. While prevailing modes of intervention would be more directed toward helping her calm down and get to what other emotions lay beneath the scream, we honor the wisdom in such moments and continue to follow the energy. What came out was a buildup of intense emotion that she had never be able to express at her father and which had been building up with Josh over the years. It was actually a very profound and, in our view, crucial moment.

These are the instances, in our work, where we feel that mindfulness alone is insufficient. **The "mind-in-the-body" sometimes needs to speak without the level of detachment we normally associate with mindfulness**. The committed relationship is full of intense, passionate emotion which too often has no outlet. Leading by following is a way of engaging the energy which is longing for expression. The idea of "right distance" from emotion as described by Welwood [(50)] suggests not getting either too far away from or too close to the feeling. There is great wisdom in this, but we believe there are times when "letting the emotion lead" is essential to an emerging new level of consciousness. It allows for a breaking of the impasse which the control patterns have established.

Helping Myrna bring mindfulness to her panic may have allowed her to manage it better. She may have even become aware of how much mistrust she had toward Josh and how it related to her dad. But without her being able to enter fully into the experience of the long-held anger and desperation it would be hard for her to truly relax the hyper-vigilance she carried. Additionally, by expressing her strong emotion it triggered in Josh his own pain of betrayal and related historical antecedents.

By following the energy we send a message that we trust the wisdom of the non-rational sensibilities in each person. We let them know it is safe to have these powerful inner states, and that it is not dangerous to release them. This is part of what we are encouraging when we talk about conflict engagement. Many couples want to know that their potent and passionate places are not wrong, evil, destructive and inappropriate. These are the cultural messages they have received from time immemorial. What they feel most relieved by is the therapist not only normalizing these fervent feelings, but the trust and acknowledgement of the validity of them.

With Josh, Marcia used leading by following after first attempting to make eye contact and helping to bring him into the present. Her words "Where have you gone?" partially brought him back as he began to accuse Myrna of not caring. His response to her was tinged with his history as we all soon discovered. Josh was vacillating between consciousness of the moment and regression into his history. Marcia employed leading by following when she repeated back to him "You don't care about me." These words seemed to carry a certain poignancy to them and sent Josh back into his history. It opened the door for him to be able to tell his story of sexual abuse. You can see in this example of leading by following that, when used effectively, it involves only a "nudge" in order to invite out into the open that which is already in the room.

Lastly, when Josh described the "punch in the gut" he experienced when he realized that the "caring" behavior by the older boy was manipulation, Marcia used this as another opportunity to lead by following. She encouraged Josh to feel into the punch in the gut. This allowed him to get in touch with how much hurt he carried and how it came to life when Myrna objectified him. By feeling the hurt, Josh was making his first attempt to "master" it. Since he had spent his entire adult life self-medicating to avoid the pain, he had never let it emerge from his gut. As it came forth he could begin to see both that he is bigger than the pain and that Myrna would not abandon him in his most vulnerable place.

Leading by following opens up a new world to couples because it engages multiple forms of wisdom. As each person begins to become more aware of a broader range of experience in each moment, he or she can begin to communicate in richer and deeper ways. When the two of us take what is given in the session we begin to send the couple a clear message not only that we see them but also that each of them have the potential to use what is available to heal and grow.

Catalyzing

Now we arrive at the level of engagement we refer to as catalyzing. While *Presencing* and *Leading by Following* both take couples away from discursive and causal modes of interacting, catalyzing alone offers them the opportunity to take quantum leaps over the edge. **As you shall see, there are crossroads in couples' therapy where, without a radical shove, the relationship will remain mired in seemingly intractable patterns.**

As we have been suggesting throughout this book, you, as a couples' therapist, need to take risks. To follow the way of water is to flow with the unpredictable. Curiosity and humility are the hallmarks of a wise and sensitive therapist. When it comes to catalyzing, courage can be added to this list. There are times when a courageous therapist will need to push the limits of comfort and consciousness to help the couple meet each other in the cauldron of forbidden truths.

In catalyzing we challenge couples to acknowledge and express exactly those things which they fight so vehemently to avoid. Take, for instance, Brenda who withholds sex, love, and even warmth from Victor. Though they have been married for six years and Brenda claimed in an individual session before couples work even began that she did not want to be with Victor, she persisted in the marriage. All the while however, she gave him next to nothing. While he protested from time to time, he was willing to settle for a vacant lot on the place where he longed for a castle.

Brenda grew up with two handicapped siblings and never was able to get from her parents the kind of loving attention her sibs received. As an adult she played out the role of the withholder and resented when others placed any demands on her. In fairly predictable fashion, her career involved working with emotionally disabled children.

One night she had a dream of the kids she worked with grabbing at her, taking her possessions and eating her lunch. She could easily feel the place where she was angry and resisted giving them anything. However, the two of us wondered about the "grabby" part of *her*. Where was this place in her with Victor? We asked her if she could feel the part where she wanted to take from him. Our catalyzing suggestion first involved her lying on a mat and kicking and demanding to be taken care of while Victor looked on.

It was much easier for her to feel her resistance to needing anything and certainly to demanding it. It was, after all, demanding, grabby energy which she experienced from her two sisters and it repulsed her. As she embodied her resistance however she began to see her father. She remembered how she longed for him to give her the kind of love her sisters received from him. It was clear that her desire for her dad got shut off and condemned to solitary confinement in some concealed place in her heart.

We then asked her to try something else as she continued to lie on the mat. We invited Victor to hold out his forearm and for Brenda to take hold of it and try to pull him toward her. We wanted her to feel into the somatic experience of reaching and taking what she wanted. Victor was encouraged to offer resistance to her tugging. As she began to make effort to pull him toward her she could feel the internal struggle between the longing for connection and the repulsion to her own neediness. Her efforts lacked any real energetic charge. She also noticed that she had great difficulty fully embodying the grabby part of herself because it could trigger the pain of not being met.

So we pushed her to embrace this disavowed aspect of herself and to make it as big as she could. We gave her some words to go along with the tugging on Victor's arm. Just as a five year old may feel about her daddy, we suggested that she pull Victor toward her and say the words "You're mine!" At first she struggled with embodying this energy but once she allowed herself to claim it, she shouted out "You're mine!" and "I want you!" while pulling and tugging at Victor until she "possessed" him. He resisted but finally succumbed to her and they fell into a tangle of arms, legs and torsos on the mat. For his part, Victor was extremely pleased to feel this energy coming from Brenda and was all too willing to oblige.

What this situation illustrates is the essential goal of catalyzing. Every one of us has competing internal impulses and they can neutralize each other if there is not sufficient permission, and sometimes provocation to fully embody one impulse. Brenda's impulse to withdraw is her control pattern and is employed to protect against feeling her need and her immense fear of rejection. Her dream informed her about the part that has always felt angry and helpless about being taken from, as well as the needy, grabby aspect of her interior world.

When we catalyze with a partner such as Brenda, we are often encouraging and challenging her to fully embrace one specific impulse—the one most exiled. We have come to refer to this as "conscious compartmentalizing." In order to circumvent the tendency to neutralize all internal impulses by the mindful, simultaneous awareness of each part, we want partners to fully and singularly take on the one piece that is most difficult to hold and reveal. In Brenda's case this was the part which longed to be loved and yearned to express itself effusively as unfettered desire and a narcissistic sense of entitlement. Or, in her words, her "grabbiness."

Catalyzing allows for a specific and focused immersion into an emotion or impulse with little or no obligation to attend to other internal realities. In this place the mentor and to a lesser degree the spouse becomes the ground for the partner to "lose control." The paramount goal of all catalyzing interventions is to bring out into the open some truthful and vital aspect of each person which would likely never surface without the invitation and provocation of the mentor. In doing so, it loses its grip.

While the concept of intuition is much maligned and infrequently mentioned in contemporary psychological literature, it is the basis for catalyzing engagements. Perhaps it emerges from limbic resonance, or the picking up on subtle cues. Maybe it is just a reasoned hunch, or a reliance on one's clinical experience. Whatever it may be, there are moments when the mentor simply trusts the non-rational, inchoate information which arises from a variant source of wisdom.

It is our opinion that everything we do, think, say, or feel is influenced by the larger field of consciousness that exists beyond our personal boundaries. In this regard there is no separate, autonomous mind. We may be reacting to visual and auditory cues and to more delicate energies which are felt in a different way. Stephen W. Porges, author of The Polyvagal Theory, [(35)] coined the term "neuroception" to describe how we sense whether another is safe or dangerous. We suggest that this pre-cognitive sensing extends beyond the simple determination of danger to include the neuroception of others in myriad ways. One's intuitions are, of course, always prey to personal projections, and countertransference. But if a catalyzing suggestion is not emerging from a place which resonates with the couple it will be summarily dismissed by them. This is the nature of the improvisational approach. There is much less danger in making an "incorrect" suggestion than most therapists fear.

Catalyzing takes us beyond Leading by Following and into a new space of making bold suggestions. **We can say that Leading by Following is primarily evocative while Catalyzing is essentially provocative.** The two of us see the role of the mentor as "caring provocateur," one who creates opportunities for each partner to step beyond the bounds of what is known or deemed acceptable. In a sense the mentor encourages the partners to give something a try and to see how it feels. This is what we did with Brenda. We catalyze to get a spouse "over the hump" and past an edge which he may not even notice until it is pointed out. It may be expressed as a prompt, an invitation, a cajole or even a light-hearted goad.

For most couples life moves along through a series of fairly non-descript moments and events. The vast majority of time is spent in self-preservation consciousness. Most days are experienced as somewhat neutral, neither very high nor very low. In the general course of life these ""normal" times are punctuated by infrequent moments of poignancy when something occurs to cause a breakthrough into deeper connection and more open and vulnerable expression. These are precious and palpable experiences of heightened consciousness and emotional expansiveness.

Perhaps in the aftermath of a bad fight there is a breakthrough into a realization of deeper levels of emotional truth. Maybe one realizes how much his partner truly matters, or she reveals a dark corner of her soul where no one has yet to travel. One spouse feels a sense of deep remorse toward her mate, or she collapses into his arms in tears of relief. These poignant moments are profoundly significant events in a couple's shared life.

Catalyzing is incorporated in order to increase the likelihood and frequency of these meaningful exchanges. So much of our passion as adults is couched in euphemisms, political correctness and sham displays of "having it all together" that most of us need a lot of help getting to the truths which result in intimate connection. When we catalyze with couples, we are pushing the envelope of intimacy. We are offering suggestions to experiment with latent energies that may be expressed through phrases, sounds, or movement.

We will routinely suggest phrases that seem to be lurking just beneath the surface of a particular interaction and which correspond to specific category of emotions, impulses, attitudes or energies.

For instance:

Category	**Phrase**
Blame	"It's your fault!"
Competition	"I'll never give in!"
Demand	"My way!"
Selfishness	"Give it to me!"
Lower Self	"I'll make you pay!"

Withholding	"You can't have it!"
Resistance to Vulnerability	"I'll never let you matter!"
Desire	"I want you!"
Fear of Abandonment	"Don't leave!'
Fear of Engulfment	"Go away!"
Lust	"Fuck me!'
Anguish	"I hate you!'
Need	"Help me!'
Surrender	"Take me!"
Control	"You have to . . . !"
Protection	"I won't trust!'
Narcissism	"Look at me!"
Ambivalent Attachment	"Come closer—go away!"
Remorse	"I'm sorry!'
Connection	"I'm here!'
Gratitude	"I'm grateful for . . ."

These are often phrases that most partners would never consider saying to each other and would rarely, if ever, emerge spontaneously. It isn't because they are not part of each person's inner experience, but that nearly all of us have long been conditioned to edit such statements. Catalyzing begins with the mentor naming the taboo expression which is evident in the shared energy field. When a mentor suggests to a partner to use a particular phrase such as "Come closer—stay away" she encourages that person to amplify it to the level of energy with which it is felt.

In such a case, one partner may stand in front of his mate and embody the energy of "Come closer—stay away!" He may pull her toward him and then push her back. Or, he may point a finger where he wants her to go, and as soon as she arrives point again to a more distant spot in the room. Meanwhile, she gets to experience with much greater clarity exactly what their relationship often feels like. It allows her greater access to perhaps her resistance to meeting his ambivalent demands. Or she may get in touch with how she collapses under the weight of his contradictory and silent edicts. The mentor may then invite her to embody her own statement. She may say for instance, "I'm not moving!" or "I'll move, but I'll make you pay!'

By identifying simple statements and amplifying them the couple exposes control patterns in their relationship which otherwise would continue to haunt the recesses of awareness. When a couple seems to be in an intractable argument for example, a mentor may suggest they stand opposite each other and simply go back and forth with the phrases "My way!"—"No, my way!" If the couple can allow this power struggle to escalate it is not unusual to see them eventually burst out laughing over the absurdity of it, as well as from having released the energy connected to it.

Catalyzing suggestions are not classically behavioral interventions in that we are not trying to teach the couple a new skill. Rather, we are often supporting the emergence of a metaskill, which, as we have previously described, is already intuitively know by each person. Full expression of emotions and impulses as well as the embodying of resistances and demands allow for the shadow energies to be released and makes space, as we shall see in the next chapter, for increasing vulnerability and intimacy.

Recently, during a workshop, the two of us mentored a couple who were on the verge of splitting up. The husband Sam kept repeating that he had tried everything but he felt that Penny would never change. His complaint was that she always had to have her way and that when he tried to offer his opinion she would refuse to listen. Penny believed that Sam was judgmental and dismissive of her. He told of how she forced the whole family onto a macrobiotic diet and how she refused to have the children immunized. She, conversely, expressed how he was derisive and insulting toward the things that were important to her.

In this session, we worked with them to *presence* their moment-by-moment experience. As Sam began to pay more attention to what was happening in the here-and-now, he began to notice how Penny would stop listening to him when he was sharing his complaints. His typical aggressive control pattern of judging her, and threatening to leave, halted when he became aware that she was not paying attention. The two of us saw how deeply affected he was by her disappearance. It was clear that what was happening was more than her simply not listening. She emotionally and energetically evaporated.

Until the moment when, through presencing, Sam became aware of Penny's disappearance, he would be desperately trying to make contact with her the only way he knew how. At this juncture we offered to him a statement which felt to us to be just beneath the surface of his reactivity. We suggested that he stand in front of her and say "It scares me when you go away." Sam slightly recoiled when he heard these words, but quickly acknowledged their validity. As he delivered them to Penny his body began to shake and she began to look frightened. After repeating them several times he said to her, "I don't want to lose you." The protective stance between them began to subside and Penny then spoke. She said she didn't realize until that moment how she would go away whenever she felt overwhelmed by Sam. This is what she had learned to do as a child when she had no other recourse.

For Sam, he had learned to challenge and threaten as a way to couch his fear of abandonment. By saying the words "It scares me when you go away" he was able for the first time to express his fear openly and honestly. Every time he would sense Penny's leaving he would express hopelessness about the relationship and threaten to leave her. It appeared that he grew up with an emotionally dismissive mother and had learned to compensate for his internal anxiety with an external show of bravado.

Often when we offer a catalyzing suggestion to a couple it results in the partners bringing forth additional internal truths. This occurred when Sam shifted his words to "I don't want to lose you." Catalyzing statements are meant to open the gates to even deeper expressions of held back realities. "I don't trust you" may open up space for the awareness, "It hurts to be disappointed." "You have to do it my way" may lead to, "I'm afraid that you won't want to give to me if I don't demand it." Often the only way a partner gets to a deeper level of truth is by having full permission to embody the first layer of the unspoken, unacknowledged interior places. This layering of expression will be addressed more fully in the next chapter.

Many catalyzing suggestions are non-verbal or primarily energetic. It has long been the experience of body-centered therapists that movement leads to awareness and allows for contact with hard to reach emotions. Thus when we work with couples we invariably encourage them to bring their bodies more actively into the session. As we mentioned previously just getting the couple to stand can have a major impact on what is occurring between them. We have spent entire sessions working with what comes up when we have a couple explore distance between each other.

Just how profoundly each partner is sensitive and reactive to the other can be brought to consciousness by having them move closer and further away from each other. Something as simple as getting them to jump up and down and make sound can result in a connection to feelings that no amount of talking would have done. Because many couples are entrained toward weak exchanges of energy, utilization of these somatic aspects of communication is fundamental to the EMM approach.

Energetic catalyzing is designed to elicit or emphasize typically blocked of disavowed internal or interpersonal experiences as well as to honor the implicit memories which cannot be fully articulated by the individual. Below are some examples of non-verbal and somatic catalyzing engagements. They are employed contextually in a session whenever it appears the couple may be on the edge of significant movement.

- With eyes closed, the partners explore each other's faces.
- One person carries the other around the room on his back.
- They both stare at each other and growl.
- The couple wrestles together on a mat.
- One partner kneels before the other in supplication.
- One of them lies down and throws a tantrum while the other watches.
- One of the partners embodies her possessiveness, grabbing and pulling her mate.
- The partners each close their eyes and synchronize their breathing.
- The mentor Utilizes music and dance to elicit emotions.
- A partner goes and hides behind pillows or a couch in a corner.

These are just a very few illustrations of possible catalyzing opportunities on a non-verbal level. There are an infinite variety of energetic catalyzing engagements. We employ them not as techniques to "get" the couple to experience something, but because the moment calls for a non-linear, right-hemisphere experience. We might offer to one partner the opportunity, for example, to hide in a corner as she recalls doing when her parents argued, or because she is experiencing an implicit body memory which is telling her to find cover. By giving her the chance to recreate this early-life situation, she may recall how she had longed for somebody to come seek her out and how saddened she was when no one ever did. Perhaps we will then invite her spouse to slowly go search for her, allowing her to experience the sensations of being missed and being wanted. Such experiences can be very tender and very healing.

Catalyzing engagements are really opportunities for you, as therapist, to step beyond the bounds of the conventional. These engagements draw from the body-centered work of Reich, Lowen, and Pierrakos who utilized energy-based interventions to unblock body armor and free up life force. Additionally, in EMM we draw from the early pioneers in family therapy and psychodrama who opened the way to shifting patterns of interpersonal behavior. By attending to what is being triggered within each partner through the crucible of the shared energy field, it is possible to create an opening for deep healing. This happens, in our estimation, because each partner is able to feel and express long-denied aspects of his/her full human experience.

It is a sort of motto of ours that in every session we want the couple to take a risk. We like to challenge them to push the envelope beyond the boundaries of their familiar haunts and to embrace some novel aspect of each person's nature. Here's a good example. Not long ago we were working with a young same-sex couple who have been together for less than a year. Amy and Ruth were in a crisis because Ruth (who had been in Alcoholics Anonymous for five years) had recently relapsed with alcohol and marijuana. As they each discussed the details of how the event affected them it was evident that Amy was trying to be understanding and Ruth was mired in self-judgment. Each in her own way was trying too hard to get past the incident.

As we probed a bit further an important back story began to emerge. Ruth had been rejected by a past lover after a nine year relationship not so long ago. In that relationship she had tried to be the good partner who never did anything to cause her lover grief. Ultimately it didn't matter as she was spurned anyway. Ruth also shared with us that when she drinks or smokes pot she becomes the life of the party. She was with Amy at the time of her recent relapse. Both of them conveyed how charming and funny Ruth was that night.

So it seemed to the two of us that perhaps Ruth was sending a clear message to Amy by drinking and getting high. We encouraged her to bring out her "big energy" by moving her body (jumping, punching the foam cube, and raising her voice.) We asked her to try some words, the phrases we gave to her were: "This is me!—Can you handle me?!" Soon the words shifted to, "I'm not so nice!" and finally Ruth began to shout at Amy "I'm a wild motherfucker!!" As Amy received this energy from Ruth she began to get excited. She also wanted to hit the cube. As she stepped forward we offered her some phrases to yell back at Ruth. The words were: “Bring it on!” “I want all of you!”

The two of them went back and forth—“I’m a wild motherfucker!”—“Bring it on!” The energy in the room rose and eventually they both started to laugh with pleasure and relief. Over the course of time they had become so cautious with each other, yet what each really wanted was to feel more vibrant and expressive. Ruth’s drinking arose as a way to protest the tepid pall that was threatening to choke the life out of the relationship just as it had in Ruth’s previous partnership.

You can see from this example that Ruth was unaware of how her relapse was a statement. She had come to believe that being caring, kind, and understanding were greater values than her wildness and playfulness. Yet Amy longed for Ruth’s wild side, a side that was more evident when they were in the Eros stage. Without catalyzing they would likely never have moved past the negatives of Ruth’s drinking. We needed to push her over the edge so she could fly. The more she could embrace the “wild motherfucker” in her, the less she needed to turn to alcohol or pot to release herself from her compensations.

The gamut of catalyzing suggestions runs from having couples pray together to seductive dancing; from having one partner straddle the other while saying “I’m in control” to one holding the other in his arms and saying “you’re safe with me.” Your challenge is to sense what is being held back and to create the platform for that energy to come to the fore. In doing so you are likely to invoke and invite more poignant moments that become integrated into the couple’s shared life experience and which create room for future forays into other withheld truths. Together we have witnessed miraculous breakthroughs in couples who seemed hopelessly mired in the safety of their control patterns.

Bridging

Past, present and an unfolding future all co-exist in each moment. Everything we think and feel exists in a broader context. Even as we *presence* we embrace all that is, all that makes us who we are. Living in the moment in a sense means living in all moments. One key aspect of healing is to decode and make sense of our present experiences and to allow the feelings that were shut off in the course of our development, to be expressed. So often what one partner thinks she feels toward her mate is a reincarnation of previously unmetabolized emotion. This is what the two of us are referring to when we talk about the 80/20% principle.

It is an active component of every couple's session. Each partner conflates the present reaction to the other with the timeless subjectivity of emotions not fully realized. One woman's anger at her partner for being worried about his health is grafted to a long history of having to care for her hypochondriacal mother. Another man's mistrust toward his partner's desire to buy a house and have a baby is intimately connected to his strong sense of being objectified and used by both parents. He's convinced the he is only loved for what he can provide.

Bridging is the fourth type of engagement we utilize in the EMM approach. Its greatest value is in giving a couple full permission and a justification for the strength of their emotional reactions, in a more comprehensive context. We are not seeking insight alone through bridging, but rather we are helping the couple to both comprehend and make room for the fullness of their emotional reactions to each other. Using the above example with the man who felt hostile toward his wife for wanting a baby and a house, bridging played a pivotal role is allowing him to express long-held resentment and mistrust. His wife could listen with a more open heart when she understood where his feelings originated.

At first he ranted about his wife's selfishness. When one of us asked him if this was a familiar reaction for him, he recounted how his parents were totally focused on his successes and had little interest in his fears and struggles. He learned to be a high achiever in order to get approval, but when it came to marriage, he finally allowed himself to "fight back." While there was some truth about his wife wanting to be taken care of, she also longed to care for him and make his life easier. But his negative narrative of her would not allow him to notice anything except the ways she wanted to take from him.

By creating a bridge to his history and his early sense of betrayal he could begin to create some separation between then and now. He could start to see his wife with greater complexity than his narrative offered. But first he needed to be able to rage at the injustice he experienced as a child. We encouraged him to express his mistrust fully. As he allowed himself to openly embody the highly protective resistance to trusting, he could, for the first time, enter into the pain of the betrayal. He screamed "I don't trust you! I'll never trust you!" These potent words, harbored searingly and somatically, needed expression. By bridging his early betrayals with his present mistrust of his wife he started a slow process of de-coupling the two realities.

We bridge in order to cross the divide between what appears to be simple reactions to a spouse and the *origins* of those reactions. Sometimes one of the partners organically makes important connections after having catalyzed an emotion or impulse. That is, it is often *through* the catalyzing of an emerging energy that a spouse will get in touch with a historical precipitant. Such is the case with Myrna who had a difficult time surrendering to her husband Lawrence. As she expressed the fierceness of an energy that we encouraged her to catalyze with the words, "I won't let you control me!" she suddenly shifted to the phrase "You can't intimidate me!"

Afterwards Myrna recounted how, as she was expressing herself to Lawrence she had an image of her mother flash in front of her. She recalled how her mother would turn the heat up in their home when her father was at work. But when he would come home unexpectedly, her mom would panic and tell Myrna to place ice cubes on the thermostat to quickly bring down the thermometer. This left a powerful impression on Myrna and played a significant role in the establishment of her control patterns. She learned to keep Lawrence from exerting too much power by constantly keeping him off guard. She would *never* be like her mother. She would never let a man have that much power. By catalyzing her resistance to being controlled she opened up space for an important memory which had surreptitiously been influencing her interactions with Lawrence for their entire relationship.

Sometimes the partners will establish the bridge and sometimes it will emerge from one of us making the connections between what is occurring in the room and what we have learned about the couple from things they have shared. As an example, Evelyn truly loved her partner Marty but she also feared that he would hurt her. She was deeply confused and distressed by this. We asked her if she could allow her body to express these ambivalent impulses to move toward seeking contact and to move away in self-protection. Marty stood on one end of the room with arms opened as if to welcome Evelyn. She would tentatively move toward him until she felt the fear, then she would back up.

The two of us recalled from a previous session how Evelyn remembered her mother as being disgusted by her. When she wanted her mother she felt a profound fear of her mother's hatred. We took the opportunity to remind her of this as she was experiencing the approach-avoidance conflict with Marty. The recollection of this reality immediately "amped up" the strength of her internal struggle. She began to run in a tight circle in a manner that is reminiscent of some autistic children we have seen. She spun around as if she could not find solace in either moving toward or moving away. It was as if she were embodying the potent struggle of her childhood dilemma. We saw this as a palpable response to a "disorganized attachment" relationship with her mom. As her mother was simultaneously the source of her deepest need and her greatest fear, she had no place to run. This got played out again and again with Marty.

By the two of us making the bridging inquiry about her mother and how it seemed to mirror what was occurring in the moment, Evelyn allowed herself to feel just how powerful her inner struggle was. She spun around, embodying the ambivalence until she collapsed in exhaustion. At that point she asked Marty to come to her. He held her as she sobbed. She told him "I want you to see how much panic I have inside me when I start to feel my need for you." This touched him deeply and he began to cry along with her. This is the type of poignant, precious moment we referred to earlier that can only occur when a couple drops beneath the control patterns they think will keep them safe.

Sometimes bridges can be made between the present dynamics and past experiences and sometimes not. It is not at all necessary to make the connections, though it often helps the couple to have more compassion, greater understanding and a whole lot less defensiveness when one can see why his partner reacts as she does. Reich was the first to acknowledge that the ability to express that which has been held down is sufficient for healing to occur. It is not essential to remember all the history. We have found though, that bridging can often help a couple move to places of vulnerability that opens the way to a genuine loving connection.

As we are about to see in the next chapter, the movement of intense and highly charged emotions is often the gateway to the tender places which are the sum and substance of the committed relationship. Presencing, Leading by Following, Catalyzing, and Bridging are the forms of engagement we utilize in the EMM approach to allow for this natural evolution from self protection to surrender into pure love. The love that flourishes as a couple begins to allow their woundedness to surface is not of an abstract nature. It is not warm and gentle. It's searing and alive with heartbreak, joy, relief, remorse, desire and formidable gratitude. To get there is the subject of Chapter Seven.

Chapter Seven

Full Self Expression

Getting the love you want involves giving the truth you have. Love is not simply the end result of "clearing out" all the messy emotions which seem to get in its way. As we see it, love is the ground upon which all internal experience rests. The intentional revealing of our secreted feelings and thoughts is love manifesting itself in the way it must. "I hate you!" is usually code for "You matter so much I can't tolerate what is happening between us." As partners learn to express their ostracized affective truths, magic happens. The condensed energy which clogs the free flow of life force is exhaled into their communal space, the space where love resides.

There's no love without need—no love without hurt, fear, resistance, protest, longing, and remorse. Even in our willingness to admit to our basest desire to inflict pain on each other there is a foundation of love. Love disappears when we deny the truth of any part of our authentic internal experience. Cruelty honestly owned is a love offering.

The range of human expression is rich and variegated. While it is not always necessary to express all that we may feel toward our partners, it is equally true that when we take the time to discover what we often overlook when confined by our control patterns, we grow wiser. In this chapter our desire is to take you on a tour of the most significant topography of the uniquely human affective landscape. By understanding the flow of each partner's internal layers of experience, from most protected to most open and vulnerable, you will begin to appreciate the value in every part of what they bring to one another.

Many of us emerge from childhood with an inviolable belief that "My feelings are too much." And so we lock them down. Yet the reality is the opposite—not that our feelings are too much but that the container, or the capacity to experience them and share them, has become too small. In other words, there is a widely held fear that certain emotions will overwhelm or flood ones capacity to remain intact. "I'll cry forever" or, "I'm afraid I'll tear this room apart" are the kinds of things partners will say in a session when invited to make contact with emotions that are on the edge of showing up. The grave concern is that "I won't be able to control my feelings." But the mistake we make as a culture is to believe that certain emotions are too big or too destructive to be fully experienced. When placed in the proper context, emotions are always absolutely right-sized. The challenge is to make room for them and to trust that the higher self or witness is capable of holding it all. To reclaim our full human capacity to feel, with an abiding comprehension that we will remain intact and actually flourish through the freedom of emotional expression is at the heart of the EMM approach.

As we discussed previously, the drive toward self expression is essential to our humanity. A relationship which is characterized largely by self-preservation consciousness is one where passion withers and routine rules the day. Self expression allows us to claim and reclaim our emotional wisdom as the pathway to our highest capabilities. The process we describe in this chapter acknowledges the vital experience of protest which all children feel when attachment is breached. It recognizes the multiplicity of internal subjective states and serves as a tool to unpack, or un-blend these states from our Core Self. Finally, it invites each partner into an acceptance of the completeness of the human condition which involves injury, reaction, repair, and transcendence.

We do not create safety in a relationship by learning to never judge, never criticize, never offend. Any strategies in relationship therapy which instruct couples to wipe negativity off the map of human engagement are destined to result in diminished affect. Safety emerges from a growing willingness to feel our full reactions to our partner's real-life ways of showing up in the world. It's not his job to be so completely conscious as to never offend me. It my obligation and my right to have my emotional reactions to his words or deeds. **Injury-free relationships are not the goal in EMM. Indeed, injury often affords us the chance to express ourselves in ways we have long forgotten.** It allows us to protest and express denied primary emotions.

Emotions are not things. They are not something one possesses. I have an iPod, but I don't *have* anger. Emotions, thoughts, and impulses are manifestations of energy that moves through us if we allow them. The full self expression template offered here evolves out of the recognition that often one emotion or reaction will flow into another when each is granted its rightful moment in the sun.

The two of us have constructed this 10 level template of emotional responsiveness as a guide to assist both couples and therapists in understanding what may be going on in a given moment as well as what may be ready to emerge. We call it full self expression (FSE). As we describe in some detail below, the top layers of the template are more focused on self preservation, autonomy enhancement, intensifying or charging the body into higher arousal, and the instinctive need to protest when connection is threatened. The bottom layers include the opening to vulnerability, intimacy enhancement, releasing or discharging of energy when arousal has run its course, and the expansiveness into empathic, loving and grateful "heart-centered" connection to one's partner.

It appears that the sympathetic arousal of the autonomic nervous system (rarely supported in the context of most therapeutic modalities which tend to bias toward parasympathetic states) may be essential to the capacity for empathy. In other words, until an individual can connect to the more charged experiences of anger, protest, demand and maybe even the impulse to be destructive, empathy is harder to reach. Just as a sociopath is not easily distressed and feels little remorse, it is likely that we dull our ability to be empathic when we shut off our stronger reactions to each other.

Couples that cannot open their hearts to each other are often unable to express their negativity. This is the reasoning behind making space for contentious feelings. In full self expression each partner is given room to bring forth an emotional "truth" as a way to discover a deeper truth. The great fear in conventional psychotherapy is that if the therapist allows strong emotions clients will get re-wounded. Yet strong emotions are the currency of the committed relationship—even though they are rarely expressed cleanly. Partners are frequently re-wounding each other, but with no consciousness of what is taking place.

Our goal is not to stop all injury. Couples do not create safety by becoming more delicate with each other. Safety is the end result of knowing that my partner does not have the power to destroy me. The expression of hot-blooded emotions, done with a conscious desire toward connection, may be difficult to express or experience, but ultimately leads to genuine safety. Through full self expression one partner reveals whatever helps the process of healing original wounds and leads to a deeper connection that can only emerge when one is fully seen.

FSE allows each person to consciously compartmentalize a particular emotion, need, or reaction without having to either unconsciously act it out, or neutralize it by allowing it to get swallowed up in a mélange of coexisting subjective states. When, for example, one partner says "I'm angry, but I'm also aware that I should have spoken sooner" or, "I'm hurt, but I know she didn't mean it," the anger gets diluted and muted. With FSE, the partner is given the air time to just hold one particular feeling state. In our work with couples we have found that this allows for a feeling to be fully released.

When any event takes place that leaves partners upset with each other it is almost always useful to unpack, or compartmentalize, the reactions. This helps them on several levels. One, it allows for the acknowledgement of parts of one's internal world which are typically exiled. Two, it creates an opening to fully embody such parts. Three, it can lead to what the two of us refer to as the "sacred shift" from one piece of subjective truth to another in a continual movement toward deeper connection.

In our mentoring work we use FSE in two ways. First, it can be utilized as a process to assist couples in breaking free of the reactive blame cycle. Each partner can write out or verbally go through each layer in order to move from the most defended to the most open and vulnerable feelings. Second, FSE is our vision for intimate connection. In every couples session we may be working with specific layers while holding a consciousness of the broader vision of opening to empathy, gratitude and connection to the ground of love. We may, for example, spend an entire session helping one partner discover and express the immature childhood needs that are enacted but never verbalized. By doing so, the individual can discover and access more vulnerable places of hurt, fear and longing.

We are indebted to numerous pioneers in body-centered therapy, as well as our own teachers and healers in our process of identifying the 10 levels of full self expression. In particular Eva Pierrakos and her Pathwork lectures, John Bowlby and Mary Main for their work on attachment, Wihelm Reich and his emphasis on energy and emotional release, Richard Schwartz and his exposition of multiplicity theory, John Gray [(11)] and his total truth process, and the transpersonal theorists who recognize that we are all longing to evolve toward our highest potential.

The 10 levels are broken out as follows:

1. Blame and judgment
2. Childhood needs and demands
3. Destructive “Lower Self” anger
4. Resistance to primary feelings and need
5. Self-affirming anger
6. Fear of abandonment or rejection
7. Hurt, sadness, or grief
8. Remorse and empathy
9. Mature need and longing
10. Gratitude, appreciation and pure love

Let’s take a closer look at each level.

Blame and Judgment

The negative ramifications of blame and judgment are so well established that it is unnecessary for us to spend too much time reviewing them. As the two of us have already pointed out, intractable cycles of reactivity pivot around reciprocal blame. This blame exchange can lead to what Susan Johnson describes as "demon dialogues." Blame wields such power that it has been the ruin of far too many marriages. In many respects it is the antithesis of empathy. Blame and judgment inure partners to the vulnerability and tender feelings that reside in their long shadows.

Sometimes blame is overt and results in very out-in-the-open reactive cycles. Other times it is more clandestine and reveals itself through cold disdain and unforgiving withdrawal. In either case couples lose each other in the turbulence of attack-and-defend. But, all that being said, we are still left with the reality of blame as a ubiquitous component of human engagement. As Jonathan Haidt, author of The Happiness Hypothesis, puts it, "Judgmentalism is indeed a disease of the mind; it leads to anger, torment, and conflict. But it is also the mind's normal condition . . ." [(13)] It is likely that judgment is a biological imperative of the human condition. We all are constantly comparing our performance to others as well as judging them against some standard. As much as blame and judgment is proscribed in couples' therapy it can never be eliminated. Part of the mirroring process involves the assimilation of behaviors and affective states which the parent transmits to the child. Every child soon learns to evaluate what she does in the light of comparison. Inevitably the child will evaluate herself in the context of her immediate world. "I'm faster than Billy." "Emily's smarter than me." In marriage too we are continually comparing ourselves to our partners.

Judgment and comparison devolves into blame as one becomes aware that one's sense of self is attached to an idealized image. We learn to find fault in ourselves and others when the standard of the idealized self image is not realized. Nearly everyone incorporates fault-finding as a tool for self improvement. Most of us have come to believe that through self criticism we will be motivated to grow.

Marital partners are experts, nay, wizards at poking holes in each other's idealized self image. Partners will blame each other often as a way to create a false sense of safety, one borne of a belief that "If my partner is better than me then I will lose her." Blame operates from the old sports axiom that "The best defense is a good offense." It is so woven into every relationship that to ignore its potent influence is to make a grave mistake.

Blame is also wedded to the tendency to want cause-and-effect explanations. As we discussed earlier, the principle of "No First Cause" challenges partners to see beyond linear causality and embrace the larger context of a given situation where blame is assigned. Over the years, the two of us have come to understand just how attached each person is to the ways they blame each other. Even while partners may outwardly agree that there is more to the story than their blame narrative, internally they hold tight. "But she *is* selfish!" "Yes, but he *is* a lousy lover!"

This unwillingness to simply let go of blame and judgment needs to be recognized and dealt with. Though there is no simple cause and effect (he may be awkward in his love—making in part as a consequence of her impatience) there is almost always a kernel of truth in each partner's blaming statements.

The two of us have found that, for many couples, there needs to be room to at least acknowledge the spoken or hidden judgments. While some may not be ready for this (it stings to hear our loved one's criticisms) for many, they either have already heard them or at least intuited them. The ownership of the judgments is both challenging and often relieving. Many times we have heard one partner thank the other for making explicit that which was unspoken, but "in the air." Sometimes, in more fragile relationships there is not enough strength to bring out the blame and judgments and we will not ask more of the couple than they can handle. Yet, often the raising of consciousness about the ways a couple blame each other is vital to opening up them up to deeper truths.

It can be helpful for a couple to bring forth the blame in either general or specific ways. For instance, we will often ask a couple who are obviously in a blame cycle to stand up and face each other and simply shout: "It's your fault!"—"No, it's your fault!" This is a good example of *simplifying* and *amplifying*. We are distilling down a convoluted argument into a simple phrase and encouraging them to bring more energy to it. As basic as it may sound, it often leads to a break in the cycle.

Good communication is predicated on the capacity to take ownership, that is, to make "I" statements when conveying feelings. Yet in this first layer of FSE we invite partners to reveal their "You" statements openly. Some specific examples of such statements include:

- "You always/never . . ."
- "You care more about golf than you do me."
- "You never want to do anything fun."
- "You're a pig!"
- "You spend money like a drunken sailor."
- All you care about is sex."
- "You're just like your mother."
- "You take me for granted."
- "You don't make an effort to look attractive."
- "You'll never change!"
- "You leave all the child-rearing to me."
- Blame in the guise of a question—"Why can't you ever remember to turn down the heat?"

When working with blame we will always remind couples that it is only the outer protective layer of their emotional world. It serves to protect them against more vulnerable primary feelings. We will tell them that in your partner's blaming statements there is probably something for you to learn, even if they are expressing it without care or compassion. We also tell them that blame is often easier to express than need and that underneath a partner's criticisms there is a need.

Blame is a distortion of the child's need to protest an infringement of attachment and therefore is connected ultimately to a desire for connection. This can easily be lost in the natural response to blame which is to defend. But it helps to place blame in this larger context in order to assist couples in moving past the sting of its energy. By exposing blame to the light of reality it can begin to lose its grip on an individual's negative narrative.

To work with blame we may utilize the following interventions:

- Allow both partners to describe their respective blame narratives fully. This helps you, as therapist, to identify control patterns and allows for a buildup of energy that may support a subsequent release into primary feelings. When people maintain a silent stash of judgments, as we have suggested the narrative becomes self reinforcing. By helping each partner to simply give voice to their inner criticisms they are able to "put a little distance" between the judgment and the larger truth. To have each partner say, "I judge you for . . ." immediately shifts the energetic charge around whatever the criticism may be.
- Energize and embody the blame but only with each partner's conscious awareness that they are expressing merely a piece of truth at best. While this is not recommended for fragile relationships, or one's where there is serious psychological injury, it can potentially be the first step in a healing process for partners to consciously own and emotionally release the potent charge of blame. When John Gottman [10] speaks of disdain as one of the great destroyers of relationships, he is, in our view, talking about accumulated blame and resentment which never has an outlet.
- Allow for "*always*" and "*never.*" While the expression of "always" and "never" statements is considered anathema to healthy communication, we have yet to meet a couple who can stop themselves from expressing such statements. Sweeping generalizations are, of course, inaccurate and unfair characterizations of another. However, when a therapist tries to impose rules to curtail this type of communication, there is a failure to recognize the strength of the subjective and energetic realities. In EMM a mentor may make it very clear that "always" and "never" judgments are distortions and yet offer to the

couple to indulge in them as a way to expose them to the light of day. For example the mentor may invite the partners to bring out such statements as: ""You never initiate sex!" "You always have to be right!" "You will never get off the computer to be with me!" "You always side with your family!" In their "higher self" awareness, most people know that they are exaggerating their case, but having permission to express it passionately is important and often makes it easier for them to acknowledge instances when their narrative is untrue.

- Re-direct the outward energy towards disowned parts of the self. That is, to help a spouse find how the blame of the other reflects something within that he rejects in himself. For example, when one partner criticizes the other for careless financial record keeping, he may be more meticulous in this area but unconscious of how careless he can be around his personal hygiene.
- Help each partner take self-ownership of the "20%" truth part of the spouse's judgments. For instance, she accuses him of always putting her needs last. While his typical response is to reel off a litany of examples of how he has been generous and thoughtful, the mentor can ask him if there is something to what his wife says, even if he believes it is exaggerated.
- Have each partner explore what gets triggered when the spouse engages in the behavior that leads to judgment. For example—ask a partner: "What happens to you when your spouse hides out on the computer?"
- Uncover the negative intent or desire to hurt. That is, there is often cruelty or revenge attached to blame ("I want you to hurt like you made me hurt.")
- Re-frame the blaming as a response to each person's "fight or flight" energy.
- Bridge to each person's past. For example a woman says "I can't stand your constant complaining." The mentor encourages her to pound on the cube and to amplify the statement, and then asks her if she can connect the strength of her reaction to anybody else in her life.

- When you have a couple embody the blame, simultaneous expression allows each person to blame without having to receive hurtful comments silently. For example: Man—"You're a prude!" Woman—"You're a sex maniac!" Have them go back and forth so that both feel empowered and not "devoured."

We want to emphasize that the reason to attend to blame is not to reinforce it, but to reveal and release it. It is usually either explained and justified, or locked in the closet, rather than simply expressed. In part, a spouse wants to say it loudly because there is both some truth in her blaming statements and because she likely learned to suppress her criticisms from an early age. In FSE we want couples to discover what their reciprocal blame is protecting against. For instance, by getting them to be up front with their judgments they often can create an awareness of their childhood demands of each other. As long as they each continue to fear that their complaints will never be heard, they will hold on to them fiercely.

Cory turns to internet porn because, he tells himself, Maeve is so controlling in bed. He has never shared this directly with her and has chosen to redirect his energies into the non-conflictual world of cyber-fantasy. When she eventually discovered how he was spending so much of his time, she became even more controlling in his eyes.

In a mentoring session, we had him bring to her directly his judgment—"You're so damned controlling!" While this was only the outermost layer of his reactions to Maeve, it was crucial for him to bring it out strongly and cleanly. His control pattern of withdrawal prevented Cory from stepping up more powerfully in his relationship. For her part, Maeve actually felt relief when she felt him stand up to her—even in blame. Of course, she had her own blaming statement. "You're a coward Cory!" she fired back at him. As we made room for them to express these judgments there was a shift. In their shared energy field, Cory and Maeve co-created a pattern of him hiding out and withholding from her and her jabbing at him to get him to respond. For him to bring forth his judgment, the control pattern immediately began to disintegrate. We will continue to follow this couple as we move down through the layers of FSE.

Owning Childhood Needs and Demands

As we discussed previously, our childhood needs often get confused with the actual adult needs for authentic human connection. This can prove disastrous to a committed relationship. The Imago model developed by Harville Hendrix and Helen Hunt [(14)] emphasizes the critical significance of each partner's attachment to the images formulated in the parent-child bond. These images, usually unspoken, show up as demands and expectations partners place upon each other.

These demands result from one of two possibilities. First is the demand for a spouse to live up to an idealized image of a parent. Such is the case when, for instance, a woman idealizes her dad and then expects her partner to adore her and take care of her the way she imagines her daddy did. Second, when there was a harmful, painful, or otherwise difficult relationship with a parent, a partner may place a demand upon the other to create a safe and injury-free world, to give him what he failed to get as a child. For example, a man was ridiculed by his father and he holds a demand that his partner never criticize him and that she bolster his self esteem in ways that he cannot do for himself.

When the childhood needs are played out in the drama of everyday affiliation they can have a ruinous effect on the potential for a passionate and sexually alive adult relationship. Each person succumbs to the pressure to meet the other's archaic demands to be rescued. Each becomes the other's transferential solution. This devitalizes the erotic, ecstatic, and creative energies which are the soul of an exceptional marriage. So many couples we have worked with are burdened with re-parenting each other. They are largely unaware of how much energy goes into meeting each other's unmet childhood needs.

In full self expression we strive to make the implicit demand openly explicit and alive. It is likely that for most of us in committed relationships we will never fully transcend the deep desire for our partners to give us what we have trouble giving ourselves. We will always want the "knight in shining armor" and the "earth mother." We may crave to be swept off our feet, or to have a lover who forever finds us the most attractive person on the planet. By allowing for these yearnings to come out of the closet, however, they lose their potency.

Bringing forth each person's fantasies of what they want from each other liberates the relationship from the confines of mutual rescuing. We encourage couples to bring forth their respective demands openly and fervently. Often these expectations are politically incorrect and therefore assiduously avoided. Examples of what you may hear include:

- "I want you to anticipate my needs without my having to ask."
- "Don't have any interests outside our marriage."
- "You can have no demands of me."
- "It's your job to always make me feel secure."
- "Don't ever criticize me."
- "You have to always take my side in a conflict with my family or friends."
- "It's your job to clean up after me."
- "I need you to make lots of money so I don't ever have to worry."
- "You can't have needs that interfere with mine."
- "You are not allowed to be attracted to another."
- "Don't ever give me reason to mistrust."
- "Tell me every day how great I am."

These are the covert immature needs that speak to a long-denied narcissism which every child possesses. Each and every one of us looks to our partners to provide us with something we believe we cannot do without. Though one may couch a childhood demand as a real need—"I need you to make me feel special"—there is inevitably the unspoken "or else" bringing up the rear of such requests. So, "I need you to make me feel special" is tacitly followed by, "or else I will . . . (take your pick: "complain ceaselessly", "never feel safe", "compare you to my father/mother who was perfect," "be devastated," "search elsewhere until I find it." and so on)

Most couples really want to know each other's childhood demands. There is often a sigh of relief as partners expose these unsavory truths to each other. When they remain underground they create a limbic dissonance which only dissipates once the truth comes out. As relational creatures, we can feel the pull of our partner's expectations and we naturally want to meet them. As we learn the details, we are freed up to make the distinction between a need that can be met and one that is not part of our jurisdiction.

"I need a hug" can be an expression of a tender child part which one partner can readily meet, if the asking partner recognizes that the other is not responsible for all the missed hugs from childhood. When a partner is unwilling to give the requested hug, it might be because he senses that the appeal is really a form of control. Her plea for a hug is coming as a way to bypass an emerging conflict—a form of damage control. When he refuses, she gets to look at what the demand behind her request really is. So "I need a hug" may really mean, "Don't be mad at me, I can't handle it." Giving the hug under these conditions stifles the growth opportunity that the emerging conflict offers. It turns the partner into a two dimensional caregiver. It creates limbic disharmony and curtails the possibility for genuine needs to be met. If the partner can avoid succumbing to the immature need, he changes the nature of how the couple relates. The difference can appear very subtle between a request for soothing and a demand to not be angry. This is why it can be helpful to bring to light these vestigial needs from early life

Unpacking childhood needs from true relational needs as two adults, helps couples to see each other in reality. The mentor works deliberately with couples to tease out the antiquated from the present. The types of interventions a mentor may use with childhood demands include:

- Have each partner reveal their secret expectations and demands. Each can take a few minutes. Give them room to express it loudly and vehemently.

- Uncover the "or else" behind each demand ("You must never look at another man, or else I will criticize you mercilessly.")
- The "or else" actually has two components, the first has to do with control patterns. As in the above example "I will criticize you mercilessly" is an aggressive control pattern. The second "or else" is related to the more vulnerable primary feelings or self judgments. For example, "You must never look at another man, *or else* I will have to feel my inadequacy, or my terror that you'll want somebody more than me."
- Explore what the fears are associated with each childhood need.
- Exaggerate the needs to absurd fantasies. (I want you to tell me I'm the most beautiful person on the planet 100 times every day." Or, "I expect you to always be ready to do whatever I want the moment I ask."
- Energize the entitled child with statements such as "My way!" "Give it to me!" or "Look at me!"
- When one person idealizes a parent, help him to bring forth the ways he compares his partner to that parent.

Corey and Maeve each carry into their relationship childhood needs which they displace onto each other. Maeve has two competing implicit needs of Corey. First, is for him to make her life easier by making plenty of money and second is to not be too powerful or demanding of her. She will often compare him to other men, saying, in essence, "Why can't you be more like so and so?" Likewise, she will find reasons to be dissatisfied with his lovemaking. Because she had a father who she idealized on one hand, but who was also sexually provocative on the other, she held a demand that Corey be both a rescuer and non-threatening.

For his part, Corey grew up in a household where emotions were never expressed. He would often try to placate Maeve in order to avoid conflict, which he found difficult to handle. His leftover childhood need was for Maeve to never be upset with him and to never place any demands on him. He would seek solace on the internet when he felt any pressure from her to take care of her.

By having each of them express their respective demands openly, they each got to see what was often driving their interactions, particularly her aggressive and his passive control patterns. Maeve expressed her expectation of Corey, "I want you to make my life easy by making lots of money and by placing no demands on me sexually!" Corey retorted by bringing forth his own covert demand, "I want you to be happy all the time and rely on me for nothing!"

To hear each other bring to the surface their non-verbal edicts was validating to both Corey and Maeve. They both intuited the others early narcissistic demands and hearing each other take self ownership of them was gratifying. Maeve knew that, despite Corey's words to the contrary, he resented her when she was anxious, depressed, ill, or otherwise not on the top of her game.

Simply reading these words may make the expression of early needs sound absurd, or worse. The actual experience of couples expressing taboo, and sometimes shame-inducing secret demands, however, is usually quite liberating. Sometimes when we have couples do it in group settings, the results are infectious. Every couple wants to get up in front of the room and passionately own their demands. Because, once exposed, these demands are often seen as "young parts" which are not so terrible after all.

While some couples are not yet ready to own their childhood needs, more often than not partners will both gain insight and ultimately feel relief from bringing these truths into the relationship. **We hold our partners hostage when we blend and confuse our immature, egocentric fantasies of who they should be with the reality of who they are**. The radical acceptance of our loved one's "otherness" will first require us to uncover all the ways we insist upon them being as we desire them to be.

Destructive "Lower Self" Anger

In Going All The Way we wrote: "One of the most perilous places to travel in the long-term committed relationship is into the realm of our destructiveness. This is such a terrifying undertaking that it is almost universally avoided. The vast majority of spouses are not even conscious of the negativity that each possesses. We frequently hear from couples we work with, 'I don't hate him,' or 'I would never want to hurt her.' While this is ultimately true, it is also true that, at certain moments, cruelty, hate, and destructiveness do exist. The absence of awareness does not make this less of a reality." [(8)]

The invitation for couples to own their worst places is certainly controversial. Indeed, it can prove harmful for one partner to tell another that she hates him and wants to punish him. Unless such words are placed in a larger context—one of exposing the negative current in order to move past it toward an open spirit of undefended, non-neutralized love—it may cause a "heap o' hurt." As a consequence of the indiscriminate encouragement of confrontation and open expression of anger in the '60's and '70's, the pendulum has now swung to an almost total bias toward parasympathetic states. But we believe the swing toward "more consciousness/less energy" has, in effect, resulted in throwing the baby out with the bath water.

Whether the expression of deep negativity is toxic or tonic depends largely on the intention behind it. When a couple is engaged in the chaos phase of a conflict, hurtful and wrathful words, sentences, or paragraphs may fly back and forth. But usually these are in the form of insults, putdowns and demeaning descriptions. In such a case, the couple is really still in judgment and blame. Vicious descriptors often signify an underlying *intention* to cause one's partner to suffer, to shake him up. But it is very different to act upon one's desire to hurt the other than it is to consciously own such intent. The goal of this third layer of FSE is for partners to be able to take full ownership of the usually cloaked desire to inflict suffering.

The two of us have found it useful to delineate three derivatives of anger. First (and most universally applied) is blame and judgment. Perhaps upwards of 90% of what gets identified as anger is expressed as blame and judgment. As we discussed earlier, when a couple is mired in a cycle of reactivity the energy rarely shifts into more vulnerable spaces. This is why anger gets such a bad rap in therapeutic circles.

The second derivative is the destructive impulse which resides in most human beings. While this "lower self" energy is typically disowned and banished to Bogeyland, its influence is enormous. This destructive current, or lower self, emerges when a child is forced to suppress his natural tendency to protest. When a child encounters a world where his needs and impulses are frustrated, he will organically want to express displeasure. If he is not free to express it he must learn to restrain this very innate urge. Lower-self energy festers in this environment where frustration is unwelcome. The child learns to adapt, but inwardly develops resentment and hostility toward those who deny him his free expression. He begins to embrace the lower-self mantra "I don't get mad, I get even." **When an individual does not feel free to express his natural distress and frustration, this energy transmutes into a covert rage against authority.** This is the second derivative of anger.

Third is what may be called "self-affirming anger." This is the primary feeling that allows us to protest, protect, and preserve our autonomy. By and large it does not get expressed directly and clearly in most relationships. We will return to self-affirming anger shortly.

In the third layer of FSE we support couples in identifying and revealing their lower-self negativity. Because EMM is a body-based, expressive approach to relationship healing and evolution, we encourage couples to fully embody the charged energy connected to their negativity. Couples who are fragile or poorly differentiated are often not ready to enter this world. For some individuals who grew up in violent households, the expression of high-pitched anger is automatically seen as toxic and dangerous. Such individuals are not yet ready to make the distinction between the unconscious, uncontained expression of cruelty and the self-aware ownership of the negative current.

In our experience, however, unless one can begin to see and accept inner places where one's own hurtful impulses reside, there will be a tendency to project onto one's partner or others such negativity. If a partner cannot ultimately see her own destructive current she will, in some ways, remain trapped in a defensive posture, forever warding off evil. Embodying the lower self is really a way to become more fully human, neither victim nor perpetrator.

When partners do not acknowledge the "dark forces" within they will enact the emotional energy that fuels these forces. So, the spouse that perpetrates violence by hitting, intimidating, insulting, belittling, shaming, controlling, "castrating", or mocking the other is enacting the lower self with no consciousness of its existence within. Indeed, most perpetrators (and we all are perpetrators) *feel* like victims! Talk to any abusive spouse and he will tell you how poorly he has been treated. **From victim consciousness we justify our own violent responses.** The way out is to claim our negative intentionality and its emotional expression.

The types of interventions a mentor may use with lower-self destructive expression include:

- Educating couples about strong negative energy and corollary negative intentionality. Each person needs to normalize for themselves the lower self as a universal reality and as only one part of a much greater truth. A partner will often resist acknowledging the lower self when she fears that it defines her. It is important for the mentor to help place its existence in the larger truth of multiple inner selves which include wounded, innocent and deeply loving parts.
- Having couples express universal negative statements—*I hate you!" "I'll make you pay!" "I'll get you!" "Die!"* (Note how these phrases and words differ from blaming and judgmental statements such as *"You're an idiot!" "You bitch!" "You're such a loser!"* These latter statements harbor a deeper, unacknowledged intent to cause suffering to the other, but without any real ownership.)
- Destructive energy must be physically expressed. Have partners hit along with the words. By allowing partners to, in essence, throw a tantrum, there can be a real release of long-held negativity. Because the lower self emerges

from an environment where the individual had to learn to hold back her "big energy," the ability to reclaim the somatic expression of this energy is very healing. It is often useful to have one partner lie down and kick and punch as she expresses her destructive emotion and its corollary words. The other partner can witness this and stay connected to what it brings up.

- Uncovering and expressing the specific negative intentions—"I'll punish you by withholding my sexuality." "I'll never say how attractive you are." "I want you to feel inadequate, so I'll always remind you of mistakes you have made."
- Having each person reveal the primary feelings and needs underneath their lower-self destructive energy. How has a partner been hurt, what is his self-affirming anger, and/or what is the fear?
- Exploring the relationship between victim and victimizer. Help each partner to own both polarities.
- Helping the couple to bridge the lower-self reactions and negative intentions to each one's history. Because the lower self emerges from a sense of powerlessness, can partners connect to the sense of powerlessness in the here-and-now and recognize its origins in childhood?

It is a great service to couples to give them a safe and open space to acknowledge the unseemly corners of each person's emotionality. Couples will very rarely show these interior places on their own. It goes against everything we have all been taught—"If you can't think of something nice to say, say nothing at all." Problem is, not saying it doesn't stop us from holding tight to our cruelty, destructiveness, and mean-spirited impulses. We simply turn them into judgments which bolster our negative narrative of each other.

The child who is powerless to respond assertively to an adult world that tells her to tame her frustrations and protestations builds an internal hostility. The lower-self impulse emanates from this disempowered consciousness. When a child curtails normal (self-affirming) anger she is left with an unexpressed negative intention to retaliate against authority. This unspoken (and usually unconscious) negative intention includes a desire to punish, shame, or otherwise cause harm to the authority figure. And in the committed relationship partners are readily placed in the role of authority.

Corey has learned to embed his lower-self desire to make Maeve feel unloved in an outward show of indifference. He lives in a bivalent internal world of deep immature need to know that she really wants him and an equally yawning disdain for her dependence on him. Corey desperately want to know that Maeve desires him and at the same time holds a deep concern that she is just using him as his mother once did (thus giving her inordinate authority and power.) He learned to be his mom's rescuer as a young boy and, with Maeve, had to hold back the natural impulses to *want* her like a child wants his mother.

Recently, Maeve returned from a vacation she took for five days while he was working a new job. When she arrived home Corey treated her with what, even for him, was an unusual degree of indifference. Inwardly, beneath his veil of apathy he was holding two separate and powerful reactions. First was his rage at her for "using" him, and second was his resistance to showing her how happy he was to see her. We will return to this latter reaction in a bit.

He was also judging himself for being so angry at her and consequently had wiped away awareness of this hostility. In its stead what remained was a barren coldness. This is what she encountered upon arriving home. In the subsequent mentoring session we encouraged Corey to be present with his icy indifference until he could feel what else was there. Soon he recognized his anger. But what we sensed existed alongside his outward apathy was a desire to punish Maeve by withholding his affection. Through a catalyzing intervention one of us suggested he bring out this lower-self urge to make her pay. We asked him to give it a voice as well as plenty of energy.

Corey began to pound the cube and with mounting energy expressed to Maeve, "I want you to feel unhappy! I want you to lose all the joy that you came home with." I want you to suffer like I did 'cause I had to stay home and work!" He went on, "I won't give you the satisfaction of knowing I missed you." As Corey poured out his heretofore hidden lower-self reactions, he gradually began to recognize how he turns his hostility against himself. He became aware of a part of himself that missed Maeve and was inwardly looking forward to her arrival with excited anticipation. But a cruel voice within chastised the exuberant and excited part. He saw it as weakness and directed harsh energy toward it.

So we encouraged him to turn his lower self wrath toward that part. In order to do this, Brian sat on the floor and embodied the part that was eagerly anticipating Maeve's arrival. Brian reached out toward her with open arms. Corey pounded on the cube and excoriated this vulnerable part as embodied by Brian. "You're weak!" he yelled. "Get up, stop acting like a little baby! You disgust me. You should be ashamed of yourself!"

As Corey allowed himself to fully express the disdain he had for his "needy part," he began to soften. He was able to see for the first time how he had to "kill" his own neediness in order to avoid the risk of betrayal and humiliation. Gradually he allowed himself to open to this child-like part. The session culminated with another catalyzing intervention where we invited him to fully embrace the excited part, and to run across the room into Maeve's arms as she came through the door. To show her this aspect of his inner self was deeply moving for both of them.

The seemingly virulent energy of the destructive current evaporates as it exposes itself to the individual and his partner. For Maeve, to hear Corey take full ownership of his most despicable interior forces was at first a bit shocking. But in short order it turned first to relief, because now she knew what was brewing underneath his icy exterior, and then to compassion as she witnessed how harshly he treated his own vulnerable place. Finally, she delighted in embracing that vulnerable part as it ran toward her with excitement and longing.

All this is to say that identification and exposure of a partner's destructive current is sometimes necessary on the path to more tender and vulnerable openness. Many people have a very difficult time acknowledging this piece of inner truth. It is not crucial for the mentor to push a couple into self ownership of this lower-self energy, but it is often the case that when it's recognized and expressed, a noxious cloud lifts from the air space of the relationship ecosystem. **The taboo against meanness, cruelty, and the desire to punish too often results in undercurrents of sadism and the violence of withholding.** People suffer more from innuendo, from emotional starvation, from the simmering rage of the caged beast than from direct ownership of destructive impulses.

Before we move on to level four, "the resistance to expressing primary feelings and needs," there is one more aspect of working with lower-self destructiveness we would like to address. Occasionally, when one partner is immersed in blame toward the other, and the mate is "taking an emotional beating," either of us might provoke the blaming partner as a way to re-direct the energy away from the beleaguered mate. We do this both to break the blaming control pattern as well as to create an opening for the lower self to emerge.

Not long ago, the two of us were mentoring a couple where the man Hank was constantly telling his spouse Leanne what was wrong with her as a way of justifying his threats of ending the relationship. Leanne mostly sat slumped and defeated as he enumerated her faults. Our attempts to support her in matching his energy were unsuccessful. At one point Brian abruptly interrupted Hank. Brian said to Hank, "You know, I don't think you're considering ending this relationship has anything to do with Leanne. I think it's what you always do." What followed was fifteen seconds of stunned silence before Hank re-directed his antipathy toward Brian. "You know what I say Brian. Fuck you!" Offering his middle finger he continued "Fuck you. You don't know anything about me! Who the hell do you think you are!" At this juncture Hank got up and started punching the heavy bag, which is part of our equipment, and continued to shout, "Fuck you! You're a crappy therapist!" Brian encouraged him to connect to his desire to humiliate. Hank soon yelled "I'm gonna get you! I'm gonna make you feel like the worst therapist on the planet! I want you to suffer!"

What got triggered in Hank was his own sense of shame which was evoked by Brian's challenging him. Hank's father always had to have the upper hand and was constantly telling Hank what he was doing wrong. The catalyzing strategy that was implemented involved confrontation of Hank in a way that both of us knew would trigger him. It shifted the focus away from Leanne temporarily, and made space for Hank to rage at the authority figure. It removed him from the role of reenacting his father's incessant criticisms and brought him back eventually to how painful it felt to be criticized. Brian acknowledged Hank's right to be angry and said he had a great deal of respect for him in standing up for himself.

From there, we could clarify (utilizing the concept of 80/20%) that while there was some truth to Hank's judgments of Leanne, he also did indeed have to look at what he was hoping to accomplish by constantly threatening to leave. As Hank realized that he had the respect of both of us, he grew more vulnerable and could look at his own participation in the relationship drama without shame. He could see how he had taken the mantle from his father and used criticism and threats as a way to control against the painful feelings of being unloved and disrespected, for this is what he imagined was coming from Leanne.

A cautionary note about provoking or antagonizing a client. Neither of us would utilize such a strategy until we had a well-established relationship with the couple, and we were certain that each of them knew we held them with respect. It is all too easy for a therapist's own frustrations to spill over into an "intervention." Especially in couples work there is a heightened risk of strong countertransferential reactions which result in a therapist getting "triggered. Having said that, we also believe that there is equal or greater danger in avoiding confrontation. Therapists who attempt to keep sessions gentle and soft are ignoring the potent realities of intimacy. As we suggested earlier, energy likes to be met with equal energy. Occasionally the provocation of one of the partners will actually allow that person to respond in a way that he never got to do with his parents. Hank's outburst was really directed at his father and was something he had held in for 25 years.

Resistance to Primary Feelings and Need

Remembering that control patterns are employed in order to avoid experiencing the primary feelings of self-affirming anger, fear, and hurt, the mentor can help spouses to embody their resistance. For most committed couples there is a huge investment in warding off unwanted emotions. To reveal that I am affected by you, that you can upset me, scare me, or hurt me, can make me feel weak and at your mercy. As Maeve once put it to Corey, "I don't want to let you know you matter, because then I believe you will think you got me."

When one displays to her partner her primary emotions it is profoundly vulnerable. Most couples prefer to complain or retreat into withholding than to share authentic emotions. In our work with couples we have come to realize that when partners can identify the fierce refusal to relinquish their control patterns, they are ready to begin the movement into intimate contact. Most of us do not go from blame, demand, and lower-self negativity into our vulnerability easily. Partners intuitively know that letting down the armor of resistance is an invitation into the ancient burial ground of innocent and fragile places. The catacombs of tender emotions are guarded tenaciously.

So, resistance needs to be respected for what it is attempting to do. In FSE we invite partners to fully express resistance. In doing so, the couple can release the energetic grasp of such resistance. The internal effort to resist requires a great expenditure of energy. The vitality of a relationship depends on releasing this contracted and stilted energy. To ignore or bypass the resistance to expression results in a less than fully intimate connection. Couples who remain in reflective or even mindful communication without embodiment may acknowledge the existence of primary feelings, but there is something lacking.

IN FSE, we support couples to simplify and amplify their resistance. The most basic phrase to bring this out is "I won't!" When it becomes apparent that one of the couple is fighting off a primary feeling, we will encourage that person to embody the resistance.

For example:

"I won't give you my heart!"
"I won't let you in!"
"I won't let you matter!"
"I'll never let you hurt me!"
"You can't get to me!"
"I won't let you know you affect me!"
"I don't trust you with my feelings!"
"I won't give you the power!"
"You don't get all of me!"
"I'll never surrender!"
"I won't go first!"

The two of us will invite one of the partners in a mentoring session to bring out resistance when it appears the individual is closing in on a primary emotion but is fighting desperately to protect herself. In our experience, sometimes the only way through to vulnerability and intimacy is by giving full permission to embody the "No!" The release into tender places is a sacred shift from protection of an intact sense of self to an opening into the most vulnerable sanctums of the heart. We are asking people to go back into their original wound and to entertain the possibility that, instead of being harmed again, their partner can meet them in a new way. It is a sign of respect to honor the resistance.

The "I won't!" is held in the musculature of each partner's body. Just as a child will freely express his "No!" as a full-bodied, unfettered wild release, the grown up partner too can benefit by an open expression. We will encourage one or both mates to bring the resistance fully through their respective bodies. Having them pound the foam cube, punch the heavy bag, or (often most effective) lay on a mattress and kick and scream is a powerful way to engage the tenacity of their resistance.

The stranglehold of resistance usually begins when a child is shamed, taunted, completely ignored, taken advantage of, or otherwise made to feel unsafe in revealing tender places. The greatest harm we humans experience is less from the limitations and cruelty of our environment, than from the stifling of and lack of acceptance for our natural reactions to such insults. If we are free to cry, protest, be frightened, or exhibit our need, we will readily recover from most of the negative experiences we encounter. This recovery is the movement from the sympathetic to the parasympathetic, from charge to discharge. When we learn to lock down our organic reactions our bodies begin to lose their vitality and our emotional world grows stilted. We learn, in essence, to "Get a grip."

For Corey, his resistance manifested through the subtle ways he kept Maeve "less than." He would not enjoy her humor, but he would emphasize her memory lapses, and tease her about her lack of skill on the computer. Behind this attempt to diminish her was a profound insecurity and fear that he was inadequate. What he fought hard not to feel was his need for Maeve, his deep fear of abandonment, and his hurt that she compared him to other men. As it came to light that he withheld positive regard for Maeve, Marcia encouraged Corey to fully embody his resistance.

Marcia gave him the phrase, "I'll never let you be important!" Lying down, Corey began to kick and scream, "I'll never let you be important! I won't let you matter! I won't feel my need!" The more he expressed these words, the greater his intensity grew. He built up to a crescendo of fury expending every last ounce of resistance in his body. As he exhausted his resistance, he began to get an image of his mother and how she was unable to hold him and notice his tender need for her. Corey could feel in his body how he recoiled from her and tightened against his need. He pulled himself into the fetal position and began to quietly, almost silently, cry. As his resistance melted, he could access a grief for his own emptiness. Such was his fear of opening to the grief, that he could only let a few quiet tears fall from his eyes.

Marcia checked in with Maeve and when it was apparent that she was moved by Corey's work, Marcia invited her to sit by him. This was the first time that Maeve had ever seen Corey so vulnerable. She had always worried that he really did not care for her. It opened her heart to witness the strength of his resistance, and to understand why he had to fight so hard to not let her matter.

Without his full-bodied expression of his resistance, it is difficult to imagine Corey being able to access such vulnerability.

The role of resistance is to keep us from being too exposed in situations where we could be deeply harmed. It exists not just as a mental choice to say "No," but as an embodied contraction against emotions deemed too much to handle. Many have argued the dangers of such high octane physical release, but until one has witnessed the transformative effects it evokes it is unfair to draw an abstract conclusion. We do not always have to "step back" from our experience. Sometimes it is more helpful to be "flooded" or overwhelmed by what we hold inside. Only when we do this can we learn to truly trust that we are bigger than the mercurial emotions we spend our lives running from.

Self-Affirming Anger

Anger as a primary emotion is designed to affirm our independent existence. It serves to protect us from being taken advantage of, abused, controlled, or violated in any way. In its primary state it is neither defensive nor abusive. The motive of self-affirming anger is to create enough boundaries to allow us to move toward deep contact. In this respect it is the gateway, the portal into intimacy. Without our willingness to take a stand for ourselves we cannot fully engage the other in our most intimate places.

In FSE the two of us support each partner in bringing forth the direct expression of what they each do not like about the other's behavior. While blame is laced with "You" statements ("You're always making excuses." "You never tell me what you feel.") Self-affirming anger is a clear statement of each person's upset. While much of what a spouse reacts to in his partner is entangled with historical triggers, there is still the "20%" reality of what she actually does (or doesn't do). To be in self-affirming anger is to make present what one dislikes in his partner's behavior. **To say "I don't like how you just rolled your eyes when I asked you to help me" is keeping your anger in the present. It is direct, self-owned, and specific.**

Direct feedback in the form of self-affirming anger is a rarity in most committed relationships. Partners are prone to either complain with blame ("There you go rolling your eyes again. What's wrong with you?"), or withdraw and build up silent disdain

(Thought bubble—"God, she's so selfish. I'll never ask her for anything again.") The other reaction is to ask questions rather than make a clear statement. "Why are you rolling our eyes?" is perhaps a fair question, but more likely it is not asked from a place of sincere curiosity. Instead it is a challenge which is apt to elicit a defensive response. Then the reactive cycle is off and running.

In our mentoring work we want couples to learn how to bring out self-affirming anger.

When, for instance, one partner can say to the other, "I'm angry that you just rolled your eyes when I asked you for help." Though her mate may cringe when he hears it, he is far less apt to go into defensive mode than when he hears her blame and judgments. We have also found that when one is able to express the anger this directly there is often an opening to the historical triggers—the 80%. Thus she may become aware of how her father treated her mother and directly feel her anger toward him.

In working with couples on this level we guide them to become more open and to trust their upset.

In your work with couples you can utilize the following:

- Stress the importance of "I" statements—"I'm angry." "I'm pissed off." "It upsets me when . . ." "I don't like it that . . ."
- Help both partners to stand and stay grounded (connected to their bodies) as one expresses self-affirming anger.
- Only after a clear expression has occurred is it then possible to ask the partner for his reaction to her self-affirming anger.
- You can then have her direct anger toward the original source with the support of her partner ("I hate the way you treated mom, dad!")

- Expression by proxy—partner expresses anger at original source for the spouse who cannot access it. In this case he would do the expression for her.
- Have each person uncover the "I want" that is the flip side of every self-affirming anger statement. "I want you to be honest with me when I ask you for a favor." "I want you to want to help me."

Maeve's self-affirming anger toward Corey was in response to his poking fun at her. At first she was unaware of his put-downs, but as she grew more sensitive she began to feel discomfort when he would engage in it. Her initial inclination was to get back at him by belittling him. In a moment of "leading by following" we pointed out to her how her face tightened up when he made fun of her for how she spoke. We asked her what her face was saying. She immediately saw how much she didn't like his criticism, which he camouflaged in levity. Her "face scrunch" as she became aware of it, informed her of what her mind overlooked.

Maeve was then able to directly express how much she disliked the way he treated her. By starting with the present she avoided assaulting him with over-generalized accusations. She told him, "It really pissed me off when you made fun of what I was trying to say. I don't like it. Don't talk to me that way." Corey just listened. We could see that he felt remorse for how he treated her. From this place Maeve was then able to express her fear and her hurt about this issue. We'll come back to this shortly.

Maeve, after having responded to a direct experience was then able to say to Corey, "This is not the first time you have poked fun at me. I would like you to look at what that's about. I want you to treat me with respect. I want to know that you see my gifts, not just my mistakes." As Maeve challenged him to take ownership of his captious tendencies we could tell that it left quite an impression on Corey.

The direct expression of self-affirming anger is empowered communication. It will often jolt the partner into a realization of his behavior, something to which he may have been blinded. The two of us believe that healthy, vibrant communication includes the assertive expression of what each person does not like about the other's behavior. This is how partners challenge each other to grow. There is a time for delicacy and a time for bluntness. Too many couples, in our estimation, either complain and blame or avoid conflict altogether.

While safety is essential to the committed relationship, it is not the end of the story. Couples should look at safety as the foundation for true conflict engagement. By knowing there is a commitment to truth and a respect for each other, partners can go at it with more vigor than many marital therapists give them credit for. Ultimately they cannot be treating each other as fragile, damaged specimens. There needs to be room for vibrant protest and passionate exchange. These are the transformative moments.

Let's return for a moment to the example of eye rolling. We'll continue the dialogue. She says to her partner, "I don't like the way you just rolled your eyes when I asked for help." In an exceptional relationship he might respond by saying "You're right, that was indirect of me. Truth is though, I didn't hear it as a request, I heard it as a demand." To which she may reply, "Well I find it hard to ask you openly because I'm afraid you will be annoyed with me." He retorts, "I get annoyed when I don't feel like I can say no." She comes back, "Well I don't know what comes first, your annoyance or my demandingness. But I can see the truth in what you're saying. I don't think I ever felt safe in asking for anything. So, I've learned to have an edge, to not really ask. It hurts too much to be rejected." He comes back, "Thanks for sharing that, it helps me to have a little more compassion, though I still don't like it. I can also see how much trouble I have saying no, so I comply but send off a mixed message. I would like to be more direct, but I'll probably do it again and I hope you can call me on it."

In FSE couples re-engage metaskills such as presencing, curiosity, tolerance of emotions, and grounding to improvise the above types of conflict engagement. By each person expressing self-affirming anger there is a more highly charged energy in the exchange. In remaining connected to self, each person can hear the other's dislikes and not revert to blame or false apology. Each person is strong and vital. The result, as in all good conflict engagement is that each partner deepens self awareness and sees something new in the other. What a gift!

Fear of Abandonment or Rejection

Here is where we begin to move more completely into "intimacy-enhancing" emotions. When partners in a relationship can access the fear of abandonment the energy between them softens markedly. In attachment studies a particularly remarkable phenomenon has been observed. At times children would actually place themselves in greater danger in order to make contact with the object of their connection and security, namely, their mothers. They would, for instance, run toward and past a scary stranger in order to achieve the security of connection.

In Mortal Spirit, Brian writes: "As (Bowlby) and his colleagues observed, children did not just respond with basic fear to the *presence* of something they considered dangerous, but also, to the *absence* of their mother, or 'love-object.' Not only would the children exhibit fear when they noticed mother's absence, but of even greater significance, when something scary confronted them their impulse was to go seek her out. If they were in close proximity to mother they were also less apt to be frightened by things that would otherwise frighten them . . . . Attachment conquers much of fear. Indeed, attachment is so compelling that children will actually increase their exposure to danger in order to achieve it!" [(9)]

The implications for the committed relationship are clear. Woven into much of a couple's interactions is a fundamental longing for attachment and a concomitant fear of loss. While most of us are not overtly aware on a daily basis of this fear, it nonetheless colors our interactions. The tension between the impulse toward autonomy and the longing for contact is balanced on the fulcrum of fear. As we have stated, couples fight for two basic reasons—for an independent sense of self ("I won't let you define me!") and for connection ("Please don't reject me!"). Look closely at any dispute a couple presents with and it will likely fall into one of these two categories.

When a partner can acknowledge and express fear, the scales begin to tip from the battle for autonomy to the willingness to share, reveal, and acknowledge that the other matters. **Relationship begins to happen through the tender mercies of fear embraced**. It is ultimately an act of great courage for one partner to reveal to the other basic fear as a primary emotion. Long, long ago most of us learned to mutate our basic fear in a myriad of ways. It can masquerade as obsessions, addictions, bravado, impotence, keeping busy, avoidance of commitment, people pleasing, controlling one's mate, and numerous other variants.

The simple expression of fear can be a game changer when couples are mired in their control patterns. In FSE the movement into the expression of fear is often the "sacred shift" away from fierce protection of the self into real relationship. Often a couple will need to express the autonomy-enhancing states as described above before they can soften into sharing their fears. The highly charged states of blame, immature need, lower-self negativity, resistance, and self-affirming anger can pave the way for a movement into the more humble emotions of fear and hurt.

Some key components to helping a couple express fear are:

- Attend to the body language—noticing signs of fear. Help each partner to become more attuned to their own fear signals. For instance, to suggest to one of them: "You looked frightened when you told her that you want her to stop criticizing your love-making. Is that true? Can you describe what the fear feels like in your body?"
- As we have emphasized, when couples are locked into blame cycles don't get ensnared in the debate! It helps to shift the focus to the experience of the *threat* rather than what the partner is doing wrong. You may ask, "What concerns (i.e. threatens) you about his love-making? When you get critical, is there something you are afraid of?" In other words, you support movement away from the control pattern (criticism) toward the threat which triggers it, and ultimately into the vulnerability which is

being protected. Susan Johnson's Emotionally Focused Therapy [16] is very useful in this regard.

- In FSE you can have partners name their fears as they relate to each other—"It scares me when you retreat into your books." "I get frightened when you speak to me that way." "I'm afraid you don't really want to be with me." "Sometimes I feel terror when you don't come home on time." "I get so scared that you'll judge me for putting on weight." By having each person articulate simply and directly what scares them, most often deeper connection results.
- Encourage use of simple, vulnerable words—afraid, frightened, scared, and terrified. Avoid muted expressions like—worried, concerned, troubled. While you may start with such words, it is helpful for the couple to learn how to speak in more direct and innocent language. "I'm scared" holds a great deal more power than "I'm concerned."
- Whenever possible relate back to original abandonment issues. Often it is necessary for one or both partners to do some embodied work around the terror they hold in their bodies. This can be done either with a partner observing or by being more actively involved. The release of terror (when it exists) in a partner's presence is vital to full self expression.
- Because fear is often frozen in the body, the two of us will work with it somatically and without words. Historical fears are often difficult to pinpoint, and are typically defended against by the enactment of control patterns that are designed to create a sense of safety. Many people we have worked with are "afraid of their fear." By helping them to face terror from their past through physical movement, breath and sound, individuals can overcome this "fear of fear."

When fear is connected to a deeper terror, we believe it is important to work with that partner while the other bears witness. One of us will hold a strong presence that encourages the terrorized individual to shake, thrash, scream, kick or do whatever allows her to move past the paralysis that keeps the terror from releasing. The implicit memories of traumas past can hold a tight grip on one's capacity to lead a vital life. Peter Levine writes, "Many are able to earn a living and/or raise a family in a kind of 'functional freeze' that severely limits their enjoyment of life. They carry their burden with diminished energy in an uphill struggle to survive, despite their symptoms." He continues, "The 'talking cure' for trauma survivors should give way to the unspoken voice of the silent, but strikingly powerful, bodily expressions as they surface to 'sound off' on behalf of the wisdom of the deeper self."

Most therapists, even those trained in somatic work, shy away from "taking the person back into the trauma." The concern about re-traumatizing a client surfaces again, when it comes to the specter of full-bodied expression of terror. This is, for sure, delicate territory. It is not our desire or goal to take someone back into a regressed experience of the original trauma. What we want is to empower them to know that the embodiment and expression of terror is *healing*. If it begins to surface in the context of a mentoring session we will give it room. Our desire is for the individual gripped by frozen terror to trust that who she is, is larger than any particular emotion—even profound fear. To be held, loved, and supported as the body vibrates with potent energy, is to heal. For the mentor to remain with someone as he moves through the tempest of emerging somatic states of arousal is to help him build faith, both in the integrity of his existence, and in the possibility that others will not flee when the going gets tough.

The essence of Exceptional Marriage Mentoring is not to do trauma work, but in the crucible of relationship intense emotions are inevitable. To have one's partner hold a loving presence as terror moves through an individual is often liberating to both. The reason many people believe that terror will overwhelm them is because nobody was ever there to help them ride out the storm. Terror foments in isolation. When a child has nobody to run to when she has been traumatized she has no choice but to keep the fear at bay. Without limbic resonance she is bereft. She will indeed be re-traumatized if no one is there when terror re-surfaces. So, on occasion in our mentoring work, one partner will do something that evokes the terror. This provides a precious opportunity for a spouse to fully embody that which there was never any room for. Instead of the relationship being controlled by unmetabolized terror, the couple can move into the deepest contact they have ever experienced.

As one partner learns to express his fear, the other feels drawn to him organically. We suspect it is fundamental to the human experience that all of us are impelled to protect one who exhibits fear. Thus the expression of fear promotes intimacy and creates safety. The autonomic nervous system begins to shift into a more parasympathetic state as deeper connection occurs.

For Maeve, as she moved beyond her self-affirming anger, she could express to Corey her fears. She told him, "It scares me when you close your heart to me. When you tease me I get afraid that you don't like me. I'm scared that you will not see how your words affect me." As she expressed these fears, Corey spontaneously came over and took her hands. His eyes grew tender and he non-verbally let her know that he was fully present and accepting of her.

Expression of Hurt, Sadness, or Grief

To express hurt is to feel the dagger in the heart. It is the bleeding out of all our protections, control patterns, defenses. When a human being finds her way into the pains and hurts which orbit around the core of her selfhood, she makes herself available for everything. Love, compassion, empathy, and altruism, the inhabitants of our core self, are intrinsically wedded to our capacity to feel our emotional hurt. No hurt = no love.

To feel hurt is to allow oneself to be fully affected by another. It is the inestimable openness to innocence. When was the last time you heard someone say, "That hurt my feelings"? Those simple words are invariably buried inside a morass of self-protections intricately designed to blunt the full effect of life's assault on tenderness. When we yell at a child—he cries, at least up until a certain age. Life hurts sans energetic barriers and control patterns. After we learn to put a damper on the hurts they transpose from pain to suffering. Couples who seek the help of a therapist are often suffering from isolation, insecurity, disappointment, hopelessness, narcissistic injury, and sexual apathy. Most often, they have lost the connection to the heartache of love's disappearance.

In this level of FSE the mentor's task is to help partners re-connect to the innocence and fragility of true hurt. Often it takes mucking through some or all of the above levels of FSE. While the various angers build energy and charge the system, the expression of hurt is a release or discharge. Crying, trembling, and an overall softening of bodily armor, characterize an opening to the emotion of hurt.

It is nearly impossible to truly feel hurt when fear is still locked in the body. But when the anger and fear associated with our autonomic nervous systems is given space to be released we can more easily drop down into the vulnerability of our hurts. In our innocent child state we hold no defenses against this primary emotional reaction. To reclaim our pure primary experience of hurt is essential to true intimacy. Almost always, hurt is directly linked to an earlier wound. Oftentimes, a turning point in full self expression occurs when one partner makes this "pain" connection and shares it with the other. When this is recognized, it results in a deepening of compassion, empathy and connection. Linking our triggers to our history is a big step toward taking ownership of the "stuff" we bring to the table in our intimate relationships.

In various ways, all of us were "broken" as children. **The child who feels the direct impact of being teased for having freckles, big ears, a lisp, not knowing something, dressing differently, acting too much like the opposite sex, being scared or needy, not knowing the rules, or showing little interest in sports, is in some crucial way "broken."** By this we are not suggesting that broken equals defective (as you might describe a consumer product). Brokenness, in this context, is a metaphor to help underscore how really human we are beneath the control patterns that help to keep us operating in a world that can be harsh. It is not the core self that gets broken, but our relationship to our innocent, tender nature. It is exactly here that the seeds of adult intimacy can be sown. We all carry the hurts of ridicule, rejection and recrimination. It is often in the exposure of our brokenness to our partners that tenderness and intimacy emerge.

Committed partners bring their brokenness into their relationships. Control patterns serve to protect against the re-experiencing of each person's most painful places. A pivotal juncture in FSE happens when one partner can allow the hurt to be felt. This is not just an intellectual recognition of bygone insults. It is the fully and presently experienced "thud" which reverberates throughout the body. It is the punch in the gut, the slap in the face. This is why we call it hurt.

As we noted above, Corey was able to release a long-held grief that surfaced when he allowed himself to claim his resistance to letting Maeve too close. Subsequently he was able to share with her how hurt he felt when she rejected him sexually. His keeping her at a safe emotional distance allowed him to avoid this hurt for many years. When she sexually rebuked him he would convince himself that she was not that attractive and would secretly fantasize about other sexual encounters outside his marriage. This is how he controlled the access to his genuine hurt.

The fear of losing her surfaced when he could no longer maintain the façade of indifference. Much like a child from an environment of ambivalent attachment, he was outwardly nonchalant but internally frantic. The even more vulnerable connection to his hurt broke through only after he fully allowed himself to express this fear. In his pain, he could reveal for the first time how much Maeve truly meant to him. Corey told her, "It hurts me very deeply when you push me away sexually. I feel a deep pain in my body. Sometimes I want to cry when you are distant. I feel awful when we are not close. I remember how much it hurt when my mother showed no interest in me."

We want to emphasize here that it is not the spouse's job to make up for ancient hurts. Nor is it her responsibility to even admit culpability. We encourage the listening spouse to take breaths and "listen with the heart." Even though she might see things differently and want to defend, we will ask her to hold such internal reactions and to let go, if at all possible, of any sense of needing to either take care of her mate or defend against what he is saying. More often than not the listening party will easily open her heart (as Maeve did) when true hurt is expressed.

In this intimate space there is no need to discuss "better" ways for her to respond to Corey when he approaches her sexually. As it turns out, part of Maeve's resistance to Corey was about *how* he approached her. In the shared energy field of their interaction, he would move toward her tentatively and meekly. She interpreted this as her having to reassure his "little boy" that she wouldn't hurt his feelings. She was not conscious of this until he shared how hurt he was. His ownership of this hurt helped her to feel the "No" to caretaking him. His tentativeness did not *cause* her resistance, but it *influenced* it. Corey's expression of his hurt opened up deeper awareness for both of them. From here both could consider various other responses to sexual engagement.

Some common ways to support the movement into the experience of hurt:

- For couples to access their hurts each partner needs to feel safe. To feel safe they must clear out the energy of the autonomic nervous system (fight or flight). This means it is almost always necessary, with few exceptions, to express the charged energies of the above layers before each person can release into his/her pain.
- Have partners utilize basic phrases such as—"It hurt me when . . ." "I feel so sad when . . ." "It breaks my heart . . ." Of course these phrases are not just expressed mechanically. When it is clear that there is an opening to the pain and vulnerability it can be enormously supportive to suggest the words that one partner may be searching for or need encouragement to express.
- Often one partner can access hurt more readily than the other. It may take time for the more controlled spouse to let down his/her guard. The tenderness, acceptance and understanding of the mentors can allow the more controlled person to gently enter his/her pain. When one has been shamed for exposing weakness, the trust in both the partner and the mentors must be earned.

- You can use softer techniques including touch, (of heart, belly, a hand), encouragement of soft sounds, lying down, emotionally evocative music, etc. Sometimes people resist entering into their hurt because they rightfully don't want to perform. It's important to convey total acceptance for their not expressing hurt. The felt sense of acceptance has led many clients into the pain of their childhood when they were not accepted unconditionally.
- It can also help to support a partner in embodying her resistance to trusting her mate. Sentences such as: "I'll never trust you with my pain" or, "You don't get to see my hurt", often will "grease the skids" to an opening to vulnerable places. Many times individuals move back and forth between expression of hurt and protection. It is not easy to remain wide open to one's partner in such a tender place.
- It can be useful to ask the question, "Can you connect this pain or hurt with any you might have felt growing up?" Connect the pain to an actual age the partner was when he was hurt. You can then say, "So when (name of partner) does that, your 7 year old part really feels terrible."

Remorse and Empathy

It is easy to find advice on forgiving. Forgiveness is often considered the sine qua non of healing. Yet there is precious little written about forgiveness' soul mate, remorse. To open up to genuine sorrow is a rare and beautiful experience. To get there often requires the expenditure of all those energies marshaled to protect and defend ones integrity. The flow of FSE takes us to remorse only after an individual has moved through the autonomy enhancing emotions and is able to express his fear and hurt. It is not easy to enter one's remorse unless one is heard. What prevents most of us from actually feeling remorse is that we need to know that our own suffering has been witnessed and accepted first.

Remorse is the empathic awareness of how my actions have impacted you. It requires an openness to crossing the divide between my experience and yours. Most expressions of sorrow in committed relationships do not meet this standard. The "I'm sorry!" that is apt to erupt in the midst of a dispute is more one of damage control than genuine remorse. The intention behind this brand of sorrow is to stop the other from being angry, hurt, or disappointed. This is a qualitatively different internal state than one where a partner can truly see how her actions (or inactions) have contributed to her mate's pain.

We have placed remorse below pain in FSE because it has been our experience that when one partner has been able to express his own pain it can sensitize him, soften him, so to speak, to his partner's hurt. It is a very simple equation—the more tender a partner can feel toward himself, the more empathy he can experience to his loved one. **Remorse puts the significant in "significant other."**

Whereas remorse is directed toward other, guilt is self-directed. Most committed partners confuse these two. Guilt is self judgment, remorse is shared pain.

Guilt is characterized by statements such as the following:

- I feel terrible.
- I really screwed up.
- You must hate me.
- I can't believe I did it again.
- I'll make up for it.
- I feel like an idiot.
- I'm sooo sorry, don't be mad.
- I'm a loser.

Whenever one partner attempts to curtail the other's response to something he feels guilty about, he is engaging in a control pattern. Listen carefully to the intention behind any expression of sorrow. If you, as the therapist, feel that such expression is shutting down the flow of emotion and life force then it needs to be challenged. It is much better to bring the guilty partner into the truth of what is occurring beneath the expressions of sorrow or "my bad." What he is often really saying is: "Please don't be mad at me, I am so self-hating in the moment, I can't take it. I'm afraid you don't love me because I don't love myself. Please don't abandon me the way I am abandoning myself." Mentors will often catalyze such statements. That is, they recognize that it may never occur to the guilty partner that such sentiments exist behind the "I'm sorrys!" so they will be offered by the mentor to "try on."

Real remorse is entered as one person has opened her self-compassion to her own "brokenness." When she can feel and accept her own pain, she gives life and breathing room to humility. She understands that both she and her partner are flawed humans who are capable of hurting each other. She comes to the deep wisdom of "I know I hurt you because I know that I am hurt by you." This is a truly remarkable illumination. She encounters her humanity through the parallel awareness of her capacity to be simultaneously hurt and hurtful.

The truly remorseful person does not ask for forgiveness. He simply takes ownership for his actions. He does not ask for anything. This is the great gift in remorse. It says to the other, "I see how I have contributed to your pain. I feel you in this place. I feel pain for your pain. I don't ask anything of you in this place. I want only to stand together with you in the truth of my own contribution to violating your most tender places."

When Marco expressed how hurt he was by Sylvia's ongoing judgments of his competency, and he saw how she was able to move beyond her justifications he suddenly became aware of how deep his pain ran. He told Sylvia "When you judge me that way I feel like I have lost you, like you hate me." I feel like your love for me is tentative and conditional and that I am always on the cusp of losing you." As he could feel the depths of his own fear and hurt, and felt her with him, Marco spontaneously saw how his response of withdrawal from Sylvia caused her so much pain.

He "got" for the first time that when he pulled away (passive control pattern) he wasn't just protecting himself but he was also punishing her. He knew that one of her great hurts in life was that she never felt protected. Her judgments of him (active control pattern) were the ways she learned to protect herself when nobody else was around to do the protecting for her. She became a fierce warrior whose main weapon was criticism. But Marco was now able to see past the criticisms, understand that she was protecting a "broken" place, and accept how his withdrawal contributed to her pain.

So with authentic remorse he could stand in front of Sylvia and tell her, "I see how my withholding my heart from you causes so much pain. I am truly sorry for hurting you. I'm aware of the place in me that has wanted to hurt you. I'm really sorry Syl." Upon receiving his remorse, Sylvia let go of all remnants of her protector (she now felt protected by Marco) and sobbed for the first time since she was a child. And the last time she cried so deeply was as a child by herself in her bedroom, where nobody would know.

Some possible ways to support the movement into remorse

- When a spouse has accessed her hurt, invite her to express sorrow for her part in the couple's distress. "I'm sorry that I attack you when you withdraw." "I'm really sorry that I don't acknowledge all the wonderful things about you." "I know I hurt you when I make fun of your weight." "I see how much it hurts when I threaten divorce."
- Keep the expression as sorrow or remorse rather than guilt, as in—"I feel terrible that . . ."
- Help each partner reclaim the part of themselves that has acted from cruelty, fear or self-protection without self-judgment. "I know I can be mean." "I see how my complaining affects you." "I have a part of me that wants to shit on everything." "I see how I sometimes want you to feel inadequate and how it shows up in my criticisms."
- It is often very powerful to invite the remorseful partner, after expressing the remorse, to hold his mate in his arms, on a couch or the floor where she can give herself over to him fully. Frequently deeply loving statements such as "I don't want to hurt you anymore" or, "I want to protect you" will spontaneously emerge during such an embrace.

Maeve eventually was able to appreciate how her expectations and childhood demands of Corey put him in a double bind. The message she communicated was, "It's your job to take care of me, but don't be too strong." She could see how hard he tried to please her and how afraid he was of her disapproval. Maeve compassionately expressed to Corey: "I'm so sorry for what I put you through. I know I can be such a bitch sometimes. I see how hard you try to make our world safe and secure, and I'm sorry that I make it seem like it's never enough." Hearing her and feeling the authenticity in her heart moved Corey deeply. Having grown up as the "star" who everybody could count on, he learned to never trust that anybody could be there for him. When Maeve could own responsibility for her demands and expectations, Corey was given a profound gift.

Opening to Mature Need and Longing

For so many couples in long term relationships the little slights, unreasonable demands, hidden cruelties, interlocking insecurities, behaviors that trigger historical reactions, and the cumulative effect of the control patterns result in highly entrenched negative narratives. These narratives have a potent effect on how each person comes to perceive the other. For Corey, he gradually came to view Maeve as a self-centered, weak, ungrateful child, whom he was forced to take care of. Maeve's negative narrative portrayed Corey as a miserable, hostile, martyr who was incapable of relaxing and enjoying life and who blamed the world for his misery.

The long term effect is that the awareness of the importance of one's partner becomes substantially diminished. Many couples who have come to us for mentoring are either operating from these immature demands and expectations of each other, or are leading parallel lives where there is little awareness of the true need for each other.

Mature need, as opposed to the childhood demands that are often mistaken as authentic needs, involve the capacity to let another person really matter. **The openness to the realization, the fully felt, embodied appreciation for a partner's existence**

in one's life can be downright terrifying. The determined and sustained resistance to feeling the strength of one's need for another is motivated by a penetrating awareness of just how far reaching this need truly is. Even though, as David Schnarch emphasizes, we need to become self-validating individuals, we are never free of our profound need for each other.

It is rare indeed to hear one human being say to another "I need you" free of shame or demand. This is innocence supreme. The over-emphasis of independence and individuality has resulted in a disavowal of vulnerability. The two of us come to refer to the capacity to open to need as "mature innocence." This is the innocence of one who can acknowledge how important his partner really is.

Mature need has nothing to do with getting the other to do anything. Partners don't need one another to buy flowers, talk more, clean up the bathroom, get a better job, stop giving the kids treats, or change hair style. Often one partner will believe that the relationship is contingent on the need for the other to change in some specific way. These are really preferences and may be "deal breakers," but they have nothing to do with mature need.

"I need you" spoken from the consciousness of appreciation for another's existence in one's life, involves the acceptance of the other's "otherness." Beyond the expression of remorse one can begin to feel how much his mate means to him. As protections melt and control patterns lose their grip, minor relationship miracles can occur. Love that once seemed lost forever is rediscovered and is often felt on a deeper level than ever before. The heartfelt, limbic-activated apprehension of exquisite connection that occurs when all the angers, fears, hurts, and sorrows are released is truly a peak experience, an ecstatic celebration. These are the exceptional experiences that fuel the relationship and motivate both partners to live from their fullest truths and greatest good. When the barriers (constructed over decades to protect one's integrity) begin to dissolve, love can prosper.

Some options for supporting the opening to mature need:

- Support the innocent expression of mature need and when appropriate offer catalyzing statements such as: "I need you in my life." "I am so happy that you are in this world together with me. "You matter so much to me." "I thank God for you." "Meeting you is the best thing that ever happened to me." "I need you so much." This is best done with partners standing and facing each other at a distance of four to five feet. This increases the likelihood that both giver and receiver can openly feel what's being expressed.
- Work non-verbally and energetically to help partners embody mature need. For instance, have one spouse kneel before the other with open arms. Or, you can encourage one partner to amplify an emerging awareness of mature need by shouting, singing, or dancing for the partner.
- If a spouse is opening up to her mature need, you can have her stand facing her partner and breathe deeply as she feels her need and appreciation. Let the feeling fill her body until she has an impulse to do or say something to her mate. Playing evocative songs can enhance the opening to genuine mature need.

Gratitude, Appreciation and Pure Love

In our mentoring work we often hear from couples statements such as: "I know that I love her, but I can't *feel* it." The verbal acknowledgement of love is often flat or tentative. When the heart is protected and there are withheld resentments, active negative narratives, banished demands, carefully guarded vulnerabilities, or shameful avoidance of remorse, the expression of love is stilted. As partners take the space to bring out their respective emotional flashpoints and know that each has been heard by the other, they make room for embodied love to spring forth.

One of the most prominent reasons partners experience difficulty inhabiting their love is the reluctance to be passionate in every form. **The prohibition against hate leads to the inhibition of love**. Many spouses will say "I don't hate him, that's not who

I am." Yes, it's true for all of us that, in our higher selves, we do not hate. But, as the two of us have emphasized throughout this book, most people tend to disavow those aspects of "self" that are considered taboo. It can be challenging to identify that a certain part, voice, or energy exists within when it runs counter to one's values, self-image, or belief system. So the part that can and does hate is shunned, and its disappearance leads to a diminished capacity to fully embody the expansive feelings of love, joy, empathy, altruism, and creativity. When partners have permission to let out the charge in the body that is captured in the word "hate," it frees up the entire somatic system to relax, to soften, and to discharge. Then the physiological experience of love can truly occur. The person who knew he loved, but couldn't feel it, can experience it as a living, vital reality.

While many professionals in this field disagree with the premise that energy can "release" by expressing negativity, we have witnessed something quite different. In our work we have seen firsthand the clear connection between expressing highly charged, so-called negative emotions and the opening to palpable tenderness and love. The lore of make-up sex seems to carry a validity which belies the belief that expression of anger and hate is always harmful. The somatic mechanism may not be entirely clear, but experientially the road to heaven is sometimes paved with "bad intentions." And when these are free to be expressed, partners in relationship often will exhibit demonstrably greater emotional kinship. Eyes soften, skin glows, lips grow fuller, words seem to match the energy being put forth through a partner's entire being. Two people who may have spent decades in what Schnarch refers to as the "comfort-safety cycle" and what we have been calling control patterns find "true love" in the throes of wild and sometimes edgy emotional expression.

The pattern of protest, despair, and accommodation detailed in attachment theory is often replayed in the committed long-term relationship. The control patterns are the couple's way of accommodating to the messiness of protest and the abject pain of despair. Through FSE, we open the channels for each person to reclaim this natural, biological and neurological need to protest. **Couples who are unwilling to raise their voices are also afraid to openly let love run throughout their bodies.**

The embodied experience of love and its correlate gratitude, happens organically when each person has developed the emotional freedom of full self-expression. Working with FSE is not about adopting a plastic behavioral strategy which, if practiced diligently, will recondition you into a loving being. FSE is only an explanation and a "permission slip" as it were to reclaim one's rightful emotional depth and breadth. Love really is not a separate or final "step." It exists in all levels of FSE when they are divulged with the intention of healing and creating intimacy. Love is the collagen which binds together all emotion.

When committed partners can unpack each piece of the emotional jigsaw puzzle, the liberty to love, openly and unabashedly, is unleashed. In this last layer, when someone has crossed the divide from blame to self-responsibility, from lower self to remorse, from demand to mature need, there is a spaciousness that is created in the heart which begs to be given to the partner. No special interventions are necessary here. We simply encourage one mate to share with her partner not just generalities of love, but to make it personal and specific. In our work with John Gray in the early 1980's he underscored the importance of being precise in the expression of love and appreciation in his "Total Truth Process." FSE is in many ways a more comprehensive exposition of Dr. Gray's Total Truth Process.

For Maeve, she made a deeper connection to Corey through encountering and expressing her cruelty, unfair demands, fears, hurts and remorse. She was able to make authentic contact with how much he mattered and how much she truly was grateful for who he was as a separate human being. Love begins perhaps with the realization that someone outside oneself exists—as a distinct being. Maeve openly expressed to Corey, "I love how you stay with me no matter what. I so appreciate your willingness to discover the truth. I love you for hearing all of my difficult emotions. Thank you for all you do to make our life comfortable. I love your sense of the absurd and your curiosity. You are a beautiful man."

These words are not a formulaic contrivance. They are a representation and an articulation of an honest and heartfelt experience of love. When a couple arrives at this juncture in an intimate exchange, it is fair to say that they have attained an ecstatic state. The full experience of love is an ecstatic connection to a reality that is larger than our human capacity to fully comprehend. It opens the relationship to its highest potential. This is our deep desire in the work we do with couples. As two committed human beings awaken their bodies to fully feel all there is to feel in this intense experience called life, they are free.

Ecstatic experience is essential for all of us in order to release our higher-self gifts. We cannot live in the ecstatic state perpetually, but we can cultivate the conditions to elicit it much more often than typically happens. Love and gratitude are expressions of ecstatic energy. As a couple finds a way into the ecstatic experience of love, inspiration begins to emerge. The inspired, creative potential of the exceptional relationship is truly something worth the effort to attain.

From a transpersonal perspective, the flow of our interior experiences is evolutionary. Individuals often need to express internal states which result from less consciousness before they can embrace "higher order" emotions which require a more expanded awareness. Thus we can view FSE as an evolutionary process comprising four distinct stages:

1. Blame, childhood need, and lower self emerge from an immature consciousness based in a belief that one is dependent on external forces.
2. Self affirming anger surfaces from a more empowered consciousness which takes form through a burgeoning awareness of one's capacity to manifest and have agency over one's immediate world.
3. As consciousness continues to evolve one opens to the world of interdependence. Here, one feels the more vulnerable and intimacy-enhancing emotions of fear and hurt. The awareness of interpersonal connection and mature need is a higher order consciousness.

4. As one embraces that incontrovertible truth that another person matters, there is an evolutionary progression toward broader compassion, gratitude, altruism and felt sense of unity with something larger. This opens one to a longing to express one's full potential as an act of generosity.

By moving through layers of emotion we cross the divide from protection and isolation to embodied intimacy and ecstatic connection. This "wisdom path" carries us through the entire range of affective possibilities in such a way that each person is freed to experience life passionately. Partners can support this movement from defended to expanded when each can encourage the other to emotionally "go all the way." Brian expresses this in the following poem:

Touch Me

Touch me where I'm numb.
The pointed barbs of your exasperation
disturb my somnolence,
and cause me to respond
to the alarm that warns
of impending soul demise.

Touch me where I complain.
Fight back in a way that
challenges me to enter into
the treacherous terror of
my own culpability.

Touch me in my need to scream.
Provoke me in such a way
that welcomes my insurrection.
Help me to feel the beauty in my
protestations so that
I can enter the pain which
they so vehemently protect.

Touch me in my fright.
Let me know that my fear
Is smaller than
your willingness to hold it.
Show me your trust
in my capacity to fully
enter my most fearful places.

Touch me in my sorrow.
Let our hearts join
in the shared experience
of love's inevitable fiascos.
Requited remorse is met
with trembling forgiveness
in a holy and healing exchange.

Touch me with your ecstasy.
As separateness dissolves
into the wild, unschooled
expression of delirious delight
in our shared awareness of
one another's true nature.

Chapter Eight

Exceptional Sex

Sexual expression is a profound human longing which can find its home in the committed relationship. Sexuality has the potential to cut through all the myriad ways couples attempt to keep themselves separate from each other and the vibrantly alive energy they are endowed with. Working with couples on their sexual relationship can be both challenging and immensely gratifying. This chapter builds on what you have learned up to now and invites you to be more expansive in working with couples' sexuality.

Let's start by making a distinction between *great* sex and *exceptional* sex. Often couples have a notion of what they would describe as great sex. Invariably it involves a loosely defined script which includes heightening arousal, maybe some particular types of sex play, uninhibited sexual contact, powerful orgasms, and mutual afterglow. Great sex is what couples strive for and fantasize about. When it happens it can have a lasting impact on the couple's level of intimacy. The problem is, great sex does not happen as often as most couples would like, and generally it cannot be orchestrated through the use of techniques. There are too many other human factors which confound the ability to achieve regular great sex.

Conversely, exceptional sex takes us in a different direction. In Going All The Way, we said this, "Exceptional sex may not look like the popular notion of pulse-pounding, heart throbbing, high-on-the-Richter Scale, orgasm-centric intercourse. While that scenario may occur, it is not the essence of exceptional sex.

When couples have been married for ten, twenty, thirty, forty, or more years, sex must evolve along with the relationship." [8] What we are suggesting, is that exceptional sex is an adventure into a world where anything is possible. In exceptional sex, it is hard to know who will show up. There is room for all the various energies existing within each person—innocence, power, playfulness, insecurity, selfishness, generosity, worry, distraction, over/under arousal, seductiveness, surrender, resistance and much more.

It is sad though, how even sexuality has been shackled by the emphasis on performance over spontaneity, and approval-seeking over curiosity. In helping couples to entertain a broader notion of sexuality, we have witnessed a palpable relief as partners learn to let go of internalized expectations. In exceptional sex it is no longer a failure when a man loses an erection, or a woman cannot reach orgasm. These are part of the experience. When couples redouble their efforts to overcome these challenges they only move further away from exceptional sex. Instead, we invite them to make deeper contact with each other in the experience of a flagging penis or frustrated pelvis.

When partners can meet each other in the moment where they might normally cut off or disappear, the sexual encounter continues rather than aborts. **To invoke exceptional sex, partners need to eroticize even their frustrations and insecurities.** We'll come back to this later. Sexuality goes way beyond a hard cock and a wet pussy. At its essence eroticism is the openness to desiring everything your mate has to offer. What prevents this from occurring often has to do with the ways each individual personalizes the other's behavior. For many, the narrative "I'm not desirable enough" is never far away and will surface when sex does not go smoothly.

Julie had been unable to achieve orgasm with her newlywed husband Kurt. While she could climax through masturbation, she had convinced herself that she looked ugly when she was in the throes of orgasm. Her self-consciousness held her down. She learned from her mother, who herself was sexually abused by Julie's grandfather, that to lose control was disgusting. Thus she would experience a "yucky" feeling in the pit of her stomach every time she began to approach climax with Kurt.

Julie dressed in ways that would not draw attention. She wore her hair short and donned only jeans and baggy tee shirts. She did not want to embrace her femininity. She often questioned her desirability, even in the face of Kurt's obvious attraction to her. To identify herself as a sexual being was difficult. In our mentoring work with Kurt and Julie we had them both open up to each other through breathing and pelvic rocking (where the pelvis is brought back on the inhalation and forward on the exhalation). As Julie began to have the yucky feeling in her gut we encouraged her to give it words. She described the sensation as telling her "sex is disgusting and I am disgusting for starting to become aroused."

By asking her to tolerate the sensation and stay with the breathing and pelvic movement she became more acutely aware of her fear of losing control. She believed that she was bad for having sexual impulses. Often a partner will shut down the flow of energy by curtailing the breath or tightening the muscles wherever there is discomfort. It can take a great deal of encouragement to keep the energy moving when the body's habit is to constrict. But Julie was determined to stay with the movement and the corresponding sense of disgust. She and Kurt kept at the pelvic rocking until something shifted.

Julie got in touch with a voice which was saying "I am desirable." So she started to express it to Kurt, who spontaneously said "Yes!" Their bodies began to move in synchronicity, their energies entrained. Each started to feel more alive. We offered Julie a catalyzing suggestion to change the sentence from "I am desirable" to "I am desirous." By shifting the focus from how others might view her (desirable) to her own capacity for desire (desirous), she played with embracing her sexuality. This brought them into a delighted place with each other and ended with them dancing together.

The idea of exceptional sex, then, is to move with the truth of whatever shows up, until it transforms. Many people harbor shame around certain aspects of their sexuality and attempt to circumvent these inner realities rather than allowing them to be part of the sexual experience. Sexuality will atrophy when couples learn to avoid all the places that do not feel safe. Safe sex equals sparse sex.

Exceptional sex encourages "erotic plasticity" where partners can expand the limits of what turns them on. There is such deep conditioning about what is acceptable and "normal" that many folks never allow themselves to explore their full potential. In EMM we encourage couples to bring forth those places that lie dormant, exiled, or locked inside a fortress of shame. As we move through this chapter we want to invite you to expand your own limits and reevaluate where you hold unexamined beliefs about what is healthy or normal.

In the remainder of this chapter we will cover the following:

- Sex as communication
- Sexual control patterns
- Sex in the session
- Eroticizing everything
- Conflict and sex
- Inviting all parts
- Welcoming the trauma
- Active and receptive energies
- The erotic spectrum
- Sex outside the relationship
- Alternative sexual preferences

Sex as communication

The value of sexuality in a committed partnership goes far beyond the capacity to achieve orgasms. Sex is a paramount form of communication which allows a couple to "speak" to each other in the most intimate of ways. One of our favorite pieces of advice we share with the couples we work with is, "Less talk, more expression." Communication through verbal discussion carries far too much weight in comparison to the intimate dialogue of touch, smell, taste, breath, movement, and non-linguistic sound. If a picture is worth a thousand words, open sexual connection is worth a million.

While words are important, and can enhance the intimacy in sexual contact, they also can be a huge distraction and deterrent. Talk is a poor substitute for experience, and sexual encounter is a supreme form of shared experience. As we discussed in the previous chapter, a major goal of the EMM approach is to elicit ecstatic experience. Talk will rarely, if ever, result in ecstasy. Sexuality, conversely, is one of the most readily accessible avenues into the ecstatic. Sexual fulfillment gives life color and texture in a way that is hard to match.

Additionally, sexuality gives a couple the opportunity to explore various parts within each person that generally cannot be revealed elsewhere. Sex play can allow each individual to discover and embody divergent interior "selves" that long for expression. The person who is always in charge in the outer world may long to be submissive; the demure individual may want to play the "slut"; the serious individual can become more playful; the stud can enact the innocent, naive virgin; the gentle soul can get a bit rough. This is the great opportunity afforded to couples through their sex lives together.

Sexual control patterns

Often, however, couples slip into control patterns which can strip the sex of its liberating potential. Control patterns operate whether one is in a business suit or lingerie. In the sexual relationship, partners will usually gravitate toward styles of interaction which are motivated by avoidance of vulnerable, shameful or intense energies. Because sexuality practically requires partners to show up in ways that breaks through the façade of everyday life, control patterns are bound to be part of the landscape. There is a magnificent fragility in revealing desire, passion, one's naked body, lust, fantasy, and specific erotic interests. Consequently, many couples create highly routinized and predictably choreographed styles of sexual involvement. Things get stale when control patterns dominate.

Passive and aggressive control patterns are evident in bed as in life. One partner may be critical of the other's touch, actions, smell, or look. Another may be highly controlling of how the experience must unfold. Yet another may go through the motions but fail to bring much of herself to the sexual encounter. Or, one may find a thousand reasons to avoid sex altogether. Whenever a spouse's behavior (passive or aggressive) is motivated by an intention to keep things safe there is a control pattern at play. It is nearly always helpful just to have each person describe what might happen if they changed the pattern.

Typical examples of sexual control patterns include:

Passive End of the Spectrum
The individual who,

- Rarely or never initiates sexual contact
- Has difficulty asking for what is pleasurable
- Keeps arousal at "manageable" levels
- Keeps sex "nice"
- Has difficulty setting boundaries—either says yes or no automatically
- Energetically disappears (dissociates) during sex
- Exhibits difficulty achieving orgasm or maintaining an erection
- Harbors silent judgments of partner
- Avoids experimentation

Aggressive End of the Spectrum
The individual who,

- Badgers, uses guilt or intimidation in sexual initiation
- Acts out through affairs, prostitution or excessive pornography
- Violates sexual boundaries
- Rigidly controls the sexual encounter
- Is openly critical of partner's performance
- Uses sex to manipulate partner
- Compulsively "needs" sex for validation of attractiveness or worth
- Has great difficulty bringing tenderness into sex
- Energetically disappears after sex—cuts off from partner

Giving up habits of sexual interaction is no easy task for most couples. More and more we see couples who let their sex lives fall by the wayside because challenging these habitual ways seems too onerous. To break free of routines is frightening for many couples. Being naked in one's body, desire, need, and sexual behavior is an extremely vulnerable undertaking. In such a place lovers are supremely susceptible to being hurt in ways that cut to the quick. An errant laugh, frustrated sigh, snappy complaint, or injudicious observation can send a partner reeling in hurt or shame. Sexual encounter brings us back to a child-like innocence where the heart is as nude as the body.

Sexuality is fraught with powerful emotions. As we approach pleasure, passion, ecstasy, and unfettered desire we also encounter the cultural and familial backlash of fear, disgust, guilt, and repression. Most of us in committed relationships were raised in environments that did not send clear and accepting messages about sex and bodily pleasure. Even the most caring and well-intentioned parents held wildly ambivalent reactions to a child's sexual explorations. More often than not, parents passed along their own confusing and fragmented relationship to their sexuality.

One's parents could be both, repressive and voyeuristic, shaming and subtly encouraging, fearful and playful. Those of us with children know just how difficult it is to embody healthy sexuality with them. It is no small wonder then that most committed couples learn to manage the confusing array of impulses and feelings through the employment of control patterns.

Sex in the session

The challenge in couple's work is to confront these potent realities in a way that allows couples to have an experience beyond their normal routines. Instead of just talking about what they can practice at home, in EMM we help couples to explore various energies within the session. To bring sexuality into the room is, of course, a delicate proposition. Some couples can barely talk about sex in the presence of others. Others hunger for such discussion and really appreciate an open and candid exploration. We have worked with many couples who describe how disappointed they have been in previous couple's therapy where the subject of their sex lives was given short shrift.

In the EMM approach working with erotic energy within the context of the session is integral to what we do. Without removing clothes or engaging in specific sexual acts which are not within the purview of a mentoring session, we support committed partners in opening up to their erotic capacities. Couples may engage in a variety of erotic exchanges without crossing specific boundaries. It is always at the discretion of the couple. As in the example of Kurt and Julie, we suggested to them the exercise of standing in front of each other at a distance of about four feet, and synchronizing the movement of their pelvises with their breath. This is something they both were open to exploring. Just as in every other area of a couple's relationship, we utilize the session to actively experiment with newer ways of relating.

Our goal is to help couples to awaken their bodies and to entertain original ways of being with each other in their sexual involvement. If one partner has a highly dominating control pattern, we may ask the more compliant mate to get on top of him, hold him down and declare, "I'm in charge!" Doing this in the presence of mentors accomplishes two things. First, the couple gets to step beyond their structured style of interacting in a safe environment in a way they are unlikely ever to do on their own. Second, mentors can witness and give feedback about how the couple embraces these novel interactions. The mentors can also suggest further catalyzing interventions which may take the couple even deeper into a more open and expansive erotic exchange.

Fundamental to the EMM approach, then, is the active engagement of the body and emotions in the process of helping the couple to embrace new and unfamiliar energies within the context of the mentoring session. In the words of Esther Perel, "Cleverly, our bodies remember what our minds may have chosen to forget, both light and dark. Perhaps this is why our deepest fears and most persistent longings emerge in intimate sex: the immensity of our neediness, the fear of desertion, the terror of being engulfed, the yearning for omnipotence." (34) From this vantage point, exceptional sex must make room for highly divergent energies to come into play. Better sex is really about each person discovering and sharing more of who they are.

The passive partner who tells her controlling mate, "I'm in charge!" gives them both the opportunity to feel what happens when they step outside of the habitual dance. He may find that it both scares him *and* brings a sense of relief. She may get more turned on and also notice how she can judge her own aggression. All good news! In our experience most couples truly want to have a richer sex life, but nobody ever gave them the compassionate permission to entertain more expansive roles with each other. While there are a minority of couples who have vibrant and delightful sex lives (some that we know should be giving workshops!) most relationships struggle.

In addition to the confusing social and familial messages around sexuality, there is a cumulative effect of the slights, rejections, criticisms, libidinal differences, over-caution, and the drift away from eroticism toward functional interaction which characterizes most marriages. Thus, many relationships inexorably evolve into business enterprises, or mom and dad partnerships. Reich was perhaps the first to suggest, "Sexual partnership and human friendship are replaced by fatherliness or motherliness . . . in short, by disguised incest." Partners in long-term relationships routinely fall prey to sexual avoidance when arousal requires confronting all that gets in the way.

Morris is a middle-aged attorney who is always the "good guy" to everyone he meets. He tries to see all sides of a conflict and never quite takes a stand. His wife of 31 years, Katy, complains bitterly about how Morris isn't emotionally available and is pre-occupied with work and money. After five sessions, Katy brings up her unhappiness about their sex life. Morris never initiates and, according to Katy, if it wasn't for Viagra they may not still be married. She says he would rather read a legal book than one about sex. Morris acknowledges the truth in what she says. He passes his sexual apathy off as part of his New England upbringing. He tells us that he avoids initiating because he has trouble letting go of work worries and he's afraid that he won't be able to please Katy.

In the shared energy field that is created around sexual engagement it often appears that one partner wants sex frequently and the other rarely. While there is often a legitimate difference in sex drive between committed partners, these positions can become exaggerated. In Katy's case, she believed she would have sex every day if Morris was game. Morris described himself as not even harboring sexual fantasies. He only masturbated once in a "blue moon" and never used pornography.

So, the less Morris expressed sexual desire, the more Katy wanted it, and vice versa. The two of us questioned Morris about what might please him sexually. Because he displayed such concern about pleasing Katy, we wanted to bring into the equation the possibility of "sexual selfishness" for him. Katy immediately chimed in, "He never asks for anything!" It was becoming clear that Morris was extremely cut off from his lust and his aggressive impulses to "take" for himself. She was in control, and that was that.

We invited the two of them to stand facing each other and for Morris to presence what was happening to him while Katy demanded more from him. Katy was very willing to bring out her demands. "I want more sex." "Where are you?" "I'm frustrated." (Katy was amplifying her control pattern of badgering Morris). We asked him to simply notice how he reacted to Katy's exhortations and complaints. At first he was only aware of feeling "shut down." Brian asked him, "Shut down to what?" As he stayed with his experience, he finally declared, "I don't want to feel how pissed off I am! I want to tell you to shut up." Marcia suggested he bring these words out even more strongly (amplifying his control pattern of resistance). So, back and forth they went—"You're not giving me enough sex!"—"Shut up!' From an energetic standpoint, both of them were building bodily arousal, or charge. While this comes easier to Katy, for Morris it was setting a precedent.

As we discussed early on, energy loves to be matched with equivalent energy. When a highly aroused person is met with a flat or rational response, it is particularly frustrating. As Morris "met" Katy's energy she grew more animated, less critical, and seductively playful. Morris had more difficulty owning his resistance and concomitant aggression. We gave him support and let him know that this was an important first step. Marcia asked if he could feel any pleasure in resisting Katy. He acknowledged that it felt good to say out loud what usually came across non-verbally.

Brian suggested to Morris that perhaps he shut down, in part, because he saw Katy as too demanding and too vocal. We could see that this opened a door of possibility for Morris. Brian suggested, "Why don't you try putting your hands on your hips, become aware of your balls and tell Katy, 'Shut up and fuck me!'" Marcia encouraged Katy to keep expressing what she wanted from Morris. "I want more sex!" she shouted. "Shut up and fuck me!" he retorted.

While this scenario may sound crude or absurd in written form, the real-life experience was highly positive. Within two minutes, after Morris let go of his self-consciousness, both of them were smiling and basking in erotic energy. If you recall earlier, the utilization of a catalyzing intervention is apt to be successful when the mentor can sense or intuit that an individual is ready to take a leap forward. In this case, both of us believed that Morris was open to "trying on" his sexually aggressive energy. If what we suggested was beyond what he was open to, or in some way was not right for him, this would have been immediately evident. Morris had lost connection to his erotic impulses and all he really needed was permission to claim a part of himself that he was aware existed. To entertain the possibility that it was in any way acceptable to tell his wife to "Shut up and fuck me'" required our support and encouragement.

Eroticizing everything

Eroticism is an energy that is hard to define. Words cannot possibly depict its full meaning. Its absence in a relationship leads to stale, arid and brittle interactions. In the vernacular of Core Energetics and other body-based modalities, there is no "pelvic" energy when eroticism is missing. But it is more than the pelvis involved in erotic awakening. When Morris could tell Katy to "Shut up and fuck me," he was not expressing it with disregard or cruelty. He was revealing a secret selfish place which Katy always sensed was "in there" but never honestly owned. Additionally, by expressing it from a playful place, he was appealing to the part of her that wanted to feel his solidness and authority. When a spouse can bring out these inner truths, eroticism blossoms.

Erotic energy is light, free, stimulating, playful, positively aggressive, creative, innocent and delightful. Much of the work we do with couples is ultimately destined to awaken the eros that is latent in the relationship. Far too many couples shrink back into timid and politically correct forms of sexual expression. Eroticism combines heart and pelvis, love and lust, narcissism and generosity. While couples can have sex without eroticism, it will remain extremely limited and ultimately unrewarding. Many couples operate from the axiom "I'd rather be safe than sorry." As David Schnarch suggests, "Eroticism is very personal and self-revealing—that's why partners typically hide their eroticism from each other." [(41)] When the only choices available are "safe" or "sorry" eroticism is the greatest casualty.

We mentioned above that in exceptional sex even the struggles, frustrations, and "failures" are eroticized. This means that embedded in every interaction or emotional reaction is the capacity for erotic awakening. When one partner notices that the other has gone away he can roll over in frustration (enacting a control pattern) or he can beckon her back. When a spouse asks her mate to go down on her and he hesitates, she can get self-conscious or she can presence her reactions to his hesitance. Such a moment can become erotic when two people stay with what is happening. For her to say, "It's hard for me to ask you to go down on me. When I sense your reluctance I want to pull away," opens the way for deeper contact. This then reignites eroticism. His experiencing her vulnerability might open his heart and turn him on. Perhaps it will lead to a more honest discussion about his trouble with oral sex, which may temporarily move the couple away from the sex. But this is a necessary step in finding the way back to the erotic.

Conflict and sex

The capacity to remain present through conflict is central to exceptional sex. Partners who grew up with insecure attachment have a much more difficult time staying with each other through the differences sexual encounter will inevitably evoke. Sexuality naturally stirs up very child-like need for connection and merger. In a very real way both the adult self and the tender child are present in sexual communion. Autonomy and immersion are mutually significant to the full-fledged sexual experience.

Couples who can navigate this dynamic tension are likely to have satisfying and meaningful sex. Relationships where partners can use conflict as a means to re-kindle eros are usually ones where each person is sufficiently individuated. This means that both people are capable of emotionally managing the necessary separation that is part and parcel of conflict. In EMM we encourage partners to "move toward the conflict." This suggests that rather than engaging in the control patterns of withdrawal or reactivity each person stays with the experience of threat that discordant interactions evoke. The more couples can do this the more they will realize that the real conflict is not between partners, but within each.

Simon and Billy are a same-sex couple in their late 20's who have been in a committed relationship for two years. In our mentoring work, we supported them in moving toward the conflict as it related to their sexuality. When Billy approached Simon to initiate sex, he was often met with resistance. Billy appeared to have the greater need of the two for more frequent sex. Initially Billy saw Simon's reticence as endearing and something that he could overcome with his love and encouragement. But quite the opposite occurred. Two years in, Simon felt badgered by Billy, while Billy saw Simon as uncaring and intentionally resistant. When they did have sex, Billy felt like he had to curb his energy to keep Simon from disappearing.

To move *toward* the conflict for this couple meant presencing what was behind the control patterns of badgering and knee-jerk resistance. For Simon this meant entering into his inner conflict between being afraid of Billy's "big energy" (which was reminiscent of how his cousin would regularly beat him up, and sexually humiliate him) and his own erotic desire. To live on just the one end of the polarity (the one of saying "no" to sex) was easier for Simon than struggling with his internal discord. In one particular mentoring session we asked Simon to first amplify his resistance, to make it even bigger than it was normally expressed at home. As he pounded the foam cube he shouted at Billy, "You can't have me! Stay the fuck away! I'll never let you have your way with me! "I'll never let you know I need you!" All the words (and the passion behind them) that he never was able to say to his bully cousin came out in a glorious expression of self-care.

Billy's own inner conflict involved on the one hand, his true longing to be fully met sexually, and on the other, his disdain for his "needy and grabby" part. He wanted Simon to be more sexually initiating so that he would not have to confront this needy side which he viewed as desperate and ugly. We asked him to move toward the conflict by amplifying and embodying his grabby energy—the part he most despised. He too smashed the cube and screamed at Simon, "You have to make me feel loved! It's your job to keep me from feeling insecure! "Fuck me until I love myself!"

The more each of them was able to take ownership of the *inner* conflict, and make adequate room for the voice of the most disowned part to be expressed, the less reactive and withdrawn they became. There is usually a voice in each person that needs to be heard and which has never been allocated its proper place in the couple's reiterative struggle. The eroticism in Billy and Simon's relationship increased as Billy could see how his big energy triggered an old protective response in Simon, one where his only choice was to disappear. Likewise, Simon opened his heart to Billy around how difficult it was for him to reveal his insecurity and how truly scared he was of Simon's seeming indifference. Billy recalled that as a gay adolescent, he had several painful experiences where other boys and he would have brief clandestine encounters. Subsequently, these other boys would act as if he didn't exist.

Inviting all parts

Every person in relationship has these voices, or parts, which are longing for expression but are considered too unacceptable to reveal. The mentor works to help a partner find this voice so that he can embrace and embody it. In the sexual relationship these hidden parts are particularly verboten. To reveal and express impulses, fantasies, preferences, fetishes, and desires that may be deemed perverted is no easy undertaking. Yet, as these parts are allowed to emerge most couples find a way to work with or around them.

Castration and rapist fantasies, masochistic or sadistic impulses, homoerotic proclivities, desires to have sex in risky places, and any of an assortment of fetishes, from lipstick and high heels to diapers, can be part of a spouse's hidden world. If these can be brought out in the open there is a good chance that it will enhance the couple's sexual connection. Sometimes one partner simply does not want to know what the other's secret sex world holds. Couples will find a way to negotiate how much intimacy they can tolerate in this regard. In EMM we want to push the envelope of the tolerable and discover what each partner's edge is.

Tula and Dominic had been together for 5 years when they came to us. They had reached an impasse around one aspect of their sexuality. Tula recently discovered that Dominic occasionally indulged in viewing (and masturbating to) internet pornography. She was extremely threatened by this and had a hard time imagining him being attracted to another woman. Whenever she saw him looking at another woman she would fly into a rage and accuse him of cheating on her. She wanted to have sex with Dominic often as a way to reassure herself that he was still attracted to her. Tula insisted that she herself was never attracted to another man and deemed such attraction as tantamount to having an affair.

For a while Dominic would bend over backward to reassure Tula. He too could spiral down into insecurity attacks whenever he imagined Tula with a past lover. So he tried to hide his sexual desires for other women and convince her of his unwavering fidelity. The edge for Tula involved staying with the sense of panic that would crop up every time she suspected Dominic of having attraction to another woman. This concern about attractiveness had nothing to do with eroticism. It seemed, in part, to be connected to the physical absence of her mother in the first several years of her life and observing her father bring more attention to her younger sister. Inside her panic there was a fiercely competitive place and a narrative that she would ultimately lose the competition to another woman. In her competitiveness she brought all her attention to the man and essentially shunned relationships with other females.

Tula understood that her intense reaction was not based in a present reality. But she could not stop herself from raging at Dominic when threatened. We confronted this issue on two fronts. First, we asked if she would be willing to hear about Dominic's attraction to other women. She agreed. So, we encouraged Dominic to tell her how he enjoyed the women he observed on the internet. As her anger began to surface, it was very evident how frightened she really was. We asked her if we could shift away from Dominic, have her lie down and let the fear speak to her. She again said this was okay. As she lay down we asked her what the "scared child" was trying to say. Immediately she said, "Pay attention to *me*!" As she said the words we invited her to bring out the fullness of this reaction. She was encouraged to kick and scream her insistence that her dad pay attention to her. She moved back and forth from angry demand to desperate pleading, "I want your love!" "Where are you?" "I hate my sister!" She cried and yelled as she opened to her immature need and the despair of losing out to her sister.

We encouraged her to really go fully into her exaggerated demand for her father (a healthy narcissistic protest). We gave her the words to try on, "I want all your attention! Don't even look at my sister! It's all for me!" Here was a huge edge for Tula and she embraced it beautifully. This was what she was enacting with Dominic regularly and now she was bridging it to her past. Additionally, she was embodying the full strength of her desperate need for requited fatherly love.

The second front involved giving her a suggestion to explore her attraction to other men. Her insistence that she did not feel sexual attraction to anyone but Dominic was a control pattern she incorporated in order to avoid feeling the fear and pain of his bringing attention to other women. She also did not want to feel how much she wanted her father to cherish her as he appeared to do with her sister. The control pattern was so entrenched that she truly could not feel erotic energy outside her committed relationship.

We asked her between sessions to notice other men and to simply decide whether any of them were good looking. When she came back to our next session she said there was one particular man whom she thought was handsome. We had her presence how her body felt as she described him. Tula noticed how her stomach tightened as she talked about this other man. She told us that her stomach seemed to be saying "Don't feel, it's too dangerous." She explained that if she allowed herself to feel attraction she believed that she had to act on it. In other words, there was no sexual attraction without enactment.

She was deeply afraid that she could sexually act out on Dominic and that he too would have no control over his impulses. He told her that he did not want to bring his eroticism elsewhere but that he was frightened of her potential to stray. Because his own mother was seductive and manipulative, Dominic needed Tula to need him. This is how he created an illusion of safety. But the price was high. He had to hide his sexuality, and worse, their lovemaking was saturated with childhood demands for reassurance and validation. While they had sex often and could be very erotic with each other at times, more often they were using sex as a control pattern in order to avoid the pain of abandonment.

One of the pieces Dominic worked on was separating the slavish desire to win his mother's love from his mature desire for Tula. The unspoken words he held as a component of his wish to attain the love of his mother were, "I'll make you dependent on me. I'll make myself indispensible so I will never lose you. I'd rather be smothered than abandoned!" As he expressed and embodied these sentiments, he could then feel the pain of opening to his mother's seductions and as well as the subsequent shame and rejection. After he experienced this pain and shame he was able to see how *he* had become seductive of Tula. This was a very entrenched control pattern which took quite a long time to release. Together they had co-created a world where her clinginess supported his insecurities. Their mutual immature need for exclusivity (enacted in a different form for each of them) had gradually stifled the eroticism between them.

As each became more aware of the fragile and young parts which could dominate their interactions over time, they slowly engaged in a more fulfilling sexual experience. They began to make room for the "child parts" to be acknowledged during sex as they showed up. In doing so they learned to take responsibility for the immature childhood needs that co-existed with the genuine adult desires. Tula's demand that Dominic see her as the only object of desire in the whole world became part of their sexual play. He was able to turn his surreptitious seductions of Tula into an outward display of control. He embodied his Don Juan De Marco alter-ego with great zest.

So when we talk about helping couples find their edge sexually, we can see that for Tulsa and Dominic each needed to experience the seemingly intolerable feelings of not being "enough" for the other. Tula's fright that some more attractive woman would steal Dominic's affection needed to be fully felt, owned, and revealed. Dominic's need to make Tula dependent on him as a way to keep her from straying also required exposure and ownership. By bridging the historical antecedents to the present control patterns they both began to take risks. Their sexuality became more mature.

Welcoming the trauma

There are many couples we work with where one of the partners begins to exhibit strong somatic reactions to sexual interaction. Repulsion, rage, dissociation, terror, physical contraction and an adamant refusal to being touched are a few of the common reactions that are experienced somatically. Some of these individuals can connect the present physical response to a history of abuse, but many have no specific memory. One of the great values of embodied couples work is that we can address the in-the-moment manifestations of sexual difficulties without having to ever know the origins.

Mentoring work with a couple where one partner experiences strong negative reactions to sexuality can run the gamut from very gentle exploration, to permission to bring out powerful emotions. For instance, Avery and Tim needed to tread lightly on the subject of their vanishing sex life. Avery had developed a deep aversion to being touched by Tim. If she were absolutely convinced his touch was supportive and did not carry an implied request for sexual contact, she could allow (though not particularly enjoy) it. In her individual therapy with a different therapist, she was unable to identify exactly what might be causing her somatic reaction to sexual contact. She held no specific image memories of abuse or boundary violation. Though she guessed that some early life experiences were contributing to her present-day aversion to sexual touch, she could not connect the dots.

In EMM we work with the palpable reality that each person in the partnership can feel. We begin with a presumption that the couple's energy has entrained toward specific control patterns which know no first cause. As Mindell describes it, ". . . some signals are reactive and caused whereas other signals seem to be 'entangled' as if they were expressions coming from the field between two people. One possible effect is ambiguity about who did what first or second. Each partner may feel 'I did this because you did that,' but when they try they find it impossible to tell who did what first!" [26] Avery and Tim had become 'entangled" around sexual initiation.

We began by having them explore physical distance and proximity. Avery stood still and Tim adjusted his position in front of her to offer the "ideal" space. Originally this was about six feet. Further away she felt lonely and closer she began to experience anxiety. Our goal is to help one learn to not only tolerate greater and greater contact, that is, to manage the anxiety internally rather that by relying on the good graces of someone else, but also to be able to bring out whatever the anxiety might be protecting.

Tim was encouraged to gradually move closer to Avery and her task was to report how it felt. She knew she had ultimate veto power over Tim's moving too close, but we wanted her to play with the "edges" of what was tolerable. As Tim moved to within about two feet of her, Avery could feel her anxiety begin to flood her. We asked him to back up just enough to where she felt the discomfort was manageable. As he backed off slightly she became aware of not trusting Tim. She described him as having "grabby energy." She said to him, "You have this way of pulling at me, of wanting me to take care of you." When she experienced this "grabby energy" she would begin to feel trapped and out of control. From Tim's perspective, he would feel frustrated at her resistance and would then try to force the connection. Each of them believed that they were simply reacting to the other, yet clearly neither could say where the pattern began. By continuing to explore the very simple process of distance and proximity, each was able to see that other options existed than their entrained control patterns. Ultimately what each of them discovered from this gentle process was very crucial to moving past the deadlock.

For Avery, by staying on the edges of panic, she opened up to a potent realization of a deep ambivalence or tension between the part that loves and the part that lusts. Once Tim became her committed partner her anxiety began to rise. This was not an issue of commitment, but rather a significant confusion about whether her heart can love and her pelvis can desire the same person. For Avery, never the twain shall meet. By bringing this internal struggle to the light of day, she began to see the possibility, and indeed the desirability, of both loving and desiring Tim.

For Tim, he became aware that he had several layers of reactivity to Avery. First, he tried to be the caring, cautious, and respectful man that he believed she needed. But as he engaged in this experience of slowly moving toward her, he could sense the part of him that would get frustrated and wanted to force the connection. At its extreme, this is the "rapist" archetype. While Tim was far from being the kind of person to force her against her will, the grabby energy still elicited a strong reaction from Avery. Finally, and of greatest importance to Tim, he began to feel how his forcing energy was a protection against a vulnerable place where he was deeply hurt by Avery's ongoing rejection.

This entrained pattern between them started to shift as they each could see their respective parts and moved away from the narrative of "first cause." Avery began to recognize how her "No" carried tremendous power and how, in spite of the misery it caused, also held a certain pleasure. She enjoyed the control she had over Tim.

Subsequently we invited them to raise the energy of this dynamic. We suggested that both her "No!" and his grabbiness were expressed in a "cold" way. We encouraged them to make the exchange "hotter." Avery made her "No!" more overt and powerful, and Tim met her with a demand that she respond to his overtures. She used phrases like "You can't have me!" and "Stay away from me!" Tim countered with "I want you!" and "Stop resisting me!" By making their typical pattern hotter and more overt, each was able to feel more empowered. Avery was able to feel the "No!" coming from her woman, and Tim could allow himself to feel his protest without shame.

As we stated above, we will utilize both gentle interventions as well as more powerful catalyzing suggestions when there is strong negativity toward sexuality. Strong resistance or repulsion toward sexual contact is generally a trigger response to historical sexual discordance. But, while it is helpful to be able to identify the antecedents to present day sexual aversion, in the embodied model it is not crucial to reclaiming one's capacity for sexual pleasure. As we discussed at the outset of this chapter, exceptional sex makes room for all that needs to emerge through a couple's sexual experiences.

With Holly and Laird, we started slowly but gradually encouraged them to explore more powerful interactions around Holly's sexual shutting down. Much like Tim and Avery, this couple had started out with a robust sex life but soon Holly began to shut down. While they continued to have sex from time to time, she was not into it. As with Avery, Holly had no specific memory of childhood abuse. What was clear however was that she had an idealization of her father. She described him as handsome and smart. She would often compare Laird negatively to her dad.

As we progressed in our mentoring work with this couple, we suggested a catalyzing intervention for them to try. Holly had already expressed her resistance to Laird powerfully but there was something greater that seemed to be emerging. We proposed to her that she may want to try bringing out her "killer." Together we orchestrated a scene where Laird lay down on a mattress and Holly straddled him with one knee on either side of his hips. We gave him a rolled towel and asked him to hold it above his neck. Holly was then encouraged to grab the towel and to "embody" the part of her that wanted to kill Laird. Both of them had been working with strong energy for some time and were very open to this exploration. She immediately began to wring the towel and yell "I hate you!" "I want you to die!" Soon her body began to vibrate and she told us that she felt nauseous.

Often, when the body has a reaction it is expressing something which the mind has not yet found the words for. In this instance, we gave her some words to try—"You make me sick." While still straddling Laird and choking the towel she looked him in the eyes and declared, "You make me sick!" He spontaneously repeated the words back to her. "You make me sick!" Back and forth they went, repeating with escalating intensity this phrase. As we discussed throughout the book, energy likes to be met with equivalent energy. So, though this couple was saying what some might consider a vile statement to each other, there was clearly pleasure for them in this sketchy place.

We know this interaction might sound disturbing to some, and it really does not translate well to the written word. But the wisdom in making space for this lower-self energy to emerge is that it takes away the fear and judgment of such places. When Holly got to express this taboo energy and was met by Laird, she released something which opened her up to an important awareness. Holly, through the expression of hatred, began to see how she had to shut off any negative feelings toward her father. She had sensed that he would be too injured if she didn't idealize him and keep him on his throne. Consequently, she transferred her negativity onto Laird. When she saw that he could handle her negativity and indeed enjoyed meeting her there she began a process of detachment from her father and commitment to Laird.

Additionally, this opened the door for a growing awareness of how she had split off her "heart" connection from contact with her "pelvic" energy. She started to understand how her erotic feelings for her father were disgusting to her (bridging) and how, once she began to feel her love for Laird, she also felt sexual revulsion. Learning to reconnect love and lust took some time, but by expressing her disgust she was able to discern where it truly came from.

Our sexual feelings toward a parent or sibling are considered so taboo that none of us really knows how to hold and allow such natural reactions. This results in all sorts of mayhem in our adult committed relationship. Through catalyzing, couples are given permission to embody deeply disowned and exiled parts. These internal states do not go away by ignoring them. When Holly felt sick to her stomach, it was as if her body knew what her mind did not want to deal with. By giving her the words, "You make me sick!" she could begin to metabolize the conflicted energy of love and desire toward a parent. Because, it appeared that her father had his own conflicted energy toward Holly, as a child she was left with no other option then to cut off from such confusing and intense energy.

With homosexual children a similar experience can happen with the same-sex parent. Only for the gay child it is even more difficult because s/he must also deal with the social taboo against same-sex desire. The pain and isolation is monumental. It requires a profound trust and sense of safety to bring out such socially unacceptable emotional truths.

Some couples can only approach these sensitive areas with great care and tenderness. In EMM our desire is to bring every couple to their optimal level of tolerance so that they have the opportunity to break beyond the boundaries of their control patterns and liberate their sexuality to the greatest degree possible. **Safety does not derive from the artificial construction of a world where one is never challenged to explore new possibilities. People feel safest when they know they can handle whatever emerges from within, not from asking others to treat them with kid gloves.**

Active and receptive energies

For many men, particularly as they age, achieving and maintaining an erection becomes a serious concern. In EMM we prefer to see erectile problems as a component of the shared energy field. While there are a variety of possible causes for erectile problems, for now we would like to focus on the very real concern of men inhibiting their active desire. Caring and conscious men are often the most susceptible to erectile problems because they have learned to react to any signal from a partner that tells them they are coming on too strong.

In the shared energy field there is a mythic interplay of active and receptive energies. The antipodal nature of active and receptive is often described as the masculine and feminine polarities. But in both opposite and same-sex relationships there is usually one person who tends to embody a more active role while the other embraces the receptive. It is a mistake though to imagine that active is dominant and receptive submissive. Both are potent in their own right.

Problems occur when, for instance, a woman confuses receptivity with submissiveness. This often results in a reluctance to receive the active energy. Knee jerk resistance is often the result of such confusion. Some women, consequently, can only have sex when they initiate. Conversely, a man who confuses his natural desire to reach out and to penetrate with "perpetrator" impulses will tend to over-compensate. He will often try to become the sensitive, gentle lover that he thinks his partner wants. But when both people are in touch with their uninhibited desires they can fully meet each other as equals.

Men with erectile problems are routinely inhibited in revealing their true lustiness. Over the course of time, a committed couple can fall prey to pulling back their true desires and acquiescing to the least risky sexual behaviors. Hard-ons can become an endangered species in such an ecosystem. In our mentoring work, we have witnessed over and over again men who first start having some problems maintaining erections and eventually become avoidant out of fear that they no longer can find desire for their partners. **What looks like lack of desire though is frequently a fear of exposure of a man's wildest places.**

So many men benefit just from hearing that their desire to take a woman (or another man) and just fuck, is a *good* thing. Likewise, many women are relieved to know that their secret fantasy to be taken is equally positive, and not a sign of some pathological perversion. The perversity is in the hiding, not in the desires themselves. For many men to get hard, they need internal permission to feel what Michael Bader [(2)] describes as their "ruthlessness." This refers to the part of the person that lives beyond the guilt and conditioned belief that it's his job to keep his partner safe. Caretaking is anathema to arousal. Shame of one's ruthless sexuality is a key ingredient in the recipe for flaccidity.

The receptive partner has a keen eye for lack of confidence in the partner who is trying to embody the active energy pole. If she senses a dearth of desire she will pull back in mistrust. She may test her partner, inviting him to find his ruthlessness which will reassure her that it is safe to receive him. This dance, while largely unconscious, is played out nightly in bedrooms around the world. For some individuals who embody the receptive energy pole, they will enact the "castrator archetype" by belittling and comparing a mate to previous lovers. Others will simply shut down and lower their expectations.

Sally and Anthony had been together for 28 years when they came to us. Sexual apathy had threatened to take down their marriage. It soon became apparent that neither of them was able to get aroused without the conditions being "just right." Sally had always been fearful of Anthony's "big energy" and Anthony said he "felt like a pig" when he wanted sex and Sally did not. At a certain juncture we encouraged Anthony to bring out his "pig self" and amplify it. We had them stand on opposite ends of the large foam cube and each of them began to thrust their pelvises into the cube in each other's direction.

As Anthony began to express his lust ("I want you." "Stop resisting me." "You turn me on.") Sally at first contracted and started to disappear. She seemed to not be there and was just going through the motions. When Marcia asked her what was happening she told us that she didn't believe Anthony and wanted to ridicule him. Marcia asked her what the words might be. Immediately she said, "You're full of shit! You're all talk." So Marcia instructed her to bring out the energy of this place, but to do it with her pelvis pushing back against Anthony.

When she started to do this we noticed that his resolve weakened. Brian asked him to share. He said "I think she may be right. Maybe I don't want her. After all, I do have problems getting it up." Brian suggesting to Anthony that maybe he protects Sally by keeping his penis soft, asked, "What would happen if you just let her take care of herself?" Anthony said he wanted to try again to bring his active energy, his ruthlessness, to Sally. So they began to parry back and forth "I want you!'—"I don't believe you!" This time Sally didn't disappear and the charge between them mounted. Suddenly she changed her words. "If you want me, take me!" she shouted. "Yes I want you!" Anthony exploded. "Take me!" she retorted.

As the two of us witnessed this beautiful exchange, it was vividly clear how the power of the active and the receptive energies were equal. The power in the enveloping energy of "take me" was no less than Anthony's penetrating desire to have her. We felt such respect for them as they met each other in full-bodied potency.

Whatever the sexual issues are, unless a couple can raise the energy and fully meet each other, no technique or discipline will itself take them where they need to go. As you can see from what we have discussed in this chapter, mentoring involves bringing out whatever is being held back in the presence of the mentors. This allows for the mentors to guide, course-correct, and create safety for the couple to enter dangerous waters.

Erectile problems, inability to achieve orgasm, and overall sexual apathy stand in stark contrast to the interior fantasy world of many couples. What looks like sexual disinterest or performance anxiety is often simply an avoidance of one's true sexual self. David Schnarch sees "emotional fusion," or being non-individuated, as a major factor in sexual problems between partners. To say what you want, at the risk of being humiliated is the price couples need to pony up if they want their sex lives to flourish.

The erotic spectrum

Internet porn, the so-called "soft porn" of trashy romance novels, and all levels of sex—for-hire are, in part, substitutes for revealing one's inner sexual world to a partner. For many couples, the more time they have been together the more they hide their "naughty" desires. We are not suggesting that there isn't a normal diminution of desire that occurs over the course of a long term relationship, clearly there is. But this drop-off is all too often attributed solely to this factor and with a little prodding it is also clear that the fantasy life does not drop off at the same rate. Indeed, sometimes it increases!

We work with many couples in their sixties and seventies who still long for the beauty of sexual contact. When they let hormonal decreases become the explanation for the loss of sexual interaction they easily give up. In EMM we like to talk about what we call the "erotic spectrum." One of the reasons why sexual apathy and inhibition settles in is because couples often have a rigidly defined idea of when sex begins. A couple will be relating to each other from reflective consciousness (that is, from the neck up) for weeks and then suddenly attempt to awaken their genitals. This compartmentalizing of sexuality is a big problem.

The erotic spectrum informs us that sex doesn't begin when we take our clothes off, and doesn't end when we roll over in post-orgasmic slumber. If we begin to embrace the idea that sexual energy can be gradually building over many days. That it waxes like the moon. Then we can avoid the abrupt shift from head to pelvis. Likewise, the post-coital after-glow is one of slowly waning energy, and can last for several days if couples are open to noticing.

We will encourage partners to begin building charge any time they notice one another in a sexual way. There are any number of moments when one partner feels a slight attraction to the other. Most of these fall under the radar in the hub-bub of everyday life. But if a spouse notices, "Hmm, her butt looks nice in those slacks." Or "I really love his neck," these are little forays into one's own sexuality.

So we ask partners to heed these sexual snippets. If, for instance, either partner has difficulty with arousal, they can use these brief attractions to build energy. A mate can consciously begin, in his own mind, to sexually objectify his partner. When he feels an attraction he can allow himself to imagine having sex with her when the weekend arrives. Over the ensuing days he may play with looking at her more sexually, and fantasize about doing things with her that would really turn him on. We might encourage him to point out to her how attractive she looks. They can begin to relate to each other more erotically without any immediate expectation of intercourse. Eroticizing everyday life is crucial to sexual fulfillment. It is much easier for a couple to have a pleasurable encounter if they have been sexually engaged for days.

In addition to noticing each other as sexual objects, we also encourage partners to engage their senses with each other. In our couples workshops we often will blindfold one of the pair and have the partner engage her mate's senses with aromas, various forms of touch, small bits of fruit or chocolate, and music. We will do this in mentoring sessions also. They are encouraged to meet one another through their senses at home as well.

When a couple does have a sexual encounter that culminates with either orgasm or heightened arousal, we want for them to savor the experience as it continues over the next few days. The erotic spectrum involves a leisurely build of charge and an equivalent release and incremental discharge of erotic energy over a much longer period of time than most couples realize. The reality is that couples can be "having sex" much more of the time then they imagine if they saw this process of arousal and release as being without fixed boundaries.

Sex outside the relationship

Before we finish this chapter, the conundrum of affairs needs to be addressed. What makes a relationship an affair is its clandestine nature. People in polyamorous relationships are up front and clear about who they may be sleeping with. To pretend to be in a monogamous relationship while surreptitiously involved with another is the very definition of an affair. It is not our goal in this book to explore the merits and drawbacks of diverse, but consciously chosen lifestyles. This is certainly a valuable undertaking, but not central to our objective here. In our estimation, affairs are a separate category and important to address because of their profound impact on committed relationships. Affairs can occur for many reasons. The most notable include:

- Control pattern affairs—designed to avoid feelings of rejection and abandonment.
- Affairs associated with sexual compulsivity—also used to ward off intolerable feelings and often a way to discharge intense sexual energy associated with early life overexposure to such energy.
- Affairs that are primarily emotional in nature—the object of the affair gives the individual something he feels he can never get from his spouse.
- The affair with an early-life romance—such affairs are often sought out to heal something which has remained unfinished, sometimes for decades.
- Eros affairs—those who mistake eros for mature love will perpetually seek out erotic contact in the erroneous belief that they have finally found their "soul mate."
- Transition stage affairs—when a couple enters the developmental crisis of the Transition Stage, an affair may occur as a way to shake up the relationship and tell the partner "we are in trouble!"
- Tacitly accepted affairs—where one partner employs a "don't ask, don't tell" policy because that person has become sexually avoidant and knows that the other still "needs sex."

Each of these would be addressed in mentoring differently. Whenever there is an emotional connection to a third party the challenge in couples work becomes much more complex. Most often, the person having the affair needs to make a clear decision to bring all her energy to one or the other party. But this may not occur easily. The affair often gives the individual a sense of power that she never felt before. Her mate is more vulnerable and frequently (though certainly not always) treats her better. He gets motivated to try harder. For her to consider giving up her lover elicits fear of going back to a place where she felt taken for granted. Under these conditions, the affair is serving her, and she is loathe to give it up.

In EMM we strive to bring to the surface this dynamic so that both parties can see what's at stake. The spouse whose partner is having the affair generally responds in one of a few ways. He may try to become what he believes she wants (passive CP), he may give up and tell her to do whatever she wants (passive CP), he may rage and threaten her (aggressive CP), or he may begin to connect to his authentic need for her and make a real effort to heal what is damaged between them.

Often affairs can lead to positive change, but not without a serious desire on the part of both people to work it out. In Lucy and Ron's case, his affair with a co-worker came about after five years of a sexless marriage. When Lucy discovered it, she started to feel her desire for Ron again. For some, the threat of losing a partner awakens erotic energy. Lucy's rekindled sexuality soon led to Ron ending the affair. What ensued was a year and a half of eros between Ron and Lucy. But eventually the old passive control patterns crept back in and sex withered. Only then were they ready to confront everything the affair helped them avoid.

Working with a couple who are in the midst of an active affair generally involves helping each person discover what is right for him or her. For the "aggrieved" spouse the focus may be on helping that person maintain a sense of integrity. For the spouse who is having the affair, the focus needs to be on how the affair is serving him and what he is really looking for. It is, in effect, crisis counseling.

Once an affair has ended, the EMM approach can help the couple to move through all that it has evoked. Some partners have a profoundly difficult time recovering from an affair while others seem to "wake up" and grow from the experience. While it is important to make adequate space to address the affair's reverberations in the partnership, it is paramount that the mentor attend to the couple's pre-affair world.

We view the affair through the lens of the shared energy field. The affair is often the culmination of a long history of avoidance of primary feeling. There is a real danger in allowing the affair to dominate the work. When this happens the aggrieved spouse can feel justified in remaining in blame indefinitely. Meanwhile, the guilty spouse believes he has no right to address his concerns about their marriage. He typically exhibits either a passive, submissive control pattern where he is forever apologetic for his indiscretions, or a more aggressive control pattern wherein he exhibits impatience and frustration exemplified in statements such as, "Alright, I've apologized, when are you going to let it go!?" In either case he is avoiding more vulnerable feelings. Many people initiate affairs because these dynamics had already been playing out with maddening frequency around less florid issues throughout the course of their relationship.

Though most people who have affairs are unaware of it, there is very often a lower-self destructive anger that is being enacted through the affair. While affairs erupt from multiple motivations, lower-self hostility is certainly a contributing factor. Because the destructive current is most often exiled from consciousness, few people recognize its place in the decision to have an affair. Working with the Full Self Expression template couples can begin to make space for every layer of emotion. While many therapies attempt to either go to the vulnerable feelings or to remorse as quickly as possible, in EMM we want to make room for the aggressive truth behind the enactment of the affair. While it may seem on first blush a way of justifying the affair, we have found it enormously productive for the spouse who had the affair to find her "Fuck you!" toward her mate. Working down through the layers of FSE, we support the "guilty party" in moving through blame, demand, lower-self, resistance to vulnerable feelings and all the way down to true and real remorse. But the ability to take ownership of the part that had some satisfaction in hurting her partner is often a vital step.

Remembering that the lower self emerges from a sense of powerlessness, we can see that many affairs are the consequence of one person indirectly getting back at the other. This destructive part, or energy, might be translated as "Go fuck yourself! I don't need you!" The enactment of this sentiment occurs when one is avoidant of direct conflict. **When conflict cannot be engaged in consciously, lower-self enactments are inevitable**. To change the pattern over the long haul, we believe that the destructive current needs to be brought to consciousness, and expressed. Doing so makes room to then express vulnerable feelings, remorse and mature need. This is where true power lies.

Alternative sexual expression

In EMM we want to embrace the often overlooked reality that monogamy is a choice (and not the only choice) in a committed relationship. External relationships occur with great frequency in long term relationships. Helping couples identify what they each want, in terms of sexual expression, is critical to our mentoring work. Outside sexual contact is not viewed automatically as a symptom of some pathological flaw in the couple's commitment to each other.

We are all sexual beings and we each have a need to express our sexuality in our own unique ways. The issues around sex outside of the committed relationship need to be dealt with forthrightly and compassionately. The gravitational pull toward sexual expansiveness includes a desire for novelty, variety, and freedom. Unless couples are willing to engage in these all-too-real, albeit dicey, conversations, they will often engage in covert sexual activity, or they will wither.

In Sex Before Dawn, Christopher Ryan and Cacilda Jetha tell us: "Couples might find that the only route to preserving or rediscovering intensity reminiscent of their early days and nights requires confronting the open, uncertain sky together. They might find themselves having their most meaningful, intimate conversations if they dare to talk about the true nature of their feelings. We don't mean to suggest these will be easy conversations. They won't be." [39]

In our mentoring we want to support couples in revealing these truths about sexuality and desires that extend beyond their relationship to each other. We have found that simply by opening the door to exploring this subject, couples often break through to a new level of eroticism with each other.

It is too often the case that an individual's sexual proclivities (which are far too complicated to bestow with any single causality) are exiled by shame and fear. What and whom one is attracted to is a vital part of who that person is. It is sad how often a partner will deny and disown her own inclinations and live a life starved of sexual fulfillment. We have witnessed marriages break up, not because of a partner's sexual impulses but because of the years of hiding and pretending. Betrayal is a far greater crisis than divergent sexual proclivities. Making safe space for couples to have these deep and frank discussions is essential to this work. This need is just as great for same sex couples as for heterosexuals.

As couples learn conflict engagement metaskills (grounding, identifying and expressing disowned parts, curiosity, awareness of the sacred shift) they are better equipped to confront sexual difficulties. The immense beauty of sexual engagement is that everything is right there to be revealed. Sexuality can take us from supreme child-like tenderness to sublime awakening into the ecstatic.

Despite the established sexual control patterns and supremely fragile innocence which these patterns protect against, most couples are surprisingly corrigible when it comes to stepping beyond their edges. Partners can discover each other anew through the feral desires of their fantasy worlds—and they are often amazed. The innate pull of the ecstatic beckons all of us to challenge our fears and embody our sacred capacity for pleasure and connection.

The most essential gift couples receive from sexual mentoring can be summed up in a word—permission. The mentor creates an environment where very little is barred. Sexuality is honored, the profane is celebrated, wounding is given the spaciousness to be completely experienced, and adventurousness is applauded. Exceptional sex welcomes the secrets, the struggles, the fetishes, the fears, the woeful and the wondrous. It is the acquiescence to all that is, and in this sanctified space eros flourishes.

Chapter Nine

Taking Risks

If you have worked your way through this book, by now you are keenly aware that the EMM approach is based on a willingness to explore edges—both the couple's and your own. We honor and employ the research discoveries in our field, *and* we know the limits of working only with that which has been thoroughly researched. Sometimes this work asks us to step beyond the tried and true and bring forth imagination, inspiration and audacity. EMM doesn't pretend to offer something better than other models of relationship therapy, just different. Our desire is to add to your skill base and to encourage you to be flexible, receptive and maybe sometimes a bit outrageous.

Couples that come to us and to other mentors we have trained appreciate the humanness, candor, and occasional absurdity that defines the EMM approach. Sessions can be raunchy, funny, deeply emotional, insightful, and exhilarating. In a recent session a couple in their early forties, Jermaine and Franny, came in wanting to share something important. They had been trying to get pregnant for several years and had been through four grueling rounds of IVF. Not long ago they had given up.

They came into this session, however, and told us that they were going to adopt. This news was met by us with great excitement. They too said they were excited, but there was a reluctance to fully allow the joy to surface. After we spent time exploring all else they may have been feeling, especially their fears, we ended the session with a catalyzing intervention. Because they still were inhibited about embodying their joy, we opened the window (from our eleventh floor work space) and suggested to them to shout out to the entire world, "We're going to have a baby!" After some initial reluctance they both simultaneously yelled their elation to the world (or at least to anybody in New York City who might be listening). By shouting it out they moved the excitement into their bodies. It was delightful.

Such catalyzing suggestions come from little inspirations that every therapist has, but few tend to act on. EMM is not a formula, but rather an invitation to follow your intuitive self, to explore your edge. **Our operating definition of intuition is, "The willingness to express something that you are not sure is correct.**" In every one of our sessions we will make at least one catalyzing suggestion. Some lead nowhere, others open great vistas.

As we have discussed earlier, the purpose of catalyzing is to help a couple, or one of them, step over an edge in a way they are unlikely to do on their own. The value of this is to help both an individual and the couple to evolve. Catalyzing interventions are transformative by design. Even when they fall flat, just raising them shifts something. It tells the couple you are with them on a powerful adventure of self discovery. When such interventions do work, it very often instigates a poignant moment of deeper connection for the couple. Life can be so mundane so much of the time and these transformative experiences allow couples to feel deeper, see each other in new ways, and free up dense and congested energy. The emotionally immature couple can suddenly become affective stalwarts. It is an honor to participate in this as a mentor.

This work lends great credence to the non-rational level of experience which informs all of us far more than we allow ourselves to know. The primacy of rational thought in our culture seduces us into believing we can problem-solve our way through all our troubles. This is simply not the case. **We are not looking for solutions in EMM, we are aiming for wisdom—a wisdom of the heart and body which allows us to know exactly what we need.** This does not mean we never engage in rational discussion, we do. But transformation never comes exclusively from ideas. It is the stuff of a different kind of wisdom. Just as dancing doesn't result from memorizing steps, the wisdom of intimacy too requires ongoing experience. This is the level of the non-rational, the emotive, the somatic.

Ken Wilber has discussed the non-rational in great detail. He makes the distinction between what he calls the "pre-rational" and the "trans-rational." The infant who has yet to develop discursive powers lives in a pre-rational, magical world where sensation and emotion hold sway. In the evolution of consciousness, Wilber suggests that humans can transcend the cognitive, rational world of abstract thinking. He sees meditation as the premier vehicle for achieving the capacity for trans-rational states. Says Wilber, ". . . meditation (or transpersonal development in general) is a simple and natural continuation of the evolutionary process, where every going within is also a going beyond to a wider embrace." [(53)]

Wilber cautions against confusing the pre and trans-rational states. The difference between them may be most readily witnessed when we look at the four levels of intersubjective connection. The couple that is fused to reactive consciousness is dwelling in pre-rational, sympathetic emotionalism. Though they may be using reasoned arguments, this is a smoke screen for non-rational fight-or-flight engagement. Contrast this to the couple who is able to mindfully engage in an experience of presencing. This is a level beyond reflective, narrative consciousness.

In the EMM approach we perceive of embodiment as a way to embrace both the pre-rational and the trans-rational. To both be aware of and to freely express immature childhood demands, for instance, allows an individual to fully transcend them, at least temporarily. To transcend does not mean to get rid of, but rather to move beyond being controlled by pre-rational demands. Unlike with mindfulness alone, we believe it is necessary to make space for the emergence of somatic realities which can be viewed as the wisdom of the body. Sometimes, the naive wisdom of the pre-rational needs to be exposed in order for a couple to move forward.

Catalyzing interventions encourage both pre and trans-rational experiences. In this final chapter the two of us will describe a number of catalyzing interventions which have stood the test of time and which we return to often when the situation calls us to do so. Not to be applied as a formula, these interventions need to arise from a felt sense that there is an opening in the relationship to "go for it." The effect of any catalyzing intervention is entirely dependent on the nature of the relationship between mentor and couple, or between therapist and clients.

So let's take a closer look at some EMM catalyzing interventions:

1. Switching Roles—We will utilize this intervention particularly when couples are locked in reactive spirals. There are two main options here. First, we will break into a reactivity exchange and ask the partners if they are willing to try something. We ask them to change seats, or positions if they are standing. Then we suggest that they continue the discussion/argument only taking each other's positions. This can help to move them out of sympathetic arousal and support the emergence of reflectivity. In more extreme situations we have asked the couple to switch roles with us. This really forces them to stand back and observe what they look and sound like. It also challenges them to find creative ways to break into the reactivity. There is one additional benefit. It helps us to release some of the frustration we might be holding from our efforts to address the seemingly impenetrable reactive spiral. We also get to enter their world which often helps us immeasurably.
2. Expression by Proxy—This can be an extremely effective catalyzing intervention. When we are working with a couple around historical issues, for example, of one of their parent's abusiveness, we may ask that person to bring out any anger she may feel toward that parent. Sometimes, however, she is just not ready to enter into her anger. She may be afraid of losing control, not want to look like the parent that hurt her, or fear retaliation in some primal way. In such cases we might ask her partner to express the anger for her. In expression by proxy a spouse may be banging on the foam cube and shouting "How dare you treat her so poorly! Don't ever touch her again! "She's just a little girl!" Very often such expression

is felt deeply by the mate who is watching. She may cry over feeling, for the first time, that someone is protecting her. The proxy partner feels good too about being able to stand up for his loved one.

3. Individual Focus—Less a specific intervention and more a choice we will make, sometimes we'll devote the bulk of a session to one partner's needs. Typically this involves some type of "regressive" work where we assist one in entering into an emotionally challenging place where he needs to reclaim his primary feelings. Thus we may have him working with the pain and rage of early life abuse, while his partner stands by and witnesses. This too is a strategy to break the reactive spiral. Often the focus in reactivity is on the "20%" that exists between the couple while ignoring the triggers from the historical "80%." When the strong emotions are re-directed toward the original wounding, the witnessing partner can develop great empathy—something that can never happen when she is still in sympathetic arousal.
4. Developmental Indulgence—Character theory suggests that we can become "fixated" at a particular level of development, which brings with it specific needs in the adult relationship. Whether characterological development as a theory ever gets validated through research, it is still useful to see how certain "young" needs exist in most every adult we work with. While it is not a spouse's job to heal his mate's childhood wounds, we have found it very powerful for each person to hear and embrace these early needs. So, for a partner who felt invisible as a child we may ask her to breathe, hold hands with her mate, look in his eyes and say, "Will you see me?" And we invite him to say something like, "I love seeing you." Sometimes the partner finds his own words that are spoken for his heart. We then reverse roles and have the man speak from his developmental need. So, he may say, "I need you to approve of me." To which she might reply, "I totally approve! You are amazing!"

5. Simplify and Amplify—We have discussed this idea throughout the book, but it bears repeating. Every couple's conflict can usually be boiled down to a basic statement which corresponds to an unmet narcissistic need, a resistance to feeling, a request for either autonomy or intimacy, or competitiveness. It is an axiom that couples repeat basically the same fight over and over again sometimes for decades. To distill the conflict down to its basic statement and to bring juice to it can often bring about profound results. Statements such as, "My way!" "Give it to me!" "Never!" or "I won't let you win!" are so packed with meaning and passion that the amplified expression of them can result in genuine release. We are, in essence, "cutting to the chase." All the narrative that serves as a prologue to the chase scene is rendered unnecessary.
6. Non-verbal/Non-rational Expression—Sometimes it is best to do away with words altogether (especially for couples enamored with reflective consciousness). Often we will ask partners to stand opposite each other jump around and make nonsense sounds. Or, we will ask them to make sounds that mirror their inner experience. Pre-linguistic humankind indulged in a rich panoply of vocalizations including growls, groans, squeals, moans, yelps, laughs, sighs, shrieks, snarls and much more. Each utterance mirrors an inner experience. To have couples show up in this way is often very evocative.
7. Working with Metaskills—Each metaskill already exists in some inchoate form within every partner. Helping a person to "ground," to become curious, to presence, to yield to emerging energies, or to tolerate strong emotions is to support him in becoming more whole and more alive. We might, for instance, instruct him to temporarily ignore all thoughts and bring attention only to what is happening below the neck. Or, we may ask him when he is challenging his partner with a question like, "Why can't you ever remember to turn off the lights!?" to take a few deep breaths and discover within himself his curious

nature. Then he can ask the question again from a very different interior state.

8. Resistance and Surrender—These polarities exist in every couple (and may show up in different areas). You can offer very simple interventions around these energies. For example, one partner can be invited to say, "I want you." While the other resists: "You can't have me!" or simply, "No!" Have them continue to build the energy between each other in this way until it feels right for the resisting partner to drop into surrender. "Yes!" or "I'm yours!" may be the expression of surrender. Or, you may have the person who is often more dominant kneel in supplication before his mate and allow both of them to feel what this evokes.
9. Battling Childhood Needs—As we've stated, couples get in real trouble when their secret and sometimes unconscious demands collide. For example, Ralph and Patricia had a huge fight when she returned from a week-long visit with her mother. Ralph was anticipating Patricia's arrival with some excitement. She was also looking forward to seeing him. But the moment she walked through the door it all went downhill.

   Simply put, they were reactive to each other's left-over childhood needs. Patricia came from a family where she was caregiver to her younger sibs after her mother died when she was seven. Ralph was generally ignored by his parents and learned that the only time he got their attention was when he was sick. So, when Patricia arrived home from her week away her desire was to have a little "down time." Conversely, Ralph wanted her to fawn over him, but could only indirectly "fish" for this by complaining how hard it had been in her absence.

   By giving their respective childhood needs a clear and direct voice in a session, they each could express what was taboo for them in their early life. We invited Ralph to demand, "I want you to be delighted to see me!" (rather than complain), while Patricia was encouraged to say, "I don't want to give you anything!" (rather than withdraw). As they brought these forthright reactions to each other, the tension between them eased and was replaced by a shared compassion.

10. Embodying Ambivalence—Every individual we have ever worked with holds wildly ambivalent feelings toward his partner. Many have both resistance and longing for a mate simultaneously, which can make for really chaotic interactions. Deep ambivalent feelings toward a parent are often at the root of split reactions to a partner. This can be brought into the energetic dynamic with a simple intervention. Have one spouse express her ambivalence by placing both hands on her mate. With one hand she pushes him away, with the other she pulls him toward her. Have her do this for several minutes and then explore which direction was stronger. If, for instance, the push was dominant, then have her make the pull slightly stronger. This embodied enactment often yields powerful feelings and awarenesses for both people.
11. Strategic use of Music—We will frequently use a song or instrumental piece which speaks directly to where the couple is at. Sometimes music is employed for purposes of energetic arousal and sometimes to touch the heart. Music sends a direct somatic message which supports the movement of specific emotions. Songs like Alanis Morrisette's "That I would be Good" and Sinead O'Conner's "This is to Mother You" are perennial favorites. We are continually adding songs to our library because music has become integral to our work.
12. Embodying the Withhold—Since most couples withhold positive feelings or responses to each other, we like to bring this pattern to life. To do so helps to remove it from the arena of enactment and into greater consciousness. One particular way we do this is to have one partner write out a list of positive qualities in her mate. We then have her roll it up and tie a ribbon around it. After this is done we instruct the partner to ask her to share her list, and she is

to refuse. We encourage them to escalate the exchange. Him pleading or trying to wrestle the list from her and her fighting tooth-and-nail to withhold it. If he pulls it away from with brute force, before he opens it we ask both of them to notice how it feels. This conscious embodying of a "withhold" often mirrors a more subtle expression which is typical of their interactions. Sometimes we will ask him to find other ways that brute force to get the goodies from her. She can "feel into" when she really wants to share with him.

13. Creating Ecstatic Experience—The emphasis on the struggles can sometimes be a tried and true avoidance of opening to higher vibration pleasure and expansiveness. On occasion we will devote a session to helping the couple encounter their own ecstatic energy. Through breathwork, working with charge and discharge, sensate awakening and other such experiences we guide the couple into trans-rational states of openness and expansion. We consider these non-ordinary states of being as fundamental to living a full and exceptional life together, and believe that couples do not experience enough of this in their daily lives.
14. Finding the "We"—When couples seem engaged in a seemingly intractable reactive cycle it may help to stop them and ask if they are willing to try something different. Point out how their dialogue is focused almost entirely on differences. Ask them to see if they can discover the "We" that they can agree upon. Many couples swallowed up in reactivity lose touch with the "we." For instance, "We love to go the movies." "We are great co-parents." "We have fun on vacation." Of course, you always have to watch for the "Yes, but . . ."
15. What are you Fighting for?—It can also be useful to stop a couple during reactivity and tell them, "I don't think you are fighting *against* each other, I think you are fighting *for* something." You may suggest that there is a good chance that each one is either fighting for autonomy or connection. If they can self identify which it is, have them

simplify and amplify basic statements such as, "I won't let you tell me who I am!" or "I want more of you!"

These are some examples of catalyzing interventions which are part of our repertoire. There are infinite variations and permutations of the ones we mention here. There are also untold other creative ways to take risks with couples in a manner that supports the best within them. As we have said often, couples come seeking help and they have to define the problem in some standard way in order to make sense of it. As a rule, they are unable to articulate what they really long for, which is growth and fulfillment. Every problem partners try to define for us is a holographic piece of a larger struggle to express themselves fully and authentically. You can help them get there if you expand your own sense of what is possible.

Respecting your own personality is crucial to this work. If you are more gentle and soft-spoken by nature then this is your gift, don't try to be more flamboyant. If you are more boisterous, use this energy wisely. Your own personal edge does not involve becoming something beyond your nature. However, therapists get in trouble when they cannot find the flexibility to open up to dormant parts within themselves. In other words, while we have basic characterological tendencies, we can be trapped by them and use them as our control patterns. A gentle therapist needs to develop tolerance for a "rough and tumble" client. A no-nonsense therapist needs to know how to soften to a frightened part that shows up in a client. Couples need you to be stronger than their fears, bigger than their resistances, capable of being a captain on the stormy seas of conflict.

Most of all, you need to trust yourself to follow your felt sensibilities. It is a sure thing that couples work will send you into self-doubt, cynicism, and a longing to move to Key West and open a tee shirt shop. When the going gets tough your instincts will serve you much more faithfully that a memorized stash of techniques. All you need to know is available to you in the shared energy field. Trust yourself to slow down, receive what is occurring all around and within, and learn to lead by following.

Much of what we learn in our professional education is only supplemental to our non-rational wisdom. Systems theory, attachment theory, character theory, transpersonal theory, multiplicity theory, object relations theory, and all the rest are valuable to help us understand. Yet, there comes a moment in every session where we need to meet the individuals who have come to us for support stripped of any roles, heart to heart in our raw humanity. Simply put, the couple needs us more than they need our education.

Our hope is that this book has inspired you to consider how much more is possible when you open to the intelligence of the shared energy field. The "wisdom path" of the long term committed relationship is saturated with potential. Couples look to us to encourage, inspire, and embolden them to take the risks which are absolutely necessary for creating an exceptional relationship. When you choose to work with couples you are entering a world where everything that is good and everything that is troubling about our human experience resides. The lows are lower and the highs are higher. If you are willing to travel this path with the couples who seek your guidance you will be affected to the core of your being. And this is what it takes to be of service.

References

1. Assigioli, Roberto. 1973. *The Act of Will.* New York, NY. An Esalen Book
2. Bader, M. 2009 *Male Sexuality: Why Women Don't Understand it—And Men Don't Either.* Lanham, Md. The Rowman and Littlefield Publishing Group
3. Benson, April. 2008. *To Buy or Not to Buy: Why We Overshop and How to Stop. Trumpeter Books.*
4. Bollas, C. 1987. *The Shadow of the Object: Psychoanalysis of the Unthought Known.* New York. Columbia University Press
5. Bowlby, J. 1988. *A Secure Base: Parent-Child Attachment & healthy Human Development.* Great Britan. Routledge Publishing de Quincey, C. 2005. *Radical Knowing: Understanding Consciousness Through Relationship.* Rochester, Vermont. Park Street Press
6. Ferrer, Jorge. 2002. *Revisioning Transpersonal Theory: a Participatory Vision of Human Spirituality.* Albany. State University of New York Press
7. Gleason, Brian; Gleason, Marcia. 2007. *Going all The Way: The Heart and Soul of the Exceptional Marriage.* Lincoln, Ne. iUniverse
8. Gleason, Brian. 2001. *Mortal Spirit: A Theory of Spiritual-Somatic Evolution.* Lincoln, Ne. Writers Club Press
9. Gottman, J. Ph.D., Silver, N. 2000. *The Seven Principles for Making Marriage Work.* New York. Random House
10. Gray, John. 1993. *What You Feel You Can Heal.* Heart Publishing
11. Grof, S. 2006. When the Impossible Happens: Adventures in Non-Ordinary Reality. Boulder. Sounds True.

12. Haidt, Jonathan. 2006. *The Happiness Hypothesis.* New York. Basic Books
13. Hendrix, H. *Getting the Love you Want: A Guide for Couples.* New York. Harper and row Publishers
14. Johnson, S. 1986. *Characterological Transformation: the Hard Work Miracle.* New York. W. W. Norton and Company
15. Johnson, Susan. 1996. *The Practice of Emotionally Focused Marital Therapy: Creating Connection.* Philadelphia. Brunner/ Mazel
16. Kashdan, T. 2010. *Curious?* New York. HarperCollins Publishers
17. Keen, Sam. 1992. *The Passionate Life: Stages of Loving.* New York. HarperCollins Publishing
18. Keeney, B. 2007. *Shaking Medicine: The Healing Power of Ecstatic Movement.* Rochester, Vermont. Destiny Books
19. Kegan, Robert. 1982. *The Evolving Self: Problem and Process in Human Development.* USA. Harvard
20. Keleman, S. 1975. *Your Body Speaks its Mind.* Berkley. Center Press
21. Levine, P. 2010. *In an Unspoken Voice: How the Body Releases Trauma and Restores Goodness.* Berkeley. North Atlantic Books
22. Lewis, Thomas, M.D.,Amini, Fari, M.D. and Lannon, Richard, M.D. 2001. *A General Theory of Love.* New York. Random House
23. Lowen, A. 1975. *Bioenergetics: The Revolutionary Therapy that Uses the Language of the Body to Heal the Problems of the Mind.* Arkana. Penguin Books
24. Mindell, Amy, Ph.D. 2001. Metaskills: the Spiritual Art of Therapy. Lao Tse Press
25. Mindell, Arnold. 2010. *Process Mind: A User's Guide to Connecting to the Mind of God.* Wheaton, Illinois. Quest Books
26. Mindell, Arnold. 2000. *Quantum Mind: the Edge Between Physics and Psychology.* Portland, Or. Lao Tse Press
27. Mindell, Arnold. 1995. *Sitting in the Fire: Large Group Transformation Using Conflict and Diversity.* Portland, Or. Lao Tse Press

28. Nelson, John. 1994. *Healing the Split: Integrating Spirit Into Our Understanding of the mentally Ill*. Albany. State University of New York Press.
29. O'Donohue, John. 1999. *Eternal Echoes*. New York. HarperCollins Publishers
30. Peperzac, A., Critchely, S., Bernasconi, R. Editors 1996. *Emmanual Levinas: Basic Philosophical Writings*. Indiana University Press
31. Pierrakos, John. 1987. *Core Energetics: Developing the Capacity to Love and Heal.* LifeRhythym
32. Pearce, Joseph, Chilton. 2007. *The Death of Religion and the Rebirth of Spirit: A Return to the Intelligence of the Heart.* Rochester, Vermont. Park Street Press
33. Perel, Esther. 2006. *Mating in Captivity: Unlocking Erotic Intelligence*. New York. HarperCollins Publishing
34. Porges, Stephen W. 2011. *The Polyvagal Theory*. New York. W.W. Norton & Company
35. Real, T. 2007. *The New Rules of Marriage: What you Need to Know to Make Love Work.* New York. Ballantine Books
36. Reich, Wilhelm. 1973. *The Function of the Orgasm*. New York. Orgone Institute Press
37. Reich, Wilhelm. 1972. *Character Analysis*. Toronto. Doubleday
38. Ryan, Christopher; Jetha, Cacilda. 2010. *Sex at Dawn*. New York. HarperCollins Publishers
39. Scharmer, C, O. 2009. *Theory U: Leading from the Future as it Emerges*. San Francisco. Berrett-Koehler Publishers, Inc.
40. Schnarch, D. Ph.D. 1997. *Passionate Marriage: Keeping Love & Intimacy Alive in Committed Relationships*. New York. Henry Holt and Company
41. Schnarch, D. Ph.D. 1991. *Constructing the Sexual Crucible: An Integration of Sexual and Marital Therapy*. New York. W. W. Norton and Company
42. Schwartz, Richard, C. 1995 *Internal Family Systems*. New York. The Guilford Press
43. Siegel, Daniel J. 1999. *The Developing Mind: How Relationships and the Brain Interact to Shape Who We Are*. New York. The Guilford Press.

44. Stern, Daniel. 2004. *The Present Moment: In Psychotherapy and Everyday Life*. New York. W.W. Norton & Company
45. Tillich, Paul. 1952. *The Courage to Be*. New Haven. Yale University Press[93]
46. Tolle, Ekhart. 1997. *The Power of Now: A Guide to Spiritual Enlightenment*. Novata, California. New World Library
47. Wallin, David. 2007. *Attachment in Psychotherapy*. New York. The Guilford Press
48. Washburn, M. 1995. *The Ego and the Dynamic Ground*. Albany. State University of New York Press
49. Welwood, J. 2000. *Toward a Psychology of Awakening*. Boston. Shambala Publishers
50. Whyte, David. 2009. *The Three Marriages: Reimagining Work, Self and Relationship*. New York. Penguin Books
51. Wilber, K. 1995. *Sex, Ecology, Spirituality: The Spirit of Evolution*. Boston. Shambala Publications
52. Wilber, K. 1999 *Collected Works: Volume 4*. Boston. Shambala Publications

About the Authors

Marcia Gleason, LCSW is the Co-Director of the Institute for the Exceptional Marriage. She brings 30 years experience to her work as a couples therapist, body-oriented psychotherapist, trainer, and workshop facilitator. Marcia has in depth training in several modalities such as Core Energetics and Internal Family Systems which she integrates intuitively in her work with clients. She trains therapists in the Exceptional Marriage Approach both in the USA and internationally. She also teaches in the New York institute of Core Energetics. Marcia brings warmth, creativity and compassion to her work with couples.

Brian Gleason, LCSW, is the co-founder, director, and trainer of Exceptional Marriage. Brian has over 30 years of experience in working with organizations, groups, couples, and individuals in a variety of mental health, corporate, wellness, and educational settings. Brian is a senior faculty member of the New York Institute of Core Energetics. He teaches internationally and is author of a book on transpersonal psychology – *Mortal Spirit*. Brian also enjoys a thriving private practice in the New York area for individuals, groups and couples as well as providing supervision for therapists.

Together Marcia and Brian developed the Exceptional Marriage, an experience-based methodology for working with committed relationships which allows couples to honor each partner's capacity to discover his/her greatest gifts and deepest truths. This authentic, rich and powerful journey is explored in couples workshops, professional workshops, books and CDs, including their last book: *Going All the Way, The Heart and Soul of the Exceptional Marriage.*

About the Authors